W9-CAP-540

Atlantic Encounters

Edited by Gregory Murry

Hanover, PA
Invino Academic Publishing
Copyright, 2023
All Rights Reserved

Encounters of the Early Modern Atlantic

By Gregory Murry

As most people know, in 1492 Columbus sailed the Atlantic and discovered the continent that came to be known as America, thereby connecting the Atlantic and opening up an age of exploration and encounter.

But as everyone also knows, Columbus did not discover America at all. The Vikings certainly got there 500 years before him. Polynesian explorers likely got there 300 years him. And a fleet from Africa quite possibly got there 200 years before him.[1] And all of this is to overlook the obvious; that the whole continent was already populated by the time any of these voyages took place.

Let's also note here that Columbus stumbled upon America quite by accident. He had sold the King and Queen of Spain on funding the idea by promising them a shorter route to the Indies, and he insisted to his dying day that India is what he had found.

What was different about Columbus' expedition then? Why did the voyages of Columbus create sustained contact across the Atlantic in ways that prior journeys did not? At least part of the answer lay in the fact that Columbus was his own best public relations man. As soon as he arrived back in Iberia, he sent his description of the 'new world' to his patrons. This letter was quickly translated into various European languages, and within a few years had become a best-seller, spreading throughout Western

---

[1] See respectively, Kuitems, et al. "Evidence for European presence in the Americas in ad 1021" *Nature* 21 May 2021. Carl Zimmer, "Some Polynesians Carry DNA of Ancient Native Americans, New Study Finds" *The New York Times* July 8.2020. "Africa's 'Greatest Explorer'" *BBC News*. 13 Dec. 2000.

Europe by means of the relatively new invention of the printing press.[2]

These and other accounts inspired return voyages, and European settlers soon discovered or devised various ways to generate wealth for themselves in the western hemisphere, usually by various combinations of conquest, commerce, and agriculture. For comparative purposes, think of how long it has been since humankind has returned to the moon, where nothing of commercial value has yet been found.

In roughly the same era that Columbus was crossing the Atlantic, Portuguese explorers were making their way down the coast of West Africa. In 1434, the Portuguese captain Gil Eanes discovered that by sailing away from the land, he could navigate past the Saharan coast at Cape Bojador, which unusual wind patterns had hitherto turned into a 'point of no return' for ships sailing south. This led to a set of journeys ever further down the African coast, driven at first by a desire for gold, and then later with the hope of finding a quicker route to the Asian spice trade. These ultimately culminated in a Portuguese explorer, Vasco de Gama, succeeding where Columbus had failed, sailing around Africa to make it to India in 1497.

But even before Columbus and de Gama, the Portuguese had already initiated a trade that would become as lucrative as gold or spices: the trade in human slaves. At first, African slaves were primarily utilized to do work in the European colonies near Africa. But when Europeans decided that the way to make money in the newly discovered (and rapidly depopulating) lands of America was by the cultivation of labor-intensive cash crops, like tobacco and sugar, they began exporting African slaves on an unprecedented scale and with an indifference to human misery rarely matched in history.[3]

---

[2] "The Diffusion of Columbus's Letter Through Europe, 1493-1497" *OsherMap Library*. https://oshermaps.org/special-map-exhibits/columbus-letter/iv-diffusion-columbuss-letter-through-europe-1493-1497

[3] David Arnold, *The Age of Discovery, 1400-1600*, London: 2002, 11-28.

So began the age of Atlantic encounters, which, for good and for ill, played an outsized role in producing the world in which we live today. Thus, to better understand the world of the Atlantic, as well as the stories we tell about it, is to better understand ourselves.

And as it turns out, from almost the initial moments, we have been telling two, pretty much diametrically opposed, tales.

In one story, intrepid heroes like Columbus improved the world by bringing the dual benefits of Christianity and civilization to native peoples in Africa and America. Despite acknowledging that violence occurred, partisans of this view have acknowledged the conquest of peoples as a regrettable, but often justifiable and likely inevitable, tradeoff for the advancement of civilization.

In the other telling, the Age of Encounter was a story about predatory European cultures extending an oppressively violent system to largely peaceful peoples, who had not asked for Christianity nor for so-called civilization and did not benefit from either. Men such as Columbus were not heroes, but villains--oppressors at best, guilty of genocide at worst.

This chapter will help us to think through these accounts with greater attention to the nuances and contexts that shaped the encounter. As we do so, our exploration of the period will be guided by the following key lenses:

Historical complexity. That is, we will apply the banal, but useful insight that historical events rarely have simple explanations.

Agency and contingency. That is, we will apply the understanding that the path history takes is dependent on the choices that individual people make at any given moment, but that those choices and attitudes are limited by structural and cultural forces that are outside their individual control.

In the age of encounter, complicated actors with complex motivations made complex choices---good choices, bad choices, tough choices, wise choices, short-sighted choices, evil choices, and indifferent choices. The task of this chapter is to give us a clearer insight into the contexts in which these choices were made and to probe their consequences for our own culture.

The Myth of European Cultural Superiority

One common misconception that we should probably clear up right away is the idea that Europeans extended their dominance in the Atlantic due to some sort of inherent technological or cultural superiority. That's a myth that some Europeans started telling themselves right away. The claim was then repeated for many centuries. But it doesn't really stand up to scrutiny. In 1492, European countries were by no means the largest nor most sophisticated societies in the Atlantic basin. On the contrary, in the valley of Mexico, the Aztec empire ruled over a complex society of some 6 million people, with long-distance trading structures, advanced glyphic writing systems, and populous cities that rivaled the most beautiful in Europe. The Inca were an even larger empire, extending their rule over a territory in South America that included some 10 million people at its height, almost twice the population of the Spanish kingdom that conquered it. In the Sahel, the Songhai Empire controlled an area of 540,000 miles, about 10 ten times the size of England. And further south, the Kings of Congo were establishing a highly centralized monarchy that would eventually grow to over 2 million subjects.

Thus, in terms of sheer political and organizational structure, early modern Africa and America had societies that were the equal of, if not superior to, the most advanced civilizations in Western Europe. Though it's true that Europeans had gunpowder weapons before other Atlantic peoples, an advancement they owed to China, the unreliability and slow reloading times of early guns meant that these types of weapons did not play a large part in early military conflicts between Atlantic peoples. Europeans did not take much, if any, initial advantage from gunpowder weaponry.

And though it's also true that Europeans had some of the most advanced navigational and ship-building techniques of the day, these were not so much a result of inherent genius as of savvy cultural borrowing. They had adopted most of their navigational aids from Arab sailors, and their ship-building technologies were a blend of Viking-influenced techniques from the North Atlantic and Arab-influenced techniques from the Eastern Mediterranean.[4] And anyways, we should not overstate the gap between European and other vessels; African navies were more than capable of protecting their coastlines from the violent incursions of European ships.[5]

On the contrary, Western Europe was in many respects the least promising of the aforementioned Atlantic civilizations. For one, they were relatively resource-scarce, obliged to look elsewhere for luxury foods like pepper and sugar (which won't grow in most of Europe) and obliged to trade eastward for luxury goods like silks and porcelain, which they wanted to buy long before they could figure out how to make. Acquiring these goods required precious metals like gold and silver, and Western Europe had little of these either. So, whereas other civilizations could find all they needed within their own borders, Europeans were often driven to the sea, thus illustrating one of the ironies of history, which is that disadvantages can quickly become advantages, given the right context and opportunity. [6]

Another weakness that drove Europeans to the Atlantic was the fact that they were flanked, to both the south and the east, by the habitual enemy of Christendom: The Muslim Turks. 1492 was quite the year for the King and Queen of Spain. In addition to launching Columbus across the Atlantic, that was also the year that Spain conquered Granada, the last Muslim stronghold in Iberia, thus completing a process of recapture that had begun centuries earlier and which is known to us as the Reconquista. The end of the Reconquista, however, did not mean the end of Christian-Muslim conflict. As the Portuguese pushed further down the

---

[4] Arnold, 26-33.

[5] John Thornton, *Africa and Africans in the Making of the Atlantic World, 1400-1800* (New York: 1996), 36-40.

[6] Arnold, 11-14.

African coast in the 15th century, and as Columbus sought to open a passage to the east by sailing west, part of what they were after was a path to the Asian trade routes that bypassed their Muslim enemies.

A related goal of European exploration was the hope of finding a Christian ally who could attack their Muslim enemies from the rear. These illusory dreams were fueled by the medieval version of fake news, a long-standing legend that located a powerful Christian ruler named Prester John somewhere in Eastern Africa or Western Asia, ---they weren't entirely sure where.[7]

The search for religious allies was not the only religious motivation for crossing the ocean. Modern people tend to explain away the passages in the Christian New Testament that seem to indicate that faith and baptism are necessary for salvation. But early modern peoples took those passages deadly seriously, and early modern Christians widely presumed that non-Christians could not go to heaven when they died. Thus, some Christians felt a pressing religious duty to take the gospel message to peoples across the Atlantic, a quirk of Christianity that differentiated it quite a lot from Mesoamerican paganism, from African animistic religions, and even from the rival monotheistic religions of Judaism and Islam.

In our first question then, we see both the complexity and contingency of the Age of the Encounter. This is not a simple story of a more sophisticated, technologically advanced civilization running roughshod over its neighbors in the Atlantic. In most respects, Europe was no more technologically advanced, nor more sophisticated than many of the peoples they encountered. It was not inevitable, nor even perhaps foreseeable, that they should be the instigators of encounter; Europeans had their own complex web of reasons to sail, but those reasons were largely rooted in structural disadvantages.

---

[7] Arnold, 24-25.

Communication and Miscommunication in the Spanish Conquest of Mexico

If the choice to sail to other lands was neither obvious nor inevitable, neither was the choice to fight or subdue the people that were found there. Indeed, violence was its own choice, and the escalation of violence between peoples would reach devastating consequences, but it was certainly a choice made in the context of limiting structures and complex misunderstandings.

In examining the limitations people brought to contact, one context that we should be especially attentive to is the problem of communication. I am not merely referring to the obvious problems of communication, such as those that undoubtedly occurred at the first meetings of peoples, when neither side knew the others' language and when both sides were reliant on gestures to make themselves understood. Problems like these were difficult but surmountable, because all the parties at least recognized the problem and realized that further contact would require a solution. Columbus, for instance, "solved" the problem by kidnapping native children and shipping them back to Spain to learn Spanish.[8] This remedy was undoubtedly brutal, heinous, and terrifying, but probably also effective.

Rather, I am referring to a more insidious form of miscommunication: one that results from the strategy that most humans use when faced with incorporating new information, which is to attempt to process it in ways that align with their preexisting beliefs, knowledge and opinions. Psychologists call this confirmation bias, and it was rampant in the age of encounter.

One easy way to see confirmation bias at work was in the names Atlantic peoples gave to newly encountered flora and fauna. For instance, when the Aztecs first encountered the horses of the

---

[8] Icíar Alonso-Araguás, *New Insights in the History of Interpreting*, eds. Kayoko Takeda and Jesús Baigorri-Jálon (Amsterdam: Benjamins, 2016), 30-32.

conquistadors, they called them *mazatl,* their word for deer.[9] Conversely, when Europeans had to come up with names for various new world birds, they sometimes persisted in Columbus' own confirmation bias, believing the birds to have come from Asia. That is why the French named one such bird an Indian chicken (*poulet d'inde*), and the English called it a turkey.[10]

The cultural gap could give rise to the illusion that both sides were communicating effectively when they were completely misunderstanding one another, a phenomenon that ethnohistorians call 'double mistaken identity'. One such famous case of double mistaken identity occurred during the Spanish conquest of Mexico, which will be illuminating to take some time to relate.

The basics of the story go like this. Following Columbus, the Spaniards spent over two decades exploring and colonizing the Caribbean. However, in 1517, a Spanish expedition reached mainland Mexico, and tantalized by the wealthier and more technologically advanced societies that they found there, the Governor of Cuba ordered an expedition under the command of an ambitious adventurer by the name of Hernan Cortez. When the Spanish governor thought better of his choice and attempted to recall Cortez, the audacious Spaniard set sail with his 500 men anyways, a move which severely cut off his options for retreat.

Among his first two acquisitions in Mexico were a Franciscan friar named Geronimo Aguilar, who had been shipwrecked eight years before and had learned Mayan as a captive, and a Mayan woman named Malinche, who had been sold into slavery as a child, and thus spoke both Mayan and Nahuatl, the language of the Aztec empire. The presence of these two interpreters in Cortez' company provided him with a crude sort of ability to make himself understood. Cortez spoke Spanish to Aguilar, who then translated it into Mayan for Malinche. Malinche then translated the Mayan into Nahuatl, which most of the natives in the valley of Mexico

---

[9] James Lockhart, *Nahuatl as Written* (Stanford: Stanford University Press and UCLA Latin American Studies, 2001), 223.

[10] "Turkey", *Online Etymology Dictionary* https://www.etymonline.com/word/turkey

spoke. The natives then made themselves understood by repeating the process in reverse.

Cortez's boats landed on the east coast of Mexico in 1519, at which point he met ambassadors of the great Aztec emperor, Montezuma, who lavished him with presents and politely asked him to venture no further. Cortez, who faced certain arrest back in Cuba, seems to have already made up his mind to gamble on a desperate strike at Tenochtitlan, the capital and the heart of the Aztec empire, and so he quietly instructed his pilots to destroy his ships. The message to his men was unmistakable; there would be no going back.

It remains a bit of a historical mystery why Montezuma, who could have easily killed every Spaniard the moment they stepped off the boat or at any point during their treacherous 200-mile journey to Tenochtitlan, did not take more decisive action against them, especially as they picked up allies from among the Aztecs discontented neighbors. One explanation that arose soon after the conquest, a theory now out of favor among modern historians, was that Montezuma feared Cortez was Quetzlcoatl, the light-skinned and bearded god who had been prophesied to return that very year and reclaim his throne (which if true, is a powerful example of confirmation bias at play).

But even if Montezuma did not long suffer from this misapprehension (or perhaps not at all), misunderstandings abounded in other ways. One such example occurred at the meeting of Montezuma and Cortez outside of Tenochtitlan. According to native accounts, Montezuma welcomed Cortez with the following words.

> *Our lord, you are very welcome in your arrival in this land. You have come to satisfy your curiosity about your noble city of Mexico. You have come here to sit on your throne, to sit under its canopy, which I have kept for awhile for you. For the rulers and governors [of past times] have gone: Itzcoatl, Moctezuma I, Axayacatl, Tiçocic, and Ahuitzotl. [Since they are gone], your poor vassal has been in charge for you, to govern the city of Mexico. Will they come back to the place*

of their absence? If even one came, he might witness the marvel that has taken place in my time, see what I am seeing, as the only descendant of our lords. For I am not just dreaming, not just sleepwalking, not seeing you in my dreams. I am not just dreaming that I have seen you and have looked at you face to face. I have been worried for a long time, looking toward the unknown from which you have come, the mysterious place. For our rulers departed, saying that you would come to your city and sit upon your throne. And now it has been fulfilled, you have returned. Go enjoy your palace, rest your body. Welcome our lords to this land.

A surface reading indicates that Montezuma was practically handing Cortez the keys to the kingdom, and indeed, that is exactly the self-serving interpretation that Cortez gave it. However, as scholars of Nahautl have since pointed out, Montezuma seems to have peppered his welcome with a figure of speech called inversion, a common aspect of formal Aztec discourse in which the speaker graciously veils his true meaning by saying the opposite of what he intends to communicate, a little like sarcasm if being sarcastic was a polite thing to do.

If we read the text this way, Montezuma would be saying quite the opposite, something more like, "my ancestors have sat on this throne for a long time, so don't get any ideas." Montezuma would have little reason to suspect that once his speech went through the translation process, his sly inversion would be stripped of its actual intended meaning. Nor would Cortez have had any reason to suspect that Montezuma had meant the exact opposite of what he said.

This turned out to be a lucky misunderstanding for Cortez, who mistook Montezuma for a weak and pliable ruler and so shortly thereafter kidnapped him and held him hostage. It did not turn out so well for Montezuma nor for the Aztecs. After some brief skirmishing in the city in which Montezuma was killed and the Spaniards were temporarily expelled, Cortez returned in 1520 with additional allies: newly arrived Spanish aid from Cuba, reinforcements from his native allies, and a set of tiny killers called smallpox, which by that time had killed nearly half the population of Tenochtitlan. The combined strength of the three (especially the smallpox) was enough to allow the Spaniards to take Tenochtitlan, steal much of its gold, and eventually burn it to the ground.[11]

All of this gives rise to the question of whether the Spanish victory was inevitable. Probably not, I would argue. There are few equivalently important historical events that allow us to see the twin influences of individual choice and sheer dumb luck at work. Had Cortez been less cornered or less bold, perhaps he would never have tried the venture at all. Had Montezuma been more decisive and simply destroyed or captured the Spaniards when he had the chance, we would not remember the expedition of Cortez as the gamble that toppled an empire, but as a footnote---as a reckless and risky failure.

We might also notice that the Spanish conquest was not quite the simple story of a technologically superior civilization violently overpowering a less advanced one. The main Spanish advantage was epidemic disease, which wasn't technological at all, but biological. If they had a technological advantage, it was certainly their steel weaponry and armor, which was stronger than native obsidian blades. This, however, would have been a pretty ineffective advantage if the Spaniards had not been joined by thousands of native allies.[12]

That being the case, you might say that the Spaniards conquered the Aztecs with the help of native peoples. But given the fact that the Spaniards' native allies vastly outnumbered them at almost every moment of the conquest (200 to 1 at the fall of Tenochtitlan), you might just as easily say that the native peoples of Mexico overthrew the Aztecs with the help of the Spaniards. The story, then, is not as simple as it seems.

---

[11] A very readable account of the encounter be found in Michael C. Meyer and William L. Sherman, *The Course of Mexican History* (New York: Oxford University Press), 99-137. For a cogent discussion of the problem of communication, see Matthew Restall, *The Seven Myths of the Spanish Conquest* (New York: Oxford University Press, 2003), 77-98.

[12] See Restall, 140-145.

The Columbian Exchange

The Spanish conquest thereby inaugurated one model of encounter in the Americas: the violent overthrow of native power structures. Violence, however, was not the only mode of encounter. Though the American continents shared some flora and fauna with the "Old World", America and Africa/Eurasia had been physically separated from each other for 200 million years of evolution by the time Columbus set foot on the Bahamas. This meant that contact led to sustained exchanges of biodiversity for the first time in quite a long time, a movement of peoples and goods that has come to be known as the "Columbian Exchange".

One of the major differences between the development of the old world and the Americas was the fact that old world peoples had domesticated many large animals, including cattle, pigs, horses, and donkeys. People living in the Americas had only domesticated one: the llama. On the one hand, this meant that the introduction of old-world animals was a significant boon to Americans, the most obvious of which were the new sources of dietary protein. Moreover, horses that escaped from Spanish captivity arrived on the Great Plains decades before the Europeans that had brought them. When those horses were re-domesticated by the Indians living there, it revolutionized their lifestyle---since hunting buffalo on horseback was a lot more effective than hunting them on foot.

On the other hand, the burden of living in close contact with animals, especially domesticated animals that are ridden, milked, or sometimes even cuddled, is that human diseases jump back and forth. In the process, the diseases mutate, and sometimes become more deadly. The blessings of animal husbandry thereby also gave us the curse of measles, influenza, whooping cough, smallpox, and tuberculosis, among others. Without large, domesticated animals, America had largely been spared both these blessings and these curses. Tropical America had also been largely spared the diseases that bedeviled tropical Africa, probably because in addition to lacking domesticated animals, America also lacked the large primate species which give rise to many such tropical human diseases, namely malaria and yellow fever.

Thus, the history of Europe, Africa, and Asia had been punctuated by the emergence of new diseases arising somewhere along the east-west trade routes, which were then followed by deadly plagues that ravaged the population. Those who had weak immunity would succumb to the disease and remove their DNA from the gene pool. Those who had stronger immunity would pass it on to their children. Thus, over generations, groups of people would develop natural immunities.[13]

What this meant for peoples living in the Americas is that when colonizers brought their animals and their slaves, they also brought their germs. Indeed, on his second voyage, Columbus and many of his men fell ill as soon as they took the pigs out of the hold: the natives, for their part, began to die. Whereas old-world peoples had built up centuries of hard-won immunity from some of these germs, new-world peoples had no such immunity, and the diseases spread like wildfire through the population, resulting in a cataclysmic population loss that robbed America of perhaps as much as 90 percent of its population.[14]

While this demographic catastrophe was occurring, the transmission of new world foodstuffs to the old world was gradually having the opposite effect, prepping Europe for the longest sustained population boom in history. One food that would play an outsized role in this process was the potato, a tuber plant originally grown on the slope of the Andes, but which spread throughout the Atlantic in the early modern period, both northward to the British colonies and across the ocean to Africa and Europe. Though Europeans had begun growing it in a few

---

[13] The classic exposition of this is in Jared Diamond's very popular *Guns, Germs, and Steel* (New York: Norton, 1999).

[14] A very readable and short account of the Columbian exchange in Encounter can be found at Simon L. Lewis and Mark A. Maslin, "How Disease and Conquest Carved a New Planetary Landscape" *The Atlantic* Aug. 24, 2018.

places by the late 16th century, its spread there was surprisingly slow; some people thought the so-called 'devil's apple' spread leprosy; others argued that it caused excessive farting. Nevertheless, the advantages of nutrition-packed potatoes were many, amongst which one was the fact that they grew underground and would therefore not be trampled and destroyed by passing armies. By the eighteenth century, it had caught on in many places, often as the food of the poor, to whom flatulence was preferable to starvation. "What is windiness," asked the Enlightenment thinker Diderot, "to the strong bodies of peasants?"[15]

Like the potato, other foods made the crossing. Europeans brought chickens, coffee, wheat, oranges, apples, sheep, goats, pigs, and bananas to the new world. They also brought foods like turkeys, tomatoes, pumpkins, chilies, and pineapples back to the Old World.[16] West Africans brought the tricky art of art of rice cultivation to the low countries of the Carolinas, while America exported maize cultivation back to Africa.[17] One indication of the global ramifications of the exchange is to consider the fact that the current top producing countries of the potato, chili pepper, tomato, and cocoa (all new world crops) are currently the old world countries of Russia, India, China, and The Ivory Coast, while the top producing countries of such old world crops of coffee and soybeans are Brazil and the United States (respectively).

Indeed, modern cuisine is unimaginable without the Columbian exchange. Italy makes its red sauces with the new world tomato plant. Thailand makes its national dish, pad Thai, with the new world peanut plant. Ghana makes its national dish, fufu, with the new world cassava plant. Koreans make kimchee from chili peppers first grown in America. England gets the chips

---

[15] Fernand Braudel, *The Structures of Everyday Life, Civilization and Capitalism* trans. By Sian Reynolds (New York: Harper and Row, 1979), 167-172.

[16] Guy Settipane, *Columbus and the New World: Medical Implications* (Providence: Oceanside Publications, 1995), 7.

[17] Judith Carney, *Black Rice: the African Origins of Rice Cultivation in the Americas* (Cambridge: Harvard University Press, 2002).

part of fish and chips from the South American potato. On the other hand, all the usual meats that Americans barbeque (that is, made in the Caribbean style of *barbacoa*) come from the Old World. And nearly everyone cooks rice.

New world foods were also blended with old-world foods to make new concoctions. To take one important example, Mesoamericans had long made drinks from cacao beans, which are native to the Amazon but grew well in the hot, humid climate of the Mexican Yucatan. So important was the drink to Mesoamerican societies that cacao beans were sometimes used as a currency, and the Spaniards noted that when Honduran cacao traders accidentally dropped a bean, they stooped to look for the valuable commodity as if 'they had lost an eye.' Columbus and his crew had been offered a drink made from cacao as early as 1502, though they didn't think much of it, finding it bitterly unpleasant. But as Europeans stayed in Mexico, some of them developed a taste for it, and when they brought it back for sale to Europe, they suited it to European palates by mixing it with an old-world sweetener: sugar. To satisfy the market for sugar, Europeans would establish sugar plantations across the Caribbean, Mesoamerica, and Brazil. The Portuguese would bring the plant to the narrow band of equatorial Africa, where they found it grew well and where 75 percent of the world's cocoa supply is produced today.

Along with the exchange of foods, we ought to mention that the age of Atlantic discovery also launched the worldwide drug trade. Indeed, one of the most profitable export crops throughout the period was tobacco, which natives living in North and Central America had usually smoked occasionally and in ritual contexts. Europeans first heard of tobacco from accounts of Columbus' voyage, but it only caught on after it gained a dubious reputation as a cure-all medicine. Though it had its early detractors, (including the King of England himself, James I, who saw it as a noxious and disgusting drug), this criticism didn't stop people throughout the old world from getting addicted to the stuff. Indeed, it was the commercial production of tobacco, which began in Virginia in the early 1600s, that helped that colony survive its early years. Tobacco, you might say, has been the new world's revenge on the old, since it has now killed more people in Europe and Africa than epidemic disease ever did in America.[18]

The example of tobacco and disease should give us pause in the urge to oversimplify the Columbian exchange as an unmitigated blessing. Even the exchange of foodstuffs was not without negative consequences. Sugar is a perfect example. The islands of the Caribbean and the plantations of Mexico, Central America, and Brazil proved to be extremely well suited to the production of the old-world crop of sugar. As a result, worldwide production of sugar soared in the age of encounter. Per capita sugar consumption in Britain increased by 2500 percent between 1650 and 1800. Sugar, unfortunately, brought a whole bunch of unfortunate social consequences, the least of which is that it unleashed an epidemic of tooth decay among the upper-classes. Queen Elizabeth I of England, to take a famous example, was so fond of sweets that her teeth turned black and gave off a foul odor. Most perniciously, though, sugar production happens to be extremely labor intensive, and thus the worldwide demand for sugar became a major impetus for the importation of African slaves to the new world.[19]

Sugar also proved to be easy to distill into a drink we now call rum. People living in the Atlantic World loved rum; colonial New Englanders drank it all day long, while West-African nobles shared it among their clients and paid for it by trading slaves. But a spirit with an alcohol content as high as rum predictably brought in its wake a host of problems of related to public drunkenness. So, I suppose even rum has its drawbacks.

On the other side of this equation sat corn, also a mixed blessing for early modern African societies. Unlike sugar, corn is relatively easy to produce and not so labor-intensive. Because of

---

[18] Peter Mancall, "Tales Tobacco Told in Sixteenth-Century Europe," *Environmental History* 9 no. 4 (2004): 648-678.

[19] The seminal work on sugar is Sidney Mintz's *Sweetness and Power: The Place of Sugar in Modern History* (New York: Penguin, 1985).

its hardiness, its caloric value, and its ability to be stored even in tropical climates, corn was an extremely popular import to early modern Africa. This unfortunately seems to have produced a 'productivity shock', which helped to feed the population boom that made the slave trade sustainable.[20]

Thus, the Columbian exchange teaches us that in complex systems, every advance normally comes with an associated drawback; even something as useful as corn has unintended effects.

The Transatlantic Slave Trade

In a real way then, sugar and corn were the cause and necessary conditions for the trans-Atlantic slave trade. But are these factors enough to explain why it happened? Certainly, greed and opportunity are powerful forces in the affairs of men, but were they enough to make it inevitable?

A point that weighs against the inevitability of African slavery is the successful campaign against the enslavement of natives in Spanish America. Spaniards had begun the age of the encounter with a particularly pitiless campaign of enslavement of the native peoples living in the Caribbean. At least some Spanish observers, such as the Dominican priest Bartolommeo de las Casas, looked on in horror as the earliest conquistadors had abused and mistreated the natives of the Caribbean and Mexico. Over several decades, these early humanitarians had waged what ultimately turned out to be a successful battle to end native slavery and offer some protection for native rights in the Americas. This movement culminated in a 1538 papal decree outlawing the enslavement of indigenous peoples, followed by a set of royal pronouncements in 1542 that provided greater protection for the natives against forced

---

[20] Jevan Cheniwchan and J. Moreno-Cruz, "Maize and Precolonial Africa", *Journal of Development Economics* Vol. 136, 2019, p 137-150.

labor, as well as their legal protection as direct subjects of the Spanish crown.[21]

Ironically, the success of the campaign to protect indigenous Americans' rights may have sealed the fate of African slaves. Las Casas himself, anxious to shield indigenous peoples from the abuses of a slave economy, suggested native labor should be replaced by the importation of African slaves, whom he expected would adjust well to the climate of tropical America. The demand for labor on the newly developing plantation economies of Spanish and Portuguese America was such that Las Casas' suggestion was readily applied.[22]

To the rapidly increasing demand for slave labor in America, Africa added favorable supply-side conditions. Slaveholding, as well as commerce in slaves, had been widespread in Africa for centuries and thus, there was already a robust market into which European slave traders could tap, normally in exchange for goods such as rum, tobacco, guns, iron, and textiles. Historians have placed special emphasis on the role of guns in this trade, since this sort of weaponry theoretically gave African commanders a military advantage that they then might use in warring with their neighbors to thereby procure more slaves. Thus, historians have pointed to a destructive and mutually reinforcing guns-for-slaves cycle that potentially functioned to destabilize West African politics and further open it up to the predatory instincts of European slave traders.[23]

---

[21] The name of the papal bull was *Sublimis Deus.* The name of the series of Spanish laws protecting the natives are generally called the *New Laws.*

[22] Las Casas' most famous work is often called in English by the title *On the Destruction of the Indies.* On Las Casas suggestion that Africans should be used as an alternative labor force, see Hugh Thomas, *The Slave Trade: The Story of the Atlantic Slave Trade:* 1440-1870 (New York: Simon and Schuster, 1997), 98.

[23] John Thornton, *Africa and Africans in the Making of the Atlantic World* (New York: Cambridge University Press, 1996), 116-125. Though it should be noted that the importance of this guns-for-slaves cycle is a matter of dispute among historians.

To demand and supply-side factors, we might another factor: wind. In the Age of Sail, one of the most convenient ways to get around the Atlantic was by sailing south from Europe to the west coast of Africa, catching the trade winds directly across the Atlantic to the Caribbean and finally taking the westerlies up the North American Atlantic coastline and back across to Europe. This incentivized a three-stage journey, in which manufactured goods were brought to Africa, African slaves were transported to America, and raw materials were shipped from America back to Europe: the so-called Triangle Trade. Given these climactic conditions, we might wonder how the age of encounter might have been different if the currents of the Atlantic flowed in the opposite direction.

Though here it is important to caution against an overly deterministic view of the slave trade, as if it were simply the unfortunate result of economic pressures and favorable wind patterns. At least a few European voices, including Las Casas himself once he saw it in action, awoke immediately to the horrors of the slave trade, and then were promptly ignored for centuries. Traditional African slaveholding was generally more assimilative in nature. Captured people and their descendants were usually expected to eventually gain relatively equal status among their captors and to enter their kinship group, whereas slaves transported to sugar plantations in the new world could barely expect to live more than a few years. Few could hope to ever be treated as anything more than property. In response to this new kind of slavery, some African nations did successfully limit or proscribe the exportation of slaves, though many did not.

Furthermore, though slavery existed in America, Europe and Africa for centuries beforehand (and has been vicious and dehumanizing everywhere it has occurred), it is scarcely possible to imagine how much more vicious and dehumanizing the transatlantic type usually was. Captives died *en masse* as they were marched to the coast in shackles and made to await the slaving ships from Europe. From there they were packed as tightly as possible onto specially rigged vessels and made to suffer a grueling month-long journey across the Atlantic. So inhumane were conditions in the middle passage that boats had to be rigged with special netting to keep captives from committing suicide by leaping overboard. For those who survived, the completion of the journey provided little relief. Most were destined for the sugar plantations of Brazil and the Caribbean, where life was brutal and often short. Between overwork, maltreatment, and accident, the average lifespan for a slave on a sugar plantation was four to seven years. Around 12 million people were brought to the new world in this way.[24]

From those who captured slaves to those who brutally seasoned them into their roles on plantations, the slave trade required many participants willing to exercise violence. However, one feature of the trade that is perhaps morally new and tragically modern was how it also relied on widespread, systemic complicity from people who never had to directly witness its consequences. It required, for instance, a failure of moral imagination from bureaucrats in England, who did things like order suicide netting to be added to the slaving vessels they commissioned without being overwhelmed by moral qualms about the sort of conditions that required such nets. It also required the moral resignation of consumers, from rum-drinkers in the British Colonies, to tobacco-smokers on the African coast, to chocolate-drinkers in Spain. Many of these people never even saw a slave (much less owned one) but nevertheless benefitted from slavery in the cheapness of the products they consumed. Far too many do not seem to have inquired too profoundly into the human misery that produced them. Against the argument of inevitability, then, is the perhaps naively conceived possibility that people could have drunk less rum, smoked less tobacco, and eaten less sugar.

For their part, African slaves struggled to reassert and recreate their traditional cultures, sometimes with more and sometimes with less success. To take a few examples, historians have recognized the survival of African notions of kinship, sociability,

---

[24] On of the best works on the Middle Passage is Markus Rediker's *Slave Ship: A Human History* (New York: Penguin, 2008).

and religion in many diaspora societies. There is no one who would seriously doubt the well-documented influence of African art and music throughout the Atlantic World. And of course, out of the crucible of slavery, African traditions of political liberty would live on, producing many of the most eloquent modern voices for the expansion of freedom and the guarantee of individual rights.[25]

Evangelization and Religious Hybridity

The last topic that we will cover in this chapter concerns the expansion of Christianity to non-Christians living in the Atlantic. Here again, we typically get two versions of this story. In the first, which sees the story of Atlantic expansion as a mostly good thing, the missionary endeavor was probably the most undeniably good part, since at the very least, it saved indigenous populations from the 'odd superstitions' of their native religions, such as witchcraft, cannibalism, and human sacrifice. In the second story, the imposition of Christianity was one of the worst parts of the Atlantic encounter since it tended to wipe out native cultures and since it exposed the whole project as hypocritical from the beginning. As you might now expect, I tend to believe the story is a bit more complicated than either of those renditions would have us believe.

The first thing that we need to understand about the early modern Christianity that missionaries brought to the Atlantic world is that by the time it crossed the ocean, it had largely already fractured into two competing camps, the battle lines largely forming between the champions of Protestantism in England, Northern Germany and Holland and the champions of Catholicism in Spain, Portugal, France, and Italy. The argument, first articulated and defended by Martin Luther at roughly the

---

[25] There are an increasing number of good historical studies on African culture in the diaspora. One very good one remains James Sweet, *Recreating Africa: Culture, Kinship and Religion in the African-Portuguese World, 1441-1770* (Chapel Hill: North Carolina Press, 2003).

same time as the conquest of Mexico, started largely as a theological one: whether good works had any role at all in helping Christians achieve salvation (Luther said no; Catholics said, 'sort of'). It then extended into a debate about church authority. Who or what should we look to in order to resolve such theological debates? (Protestants mostly argued for scripture, while Catholics mostly deferred to the papacy). Finally, when repeated attempts at compromise had failed, it flared up into religious violence, in a century of inquisitions, religious executions, forced migrations, civil wars, and deadly conflicts.[26]

That being the case, the missionary project of converting Atlantic populations was, unsurprisingly, a highly competitive endeavor. For Catholics and Protestants alike, part of winning meant 'winning souls'. New Catholic religious orders such as the Jesuits and the Capuchins set out to gain converts in Africa and America in order to make up for the ones that had been lost in Europe. And by some metrics, they did. Catholic preachers, who followed in the wake of the conquistadors, made mass conversions in Latin America in the first few generations after the conquest, while the Portuguese snared a major victory for Christianity in 1491, when the King of Congo converted to Christianity and urged his subjects to follow him into the faith.

For Protestants in 17th century British North America, Catholicism's lead in the game was a matter of great anxiety, though the early Catholic successes were not matched by the Protestants there. The Virginia colonists made sporadic attempts to convert natives, which had limited success. Pocahontas, for instance, converted to Christianity, but she was not followed into the faith by many of her people. More success was had in the Massachusetts Bay colony, where native converts were collected into so-called 'praying towns', whereby they might be turned into good Englishmen as well as good Christians. These experiments mostly did not survive the outbreak of war between the settlers

---

[26] The basic story of the Reformation can be found in many places. The one I find most readable is Patrick Collinson's *The Reformation: A History* (New York: Random House 2003).

and natives, though the motivating idea (expressed in the aphorism that the Indian must be killed so that the man might be saved) continued to inform conversion practices throughout American history, sometimes with tragic results.

A head start was not the only advantage Catholicism had over its' Protestant rivals. In many respects, early modern Catholicism had a lot more in common with the religious sensibilities of the peoples of the Atlantic than did its Protestant rivals, especially the Calvinist-inflected versions prominent among the English and the Dutch. Early modern Catholics practiced what anthropologists call a more immanent version of Christianity; that is, they were more likely than Protestants to see God's presence in the material world, or at least, to see the material world as a pathway to the divine. The clearest and most controversial aspect of this was the Catholic doctrine of the Eucharist, which Catholics believed became the physical body and blood of Christ during the mass, and which Calvinists, in contrast, considered a symbol. But the differences could be seen elsewhere. Post-Reformation Catholics doubled down on adorning their churches with statues and images: Calvinists tore such things down and left the walls of their churches bare. Catholics decorated their crucifixes with the immanently human figure of the dying Christ; Calvinists preferred the more abstractly symbolic empty cross. Catholics continued to invoke the saints in prayer (Saint Blaise to cure an ailing throat, Saint Anthony to find lost objects), Protestants preferred to speak directly to God. Catholic communities continued to seek and promote miracles, responding to outbreaks of drought or the plague with processions to and from local miraculous images; Protestants viewed processions as an almost unimaginable superstition and debated whether miracles even still happened. To put all of this in the language of Catholicism's Protestant critics: the problem with Catholicism was that it was deeply and hopelessly imbued with pagan idolatry. The English even had a name for it: popery.[27]

---

[27] For more on this dynamic in missionary competition, see my Gregory Murry "Tears of the Indians or Superficial Conversion? José de

On the level of popular piety, that was probably a fair criticism. Catholicism did allow for a wide range of devotions that had originally been drawn from pagan Europe. This flexibility, however, turned out to be a major advantage when trying to convert the pagans of early modern America and Africa, since it made for quite a lot of overlap. Early missionaries in the Congo, for instance, ran into a stroke of luck when they found that the cruciform was already a sacred symbol in Congolese cosmology, representing, much as it did for Catholics, the links between the world of the dead and the world of the living.[28] To take another example, missionaries among the Aztecs were both fortunate and a bit flustered to discover one Aztec ritual involved baking corn dough into an idol of the war god, then breaking it into pieces, sharing it, and eating it (as the body of the god), much like the Catholic Eucharist.[29]

Rather than, for instance, just getting rid of all these pagan practices, Catholic missionaries sometimes intentionally channeled them into Catholic observances. For instance, Congolese blacksmiths specialized in casting beautiful iron crosses that combined Christian and traditional Congolese iconography.[30] Spanish priests moved the traditional native celebrations of the dead to November, in order to coincide with All Saints Day. In a hybrid festival that combines both pre-Christian and Christian elements, Mexicans to this day construct elaborate altars (known as *ofrendas*), with the favorite goods and foods of their deceased relatives, who are thought to return to the land of the living to consume them. In such a way, Spanish Catholicism was able to reconcile (albeit uneasily), Christian concerns for the afterlife with preconquest concerns to preserve familial links between the living

---

Acosta, the Black Legend, and Spanish Evangelization in the New World" *The Catholic Historical Review* 99 no 1, 2013.

[28] Cécile Fromont, *The Art of Conversion: Christian Visual Culture in the Kingdom of Kongo* (Chapel Hill: University of North Carolina Press, 2014), 65-109.

[29] See Murry, 36-37.

[30] Fromont, 70.

and the dead. Even the most famous American religious image, Our Lady of Guadalupe, has unmistakable links to the Aztec Mother goddess Tonantzin, on whose hill she sits.[31] Church officials did draw hard and fast lines at outright idol worship, cannibalism, and human sacrifice, but in between there was a lot of gray area. As a result, Catholicism did not so much displace other Atlantic religious traditions, then, as it merged with them and created new religious forms, a phenomenon that is known as syncretism.

Some of these forms went beyond the bounds of what the Church was willing to tolerate. One such hybrid arose in Congo in the early 18th century, when a Congolese woman named Dona Beatriz Kimpa Vita, claimed to be possessed by the spirit of Saint Anthony. In this, Dona Beatriz was already combining reverence for Christian saints with the traditional Congolese (and widespread West African practice) of spirit possession. Sources tell us that she had trained as a Nganga Marinda, a shaman who invites the possession of beneficent spirits into her body to perform white magic. Dona Beatriz preached a two-fold message, one which urged the civil war-ravaged Congolese to unite under one monarch, and another which outlined a distinctively Congolese brand of Christianity, preaching salvation by a black Christ and rewriting the history of the Gospel to locate Jesus' birthplace in Congo. Her successes were short-lived, however, as she was captured by one of the rival claimants to the Congolese throne, and at the urging of Capuchin missionaries, burned as a witch in 1706.[32]

Other similar hybrids sprung up in the African diaspora communities living in the Caribbean, Brazil, and the southern United States. In Cuba, this new religion took the name of Santeria. In Brazil, Candomblé. Most famously, in Haiti and the

---

[31] This is a much disputed point, though it is worth noting that even early missionaries debated about whether the natives who traveled to Tepeyac were actually worshipping Tonantzin in the guise of Our Lady.

[32] John Thornton, *The Kongolese Saint Anthony: Dona Beatriz Kimpa Vita and the Antonian Movement, 1684-1706* (Cambridge: Cambridge University Press, 1998).

Southern United States, it took the name voodou. These new religions were based on the pantheon of spirit deities from West African cosmology, as well as the practice of spirit possession, in which the deities were invited to inhabit the body of a medium and plied with goods like alcohol and candy in exchange for their help. Probably to hide what was going on from their masters, practitioners of these religion gave these spirit deities the persona of Catholic saints. In this way, the West African cosmology (including the idea of a supreme God, who in voodou is known as Bon-Dye) was 'mapped on" to the Catholic religion. Thus, Legba, the intermediary deity between the gates of the living and the gates of the dead in Voodou, became associated with Saint Peter (who holds the keys between heaven and hell). The female deity Erzulie was associated with the Virgin Mary, especially the black Madonna of Czestochowa (a miraculous, dark-skinned Czech image of the Virgin Mary). Damballa, the serpent deity, was associated with Saint Patrick, ironically famous for chasing the snakes out of Ireland. For centuries, these hybrid religious traditions persisted uneasily with the official Catholic faith, with adherents often practicing Voodoo on Saturday and Catholicism on Sunday. Haiti, as a traditional saying goes, is today 70 percent Catholic, 30 percent Protestant, and 100 percent Voodoo. How the official Church should relate to voodou remains contentious to this day.[33]

As a final topic, we might take a moment here to discuss the sincerity of the conversions that were made. Here again, the problem of double mistaken identity rears its head. Missionaries had their own motivations and confirmation biases in assuming that the peoples they encountered were ready and willing to adopt Christianity. It appears that the missionaries' hopes were not completely ill-founded. At least some Africans and indigenous Americans were indeed ready to adopt the Christian god and the

[33] A very good introduction to the historical and sociological origins of Vodou can be found in Leslie G. Desmangles *The Faces of the Gods: Vodou and Roman Catholicism in Haiti* (Chapel Hill: University of North Carolina Press, 1992).

Christian faith, and there is good evidence to suggest that many of these conversions were sincere. The problem came in a misunderstanding about what exactly conversion meant. For polytheists, sincere adoption of the Christian God did not always seem to require total abandonment of their traditional gods. Sometimes, this only became apparent to the missionaries after many years of laboring in the vineyard. The Franciscan bishop of Yucatan, Diego de Landa, spent decades believing that he was making progress in spreading Christianity to the Maya, only to realize in 1562 that many native converts had not, in fact, given up their idols. Upon discovering this, Landa unleashed a brutal inquisition on them, in which many natives were tortured, and many Maya manuscripts burned.[34]

For others, conversion was clearly just a politically expedient thing to do. For King Nzinga Nkuwu of Congo, conversion to Christianity was a way to make an alliance with the Portuguese, but probably did not represent a full-throated endorsement of the new faith since he abandoned Christianity when he found out that it would require him to give up polygamy. His son, Nzinga Mbemba, seems to have been more enthusiastic, as he built Christian schools, campaigned against idolatry, and perhaps more signally, took only one official wife.

It's probably useful to note here that motives for evangelization were mixed too---usually neither entirely pure nor entirely cynical. If we can believe his letters, Hernan Cortez never hesitated to lecture either his native allies or his native enemies about the need to abandon their gods and convert to Christianity, a practice that probably was at odds with his military aims. It is also abundantly clear that he utilized Christianity as a convenient pretext for widescale violence and looting. Likely the motives of Jesuit, Franciscan, and Dominican missionaries who formed the first wave of missionaries were purer. It is among these religious orders that we find some of the earliest and most ardent defenders of African and Indian rights. Nonetheless, it is also among these

[34] Matthew Restall, *Maya Conquistador* (Boston: Beacon Street, 1998) 12-17.

orders that we find some of the most terrifyingly intolerant figures as well, such as the aforementioned Diego de Landa.

Thus, missionary work has an ambivalent place in the history of encounter. On the one hand, it sometimes helped to shield Africans and indigenous Americans from the worst abuses of encounter, and European missionaries were successful in rooting out practices such as cannibalism and human sacrifice. On the other hand, it also functioned as a justifying motivation for patently unjust instances of violence and conquest. As for the preservation of native cultures, Christianity helped both to preserve and to destroy them, sometimes even by the same agents. In addition to being a brutal inquisitor who destroyed some truly irreplaceable Mayan manuscripts, Diego de Landa is one of our best sources for knowledge about precontact Mayan beliefs. Finally, in many cases, we can identify pure motivations for conversion and evangelization, but it is also exceedingly rare to find pure spiritual motivations unmixed with political or economic ones. In the last analysis, how you feel about this aspect of encounter is probably at least partially conditioned by your own views on the value of Christianity in the first place.

Conclusion

In many real ways, we now live in the aftermath of the Atlantic encounter. From the foods we eat, to the places we grow them, to the ways we trade for them; from the languages we speak to the way we worship; from the music we consume to the art we produce, from the ways we think about civilization to the ways we think about freedom and liberty; from the heroes that we celebrate to the villains that we despise, we are products of the choices made in the Age of Encounter. To live as free people in the modern world requires us to look squarely and honestly at those choices, in order that we might embrace or reject them.

Ways of Knowing in Early Modernity

By: Sean Lewis

How do we know what we know? This question is central to *epistemology*, the study of what knowledge is, how it is produced, and how it is transmitted. That sounds fairly abstract (and it is), but questions of epistemology affect us every day. What will the weather be like this afternoon? How did the recent election turn out? Does this injury merit a visit to the doctor? To answer all these questions, you need to seek knowledge, but what counts as actual knowledge and authoritative sources for knowledge are topics that you might take for granted. By the end of this chapter, I hope that you do not take them for granted. How we imagine knowledge in the 21st century has been shaped incontrovertibly by how early modernity explored ways of knowing.

Premodern Ways of Knowing

Before the early modern period, in Antiquity and the Middle Ages, knowledge was inextricably linked to tradition and authority. This is not to say that individuals could not formulate their own opinions and worldviews—the philosophers, writers, and characters you've already studied are proof of this fact. But a heavy premium was placed on traditional beliefs and opinions. Consider the resistance Socrates faced by questioning the norms of Athens: when in doubt, the traditional way tended to be the preferred way. The canon of texts and authors was relatively fixed: books were produced by hand (on scrolls in antiquity, manuscripts in the Middle Ages), and thus relatively expensive. If you wanted to have a book made for you, you were going to choose something long recognized as valuable and authoritative. In the Western Middle Ages, this meant that the Bible was by far the most copied, read, and heard text, with Latin Classics coming in second (Cicero, Virgil, and Ovid were particularly popular). New works were certainly produced over the Middle Ages, but these works often authorized themselves by reference to texts that were already recognized as classics (consider Dante's use of Virgil in *The Divine Comedy*).

Authorship and authority went together, and it is not surprising that premodern knowledge also gave great deference to authority, whether that authority was a canonical author (no one beats Aristotle, right?) or a person in authority (if the king or pope says so, it's true, right?). On the one hand, this makes sense: with the spread of knowledge moving at a much slower rate than we are used to, the texts and traditions that have worked for generations (and the institutions that they support and that support them) could be taken for granted to work for future generations. If it was good enough for your beloved ancestors, it was good enough for you. On the other hand, particularly by the end of the Middle Ages, questions began to form over the nature and scope of authority. Geoffrey Chaucer's famous Wife of Bath from *The Canterbury Tales* (c. 1390) begins her prologue with the dichotomy between authority and experience in matters of marriage: "Experience, though no authority / Were in this world, is right enough for me / To speak of woe that is marriage."[35] What happens when your own experiences appear to contradict established authorities? That phenomenon would become a more frequent one as early modernity developed, leading to a shift away from authority and tradition in various ways.

Precursors: The Renaissance and Reformations

The first development in this shift was the Renaissance. While there were several explosions of knowledge and art throughout the Middle Ages (such that we can speak of the Islamic Renaissance, the Carolingian Renaissance, and the Chartrian Renaissance), the

---

[35] *The Canterbury Tales*, III.D.1-3, spelling modernized by Lewis.

explosion of knowledge and art in Italy towards the end of the Middle Ages had two major differences. In the first place, it benefitted from the fall of Byzantium by having scores of Greek scholars come to Italy with their texts—the Florentine Academy, in particular, became a leading center for the revival of Greek language, literature, and philosophy in the West.[36] In the second place, it lasted long enough to overlap with the advent of the printing press in Europe, imported from China and popularized by Johannes Gutenberg.[37] This meant that this last medieval Renaissance was associated with a relatively rapid expansion of the canon: scholars encountered new works of antiquity, both "lost" works of Latin authors, and, more importantly, the "lost" Greek texts of Plato, Homer, Sophocles, and others. These texts were "new" to Western Christendom, and encountering them gave the sense of an intellectual project that was open in new ways: tradition and authority were still important, but what happens when you find new authorities in your tradition? A new intellectual project was underway, and within 50 years of the introduction of the press, writers and publishers felt its effects: books of all kinds, but particularly canonical texts became much more widely available, and the press encouraged new writers to circulate their work through print. A corollary to this Renaissance project (which we will see in many of our primary texts) was the view that antique texts should be used to shape our *current* world: now that we have a much richer knowledge of classical texts and ideas, those ideas should be put into practice to change our current world for the better.

Keep an eye out for when authors we read cite classical texts and authors—they will do so throughout the course, and the Classics remain an important way of knowing throughout early modernity. As book production and literacy increased, knowing by *reading* became an important early modern category. By the 18th century, there was the notion of the "Republic of Letters": the claim

---

[36] See Colin Wells, *Sailing from Byzantium* (Random House, 2006).

[37] Elizabeth Eisenstein makes this case in *The Printing Press as an Agent of Change* (Cambridge University Press, 1982).

that those who are well read (regardless of faith, nationality, background, or even gender) form a kind of society, carrying on intellectual conversations across the globe. This use of texts would have highly positive effects, but also negative or complicated ones. Neoclassical arts (often inspired by Neoplatonism) have left their mark on Western arts to this day in architecture, art, drama, literature, and music. Ancient political philosophy would cause thinkers to question the status quo of social and political arrangements. On the other hand, classical treatments of "barbarians" would become a touchstone for how Europeans were to understand Native Americans. Aristotle's ideas about natural law and "natural slaves" would have a profoundly negative effect on discourses concerning colonialism and enslavement. Applying old ideas to new situations does not always yield good fruit.

The scholars of the Renaissance are called Humanists for their interest in the Humanities (literature, art, ethics, politics, history, et al.), but they were by no means "secular": the most prominent Humanists of the era were deeply religious, including Desiderius Erasmus ("prince of the humanists" and a Catholic priest), Pius II (a pope), Philip Melanchthon (a Protestant reformer), Thomas More (a saint in the Catholic and Anglican Churches), and Sir Philip Sidney (a model Protestant intellectual). It is no wonder, then, that their interest in texts and languages would be applied to the most important text of their world: the Bible. Better knowledge of Hebrew and Greek (the languages in which most of the books of the Bible were written) led to better editions and translations of the scriptures, both in Latin (the common liturgical language) and various vernaculars (before 1500 there were already French, Dutch, German, Spanish, and Italian translations of the Bible in circulation). As noted above, the Bible was about as authoritative a text as one could get, and this greater accessibility to Bibles coincided with real abuses of authority in the Church.

The Protestant and Catholic Reformations are too important and complex for this short section to do justice, but we do need some understanding of what occurred in them to understand how ways of knowing developed in early modernity. The end of the

Middle Ages saw various controversies and crises in the authority of the Catholic Church. From 1309 to 1376, the Bishop of Rome, the Pope, lived in Avignon, France, and was strongly influenced by the French king. The pope was not the only bishop who did not live in his own diocese: several bishops preferred living in more luxurious places than their own dioceses (which they were supposed to be ministering to, right?). From 1378 to 1417, Western Europe had *two* popes: one in Avignon and one in Rome, and the situation was so confusing that canonized saints took different sides. The quality of the clergy and religious took a hit after the Black Death, since holy men and women who ministered to the sick and dying had a tendency to get sick and die themselves. Late 14th century texts bear witness to corruption in the Church in this period.[38] To top it all off, the world around 1500 saw two of the least popish popes in history: Alexander VI (1431-1503), who kept mistresses in the Vatican and spent most of his energy promoting his children's political careers, and Julius II (1443-1513), who spent most of his energy conquering parts of central Italy with his army.

These problems with Church authorities coincided with an intellectual movement that ended up privileging authority to reason: the end of the Middle Ages was characterized by nominalism, a scholastic movement inspired by William of Ockham (1287-1347), father of "Occam's razor" (don't multiply causes needlessly in your explanations of reality). Nominalism is complicated, but it essentially denies the reality of universals: concepts like "justice," "human nature," or "tree" are simply words (*nomina*) that we use to refer to individual entities that are somehow similar. Nominalism *did* help effect a turn to the natural sciences (studying individual entities, rather than universal concepts), but it was utterly damaging to philosophy and theology: how can we consider questions of good and evil when "good" and "evil" are merely words, not real concepts? A pious answer to this question was faith and authority: reason might be highly limited,

---

[38] While both devout Catholic Christians, Geoffrey Chaucer (c. 1342-1400) and William Langland (1332-1386) do not mince words in their works over corruption in the Church and the State.

but we can have faith in God, the Scriptures, and the Church. Notice that at least two terms in that list were becoming quite complicated in this period.

Martin Luther (1483-1546) was born into this world and this Church, and as a university professor of theology, trained in the nominalist tradition (almost all universities were nominalist by his day). His Humanist-informed study of the Bible and his distaste for Church corruption (particularly abuses in the practices of selling indulgences, a kind of way of buying merit) led him ultimately to begin the Protestant Reformation. Luther's solution to the problems of his world was simple and elegant: go back to scripture. The problem is that the Bible is a complex collection of texts, written by various human authors, in various languages, in multiple genres, over centuries. Scholars and clergy in the Reformation, of course, believed that matters were a bit simpler (that Moses wrote the Pentateuch word for word, or that the Holy Spirit inspired texts verbatim). Even so, questions about Scripture often came down to this question of authority: whose interpretation is correct? The Catholic answer had been "what the Church says." But Luther, through his view that the text *itself* would be sufficient and sufficiently clear (*sola scriptura*) and his view of the priesthood of all believers, thoroughly denied the authority of the pope in resolving doctrinal disputes. Three months after excommunication, Luther was hauled before an imperial court (the Diet of Worms) and told to recant his opinions. Luther held firm, famously claiming:

> *Unless I am convinced by scripture and plain reason, I do not accept the authority of the popes and councils, for they have contradicted each other. My conscience is captive to the Word of God. I cannot and I will not recant anything, for to go against conscience is neither right nor safe. Here I stand, I can do no other. God help me. Amen.*

Sadly, there is no such thing as a "self-interpreting" text: it always relies on a community of interpreters. Luther found this out first-hand in an argument with one of his admirers, the Swiss reformer Ulrich Zwingli (1484-1531). Luther interpreted John 6 to mean that Jesus is truly present in the Eucharist; Zwingli read that chapter to mean that Jesus is only symbolically present in the Eucharist. While Protestant Christianity justified and encouraged individuals to read the Bible, Protestant *Traditions* formed around different interpretive communities and their answers to such scriptural controversies (Lutherans, Calvinists, Dutch Reformed, Quakers etc.). For each interpretation, Christian practices of worship might change as well – such as if or when a Christian should be baptized, or how one should confess one's sins.

Such controversies were often exacerbated by the nominalist background of Catholic and Protestant scholars. The humanist, anti-nominalist Erasmus engaged in Ciceronian probable reasoning to articulate his stance on Scripture and free will in *On the Freedom of the Will* (1524). While the Bible and experience could support either argument, Erasmus thought that it is much more probable that we have some kind of free will. Nominalist Luther answered him in *On the Bondage of the Will* (1525) with the assertion: probability is itself a problem, and the Scriptures clearly show that we do not have free will. These debates and those that followed concerning ideas of salvation and sacraments represented real doctrinal differences with life and death consequences. Getting Christianity wrong may mean sending oneself and one's neighbors to damnation, and many likewise feared that God may even punish wrongdoing or wrong belief through plague, catastrophic weather events, or monstrous births. These fears no doubt helped to justify the wars of religion that marked the period, and also justified the institution of the Papal Inquisition and Spanish Inquisition, courts entrusted with ensuring correct belief.

Ultimately, the Reformation notion of Biblical reading, simply reading the "text itself," would have important consequences to early modern ways of knowing. It started the process of individual interpretation and using that individual interpretation to challenge authority. The Catholic Church responded to the same problems with its own Reformation, culminating in the Council of

Trent (1545-65). While more traditional and authoritarian than many of the Protestant Reformations, the Catholic Reformation did mark a palpable break from late medieval ways of knowing and practicing the faith. Great Catholic reformers, like St. Ignatius of Loyola (1491-1556) and St. Teresa of Avila (1515-1582) challenged Church authorities (while acknowledging their legitimacy). Humanism in the Catholic world led to an explosion of scholarship and science, and notions of reading also became important. If we need to read the Book of Scripture more carefully, why not also read the Book of Nature more closely as well? The Reformations left Western Europe split religiously, but with renewed vigor and confidence in their own respective Christian traditions, and an imperative to support those traditions with arguments drawn from the best scholarship available. The best scholarship available would soon be more challenging to the status quo than any reformer could have imagined.

Early Modern Knowledge: Traditional

It is important to note that Renaissance Humanism and Reformation arguments set the stage for shifts in ways of knowing seen in early modernity. It is also important to note that many thinkers retained a highly traditional sense of knowledge throughout the period. The Platonic tradition held that knowledge, *episteme,* was ultimately a divine gift, provided by illumination by the Good (later God)—it was infused in one's mind by something beyond the human, and contrasted to mere human opinion, *doxa.* The Aristotelian tradition kept knowledge and opinion but added a third term (as Aristotle usually did): *endoxa,* reasoned opinion, which came from observation, experience, and what was commonly held to be true. Nothing divine was necessary: one simply had to observe and use one's own powers of reason. These traditions lived alongside one another through the Western Middle Ages into early modernity, and both were seen as valid.

Empiricism and divine illumination may seem like they are opposites, but both are evident in much of the religious writing of the period. Teresa of Avila's treatment of her visions and the Nican Mopua's account of the apparition of Our Lady of Guadalupe take for granted that the way we ordinarily know things is through our senses: that is why it is so extraordinary when something like a vision or an apparition takes place. How does Teresa know Jesus is talking with her? How does Juan Diego know that he encounters the Blessed Virgin Mary? Because they are seeing and hearing them. Skeptics of their spiritual encounters certainly could posit explanations that discount divinity (mental illness, hallucination, etc.), but most people throughout early modernity took for granted that the world has a natural order, but that natural order can be occasionally modified by a miracle. And how do we know that miracles occur? By trusting in the authority of the person who reports that miracle. Without being credulous (believing *everything* one is told), one can articulate reasons for trusting the credibility of a source outside one's own experience. Some level of trust in the authority of others remains an important part of our way of knowing: we trust that weather and traffic reports are made by credible people, and respond to them as such.[39]

Early Modern Knowledge: The Scientific Revolution

The first challenge to traditional epistemologies came from the Scientific Revolution. The Scientific Revolution is too large to be contained in a short chapter. Still, the outline is clear: it is the continuation of medieval empirical sciences, but with two vital additions: 1. Renaissance freedom to rethink old models; 2. New tools to increase human experiential abilities. These two features would challenge traditional, authoritative models of the world.

One of the first events in the Scientific Revolution was a shift away from a geocentric model of the cosmos (the earth is center of the solar system; this is what the ancient astronomer Ptolemy

[39] Robert A. Orsi has traced the persistence of this way of knowing through the 21st century in America in *History and Presence* (Harvard University Press, 2016).

taught) to a heliocentric model (the sun is the center of the solar system). This process began with a need for reformation in the calendar. When Julius Caesar reformed the old Roman calendar, he fixed the year at 365.25 days. Unfortunately, a year is actually more like 365.24 days. This small difference had a noticeable effect over the centuries: by the 1500s, it was clear that the calendar did not match the stars. Nicholas Copernicus (1473-1543) was the Polish priest, lawyer, and mathematician commissioned to fix it. Over the course of his calculations, he realized that the entirety of the celestial model would be clearer if the earth revolved around the sun. Copernicus' heliocentric model made astronomy much simpler, and, as a theory, it circulated throughout the 16th and 17th centuries, living alongside the more traditional, authoritative Ptolemaic model. To be fair to Ptolemy, what we *observe* in common experience looks an awful lot like the earth is fixed and the sun is moving around it: to this day, we talk about "sunrise" and "sunset," though we know that "earthturn" would be a more accurate term. Furthermore, Ptolemaic astronomy is good enough for basic calculations of the seasons (very important for farming societies) and had worked for generations.

Enter Galileo Galilei (1564-1642), a brilliant astronomer, mathematician, and physicist, who wedded Copernican theory to new technology. Galileo perfected the astronomical telescope of his age. He could observe things that astronomers without telescopes simply could not. When asked how he knew that there were multiple centers of rotation in the solar system (contradicting both Ptolemy and Aristotle, much to the horror of many), his clear response was: I have observed the moons of Jupiter! Galileo continued to work on empirical principles, but his empiricism—what he could observe, measure, and study—was enhanced through specialized technology which made him authoritative in his claims, in opposition to established authorities. No wonder Galileo often sought to convince his skeptics by inviting them to look through his telescope. As he wrote to his friend, Johannes Kepler, in a letter in 1610, "Here at Padua is the principal professor of theology, whom I have repeatedly and urgently requested to look at the moon and planets through my glass, which he obstinately refused to do."

Some Christians, both Catholic and Protestant, were wary of Galileo's teachings because of a few passages in the Bible (particularly the Book of Joshua, in which God miraculously causes the sun to stand still, implying that it revolves around the earth). The Grand Duchess Christina was one such critic, thinking that Galileo's new science undermined faith. What is his answer to her in his letter? He focuses not so much on her as on his critics, who apparently haven't heard of St. Augustine's *De Doctrina Christiana*, which teaches that *not all Scripture is literal* (Galileo is being *really* salty to his critics: Augustine's work had been a major authority on scriptural interpretation for over 1,000 years by that point). Passages in scripture that seem to defy reason need to be read symbolically. How does Galileo support both the claims of faith and the claims of reason? Do you agree with his stance? Galileo lived and died a pious Catholic Christian, even though the Catholic Inquisition ultimately said that he could not teach publicly and sentenced him to live under house arrest (in a beautiful villa in Tuscany, but still). Though Galileo did not see any necessary opposition between faith and reason, the epistemological problems of his *critics* set early modernity on a dichotomous path: do we accept the authority of the scripture or our own scientific reasoning? Galileo would have seen that as a false dichotomy; his later fans asserted that that dichotomy was real.

The underlying debate between the Copernican and older model of the universe, moreover, showed that ancients and moderns seemed to disagree about the very nature of the universe itself. Was the universe, as Aristotle seemed to suggest, like a living organism that propelled each of its parts towards some 'end' or *telos*? Or was the universe more like a machine, a divine cosmic clock that ticked away through eternity according to unchangeable laws? Should scientists probe the secrets of the universe as Galileo had done, by observation, experiment, and measurement, or should they take the word of Aristotle's own observations, which carried the weight of authority and custom on their side?

In the wake of Galileo's trial, one of his disciples, a man named Evangelista Torricelli, conducted a series of experiments with vacuum chambers that illustrated the stark differences of worldview. Ancient writers knew from their own observations that water would fill up a vacuum. Pump the air out of a tube, and water can rise into the empty space. This is, in essence, how every straw works. How, though, does one explain *why* it happens? Aristotle had argued that the water filled the empty space because "nature abhors a vacuum," as if nature was a person with thoughts and feelings who could either like or abhor anything. Torricelli's experiments proved otherwise. He set out to understand why, pump as one might, water cannot be lifted higher than thirty-three feet. Hypothesizing that water in a suction pump was being pushed up the tube by the weight of the atmosphere, Torricelli surmised that water stopped rising in a vacuum when the weight of the water in the tube equaled the force of the atmosphere pressing down on it. To test his theory, he filled his tube with a denser liquid: mercury, which he knew was about 14 times as dense as water. If he was right, the weight of the atmosphere should hold the mercury approximately 1/14 as high as it held the water, or about two and half feet, which is exactly what it did. Almost by accident, Torricelli had invented the first barometer. Thus, water did not rise in a vacuum chamber because "nature abhors a vacuum," but because it was being pressed upon by the weight of the atmosphere.[40] Indeed, the water was behaving according to mechanical laws, laws that could be proven by observation and then predicted and manipulated.

The final death blow was delivered to Aristotle's universe by a professor of mathematics at Cambridge University named Isaac Newton, whose wild unkempt hair and habit of muttering to himself at the lunch table made him the prototype of the kooky, genius academic. Newton was responsible for an almost embarrassing number of discoveries: he made important contributions to the science of optics, he improved upon Galileo's

---

[40] Steve Shapin, *The Scientific Revolution* (Chicago: University of Chicago Press, 1996), 37-40.

telescope, and he practically invented calculus from scratch.[41] Nevertheless, Newton's work in physics brought him immortality. His greatest moment of insight came in a flash. While sitting in his garden one day, he saw an apple fall from a tree. He had been studying the motion of the moon, and in a moment, the idea came to him: what if the force that drew the apple to the ground was the same force that kept the moon in orbit around the earth? Here were the seeds of Newton's great discovery, which he called gravity. Newton would spend the next twenty years working out the mathematics behind gravity, although work on his greatest achievement, *Principia Mathematica,* only began in earnest in 1681, when he and his good friend Edmund Halley were stimulated by the appearance of a comet blazing in the night sky.

When Newton's *Principia* appeared in 1687, it was far more widely praised than read. Yet the scientific community immediately understood its importance; for Newton was able to describe the mathematical basis behind a whole range of observed motion. Why do objects accelerate towards earth? Gravity. Why do the planets orbit around the sun in an ellipse rather than a circle? Gravity. Why do the tides come in? Gravity. Why did Galileo's moons of Jupiter appear as they did? Gravity.[42] The theory, which in its barest essentials could be reduced to a simple mathematical formula, seemed to explain practically everything. Newton had called his discoveries by the Latin word *lex,* or law. For Newton's discoveries, this made sense, since his laws were literally universal and uniform. As Newton showed, the universe behaved more like a clock, less like a person. In other realms of thought, individuals would seek to craft equally important "laws" to explain the world.

---

[41] Though Gottfriend Leibniz invented calculus at almost the exact same time, and both men quarreled bitterly about who had done it first.

[42] James Gleick, *Isaac Newton* (NY: Vintage, 2003).

Early Modern Knowledge: The Enlightenment

The fruits of the Renaissance and the Scientific Revolution developed into the so-called "Enlightenment" of the 18th century. This was a term coined by the men (almost exclusively men) who were part of the movement, and as such, it has benefitted from highly positive publicity. Who wouldn't want to be "enlightened"? If *sola fide* (by faith alone) was one of Luther's mottos, *sola ratione* (by reason alone) could have been the motto of the Enlightenment. We have seen how authority and reason have had a complicated relationship from the end of the Middle Ages into the Early Modern period, but there was always some sense that both were legitimate entities. Not so in the Enlightenment. For enlightenment *philosophes* (such as Voltaire, Rousseau, and Hume) authority was *opposed* to reason. German philosopher Immanuel Kant defined enlightenment thus: "Enlightenment is man's emancipation from his own self-imposed intellectual immaturity. Intellectual immaturity is the inability to follow your own reason without the guidance of another . . . Have courage to use your own reason! That is the motto of the Enlightenment."[43] Enlightenment thinkers were highly skilled in the art of self-promotion.

Searching out new knowledge is not a bad thing at all: people have been doing this throughout human history. As we have seen in this period, authorities sometimes need to be challenged and models revised. But by opposing authority *on principle,* the Enlightenment led to a curious phenomenon: an individual could accept or reject whether or not a person was a credible authority almost on a whim. Notice Kant's claim: as long as you are guided by "another," you apparently are not enlightened. In its most extreme forms, this would mean that one must question *everything* that came before one's self, and find out the real answers using one's own reason— in this way, Descartes's self-focused philosophical project clearly inspired Enlightenment thought.

---

[43] Immanuel Kant, "Was ist Aufklarung," accessed July 17, 2023, https://www.rosalux.de/fileadmin/rls_uploads/pdfs/159_kant.pdf , translation by Greg Murry.

Should I listen to my Johns Hopkins-trained physician or some conspiracy theorist on YouTube? Enlightenment rationalism would enjoin me to "think for myself," thus undercutting the possibility that I might not have the authority or expertise to make sound judgments on every single topic. Unsurprisingly, Enlightenment *philosophes* rejected, on principle, just about every religious authority, particularly those of Christianity.

Perhaps naturally (pun intended), the main rhetorical appeal for Enlightenment thinkers was nature. The notion of natural law is an old one indeed (we see Sepúlveda using it in his argument about Native Americans), and Newton's laws yielded great understandings of the natural world, but for Enlightenment thinkers, their own stances and conclusions were inevitably "natural." What is the "natural" form of government? For Voltaire it was monarchy; for Rousseau it was democracy. Which of these two was most "natural"? Simply use one's own reason! Part of the interpretive problem of scripture in the Reformation had a parallel in the Enlightenment: Nature and Reason supposedly yielded "self-evident" knowledge, and anyone who disagreed was obviously not enlightened. With apologies to American *philosophe* Thomas Jefferson, we very rarely see actual "self-evident" truths. Going back to Aristotle, most knowledge appears to be endoxic: intelligent people of goodwill can have different interpretations and offer different arguments about the same phenomenon. Enlightenment rhetoric thus often *stifles* debate and argumentation, as surely as nominalism did in the Reformation: my position is rational, natural, and self-evident, while yours is the opposite.

To be fair, the Enlightenment did popularize and continue the Scientific Revolution and helped to inspire the era of political Revolutions across the Atlantic world. Those are arguably good results of the movement. But in terms of ways of knowing, it introduced some difficulties that remain with us to this day. Popularizing science could easily lead to *scientism*, the ideology that scientific knowledge is the only valid way of knowing things. Actual scientists often do not hold this view (cf. Galileo), but when a person discounts religion, experience, art, or philosophy as a valid way of knowing something, that person rests on Enlightenment principles (clearly that person knows Nature because of Reason!). Furthermore, supremely self-confident white, European men of the 18th century could very easily mistake culture and convention for "nature." A less serious example would be the attempt to discover "rational principles" in drama. The so-called "unities" in drama posited that a play needs to be set in a single place (unity of place), over the course of real time (unity of time), with little change in character (unity of character)—this sort of drama was according to "nature," unlike the dramas of Shakespeare, which require the audience to imagine different scenes, time lapses, and character development. (The 18th century even saw Shakespeare's plays "improved" by rewriting them along these "natural" lines.) This attempt at making drama more "rational" led to some relatively shallow plays, but nothing more serious. More seriously, the scientific taxonomy of the natural world would lead to the "scientific" taxonomy of races and racism, with Western Europeans "self-evidently" at the top of the hierarchy. Notions of race existed prior to the Enlightenment, but Enlightenment *philosophes* made race and racism "natural" and "scientific." We are dealing with the fallout of this Enlightenment invention to this very day.

Enlightenment enthusiasm for science further led to the notion of a "Disenchanted World." *Philosophes* took for granted that the universe worked according to natural laws, and that these laws were never violated. The quintessential Enlightenment theology is Deism: the belief that a God made the universe but does not interfere with it. A common image from the period (which we already saw foreshadowed by Newton) is God as a clockmaker: once the clock is made, it can run on its own. There is no room for the miraculous in this ideology, and any religion that is open to the possibility of miracles (such as Judaism, Christianity, or Islam) is self-evidently false. Scottish *philosophe* David Hume (1711-1776) argued that miracles never occur, and less overtly agnostic thinkers simply took for granted that this is the case. Past instances of the miraculous had to be explained by natural terms, leading to scientific "debunking" of past miraculous experiences.

By the late 18th century, the notion of living in a rationalist clock became distasteful to artists and thinkers of the Romantic movement, who sought to re-enchant the world along the lines of medieval romance. The Romantics sought inspiration in Nature, but in a Nature re-enchanted by the imagination. Rather than something cold and mechanical, the Romantics found Nature to be *sublime*, able to transport us outside of ourselves in a manner akin to a religious experience. William Wordsworth, one of the major English Romantic poets, put the matter clearly in a sonnet:

> The world is too much with us; late and soon,
> Getting and spending, we lay waste our powers;—
> Little we see in Nature that is ours;
> We have given our hearts away, a sordid boon!
> This Sea that bares her bosom to the moon;
> The winds that will be howling at all hours,
> And are up-gathered now like sleeping flowers;
> For this, for everything, we are out of tune;
> It moves us not. Great God! I'd rather be
> A Pagan suckled in a creed outworn;
> So might I, standing on this pleasant lea,
> Have glimpses that would make me less forlorn;
> Have sight of Proteus rising from the sea;
> Or hear old Triton blow his wreathèd horn.[44]

Wordsworth was a believing Christian and, ultimately, a minister: to prefer to be a pagan was no small matter for him! That's how "out of tune" he thought scientific rationalism had made him and his world. Beethoven's 9th Symphony ("Pastoral") revels in the beauty and sublimity of Nature, containing a revolutionary choral movement (the famous "Ode to Joy," which

---

[44] Proteus (the "Old Man of the Sea") was an ancient sea god. Anyone who has seen Disney's *The Little Mermaid* should recognize Triton, a merfolk god of the sea.

you should listen to). While many of the Romantics were religious believers, Romanticism itself provided a *non-religious* response to the Enlightenment. Do passion, mystery, and sublimity have a place in the world of knowledge? That question remains with us centuries later. The Romantics further sought to change the world through their artistic visions, which would have profound connections to liberty: The Romantic poet acted like a secular prophet, proclaiming the immanent birth of a new reality and consciousness. Consider artists who, even to this day, seek to change our way of imagining and knowing the world through their works.

In conclusion, early modern ways of knowing were marked by a shift away from the traditional and authoritative towards the new and the individual. This process was highly complex, and this chapter's treatment of it is, by necessity, incomplete. It does explain, however, some of the deep divisions and tensions within our own world. In his provocative study of contemporary ethics *After Virtue* (1981), philosopher Alasdair MacIntyre argued that sociopolitical arguments in the Western world on such "hot button" issues as abortion, euthanasia, and the death penalty are ultimately unsolvable because while arguers use the same terminology, they are actually operating from very different ethical frameworks: a mishmash of premodern ethical ideas vs. a mishmash modern ethical ideas. This pluralism of thought plays out daily in our political debates and is a result of how epistemology developed over the early modern period.

Early Modern Ideas on Liberty

By Jamie Gianoutsos

In January of 1649, in a cold corner of the Atlantic world, the English people watched as their anointed monarch laid his head upon a wooden block below the executioner's axe. Charles Stuart, the two-decade king of England, Scotland, and Ireland, had been found guilty of treason by a parliamentary High Court of Justice. His sentence as a "Tyrant, Traitor, Murderer, and public Enemy" asserted that Charles carried the blame for the bloody civil wars fought between king and parliament in Britain and Ireland over the prior decade.[45] The plain wooden scaffold hastily constructed for Charles's death stood in stark contrast to the ornate stone colonnade palace behind it, in which Charles had hosted luxurious entertainments for nobles and foreign dignitaries on royal occasions. On the ceiling of this Banqueting House the celebrity artist Peter Paul Rubens had painted an elaborate series of pictures of Charles's late father, King James I, sitting enthroned in justice as a sage monarch on each end of the hall, and ascending into heaven with angels and crowns of victory in the center. Charles stood under this painted ceiling while awaiting his own death, stepping through the palace window out onto the platform when called by the executioners.

Charles's father, King James, had argued insistently for the idea of divine-right kingship. In a speech before parliament forty years earlier in 1609, James had declared: "The State of Monarchy is the supremist thing upon earth: For Kings are not only God's Lieutenants upon earth, and sit upon God's throne, but even by

[45] Thomas Bayly Howell, *A Complete Collection of State Trials and Proceedings for High Treason and Other Crimes and Misdemeanors from the Earliest Period to the Year 1820*, vol. IV (London: Longman, 1816), 1017.

God himself they are called Gods."[46] King James declared that monarchs stood above the law, and that they were accountable to none except God, for all political authority flowed from God through the king. Adopting metaphors that the king is father and the people his children, and that the king is the head of the body politic, James argued that subjects had no lawful nor Christian means to depose a king, nor that it was natural to do so, just as killing one's father or amputating one's head would be wholly unnatural, vicious, and destructive. Even if God allowed a brutal tyrant to rule, the people should never revolt. Their only recourse should be prayer and the repentance of sins, for in the contract between the king and his people, "God is doubtless the only Judge."[47]

After years of civil war, the imprisonment of Charles, and failed negotiations throughout the 1640s, the English parliament did in fact erect a High Court of Justice to serve as judge over their king. In his trial, Charles largely remained silent after an opening speech, in which he condemned the High Court as having no more lawful authority to judge him than "Thieves and Robbers by the highways." On the scaffold, moments before his beheading, Charles proclaimed publicly that "the liberty [of the people] consists in having government, those laws by which their life and their goods may be most their own. It is not for having a share in government;... a subject and a sovereign are clean different things."[48] When Charles laid his head on the block and the executioner slung his axe, the crowd gasped, and onlookers rushed to dip their handkerchiefs into the blood that pooled from Charles's severed neck. Newspapers reeled with descriptions of the scene of an anointed monarch beheaded, and *Eikon Basilike,* a

---

[46] "A Speach to the Lords and Commons of the Parliament at White-Hall, on Wednesday the XXI. Of March. Anno 1609," in *James VI and I: Political Writings,* 101.

[47] "The Trew Law of Free Monarchies," in *James VI and I: Political Writings,* 76-83, esp. 81.

[48] C. V. Wedgewood, *A King Condemned: The Trial and Execution of Charles I* (London: Tauris Parke, 2011), 191.

thick spiritual biography of Charles's trials and death, flew off the presses to become the top-selling book across Europe. Through word and elaborate image, the book deemed Charles a martyr whose patient suffering, unjust trial, and sacrificial death for his people mirrored the passion of Jesus.[49]

In the wake of Charles's execution, the English parliament passed an act abolishing kingship in England and Ireland and declaring all of Charles's royal children "incapable…of being king or queen of the said kingdom or dominions." The act labeled "the office of a king" as "unnecessary, burdensome and dangerous to the liberty, safety and public interest of the people," for kingship under a single person would be used to "enslave the subject…and to promote the setting up of their own will and power above the law." Now England would be "governed by its own Representatives" of the people, parliament declared, for it is from the people and their ancient laws and customs that just power is derived.[50] But England's experiment ruling without a king would not last. Just over a decade later in 1660, the late king's son, Charles II, would ride into London triumphant, pardoning all in his Declaration of Breda for the "sufferings" and "calamities" of the past decades. He made an exception for those who had condemned his father to death in the High Court of Justice; king-killers would not be pardoned but executed for their unconscionable crime. Exhausted by taxation, military rule, and instability, English subjects quite happily accepted kingship again.

Despite its failure to create a lasting settlement through this first English Revolution, the legacy of British writers defending Charles's trial and erecting a new republic would shape the course of future revolutions. Into the late eighteenth century, Enlightenment thinkers edited, reprinted, and sold volumes of

---

[49] Robert Wilcher, *The Writings of Royalism, 1628-1660* (Cambridge: Cambridge UP, 2001), 269.

[50] J. P. Kenyon, *The Stuart Constitution, 1603-1688: Documents and Commentary* (Cambridge: Cambridge UP, 1966), 339-41. For the declaration of these ancient laws and customs, they often looked to Magna Carta.

English liberty writings across the Atlantic world, wherein authors from the 1640s like John Milton outlined the rights and freedoms of citizens, defended the freedom of speech, free press, and religious toleration, and argued that just authority in government could only be derived from popular sovereignty and the consent of the governed.[51] Revolutionary thinkers from the marquis de Condorcet in France to Thomas Jefferson, James Madison, and John Adams in the American colonies read these volumes closely to find the inspiration and frameworks for their own declarations of liberty. This inheritance shaped revolutions from America to France to Haiti to Latin America but also sparked numerous controversies, debates, and unresolved questions, for writers disagreed significantly on who should represent "the people," whether all deserved rights and freedoms, and in what liberty consisted. As English, French, and American writers proclaimed themselves "enslaved" to the tyranny of monarchy, they profited from enslaving peoples across the Atlantic world in trading outposts and newly planted colonies from Africa to the Americas. These ideals, limitations, and downright inconsistencies would set into motion the central struggle for liberty in the early modern period.

Nation States, Global Crisis, and Centralization

Early modern conflicts between monarchs and their people (or their people's representatives) often arose from a variety of causes, including political, social, and economic upheaval, and even weather and climatic developments. Urban centers grew in size and influence in this period, and with increasing technological advances, swelling cities developed larger scales of social and political organization, the spread of information through pamphlets and newspapers, and corporate citizen action through

---

[51] Other significant liberty writers from 1640s and 1650s England included Marchamont Nedham, James Harrington, Algernon Sidney, Lucy Hutchinson, and Henry Neville.

gatherings, marches, protests, and public discussions in places like taverns and newly created coffee houses (with exotic drugs like coffee, tea, and tobacco). Initially, the word "citizen" just meant a free "inhabitant of a city" who enjoyed certain civic rights and privileges. Over the course of the sixteenth through eighteenth centuries, the political landscape shifted importantly as decentralized regions of Europe increasingly coalesced into powerful and centralized nation-states, and inhabitants of these polities (whether they lived in cities or rural areas), claimed for themselves the status of rights-bearing citizen.

Conceptions of "citizenship" developed alongside conceptions of the "nation-state." By the word state, historians usually mean rationalized and bureaucratic forms of governance with a monopoly on the use of violent coercion, as well as the power to tax, mint coins, regulate commerce, make laws, and declare war. While governments had certainly carried out these functions in earlier eras, early modern states grew increasingly powerful in their organization, utilizing scientific advances in "political arithmetic" to count populations, to collect empirical data, and to regulate commerce through standardized weights and measurements (although it would take the advent of the eighteenth century for fully modern conceptions of political economy to develop).[52] At the same time, the activities of early modern states increasingly became tied to an idea of nationhood, which historians generally define as a group of people who are bonded by a common identity centering on a shared sense of language, culture, history, and religion. Unlike small village communities where daily life would be shared among known people, those who make up a large national community forge "imagined communities" with thousands of individuals they have never met and will never meet face-to-face.[53]

---

[52] Ted McCormick, "Governing Model Populations: Queries, Quantification, and William Petty's 'Scale of Slubrity,'" *History of Science* li (June 2013): 179-97.

[53] Benedict Anderson, *Imagined Communities: Reflections on the Origins and Spread of Nationalism* (NY: Verso, 1997).

European nation states centralized and grew in power in this period partly because they needed to respond to significant crises of technology, poverty, food shortages, and religious conflict. To address new technologies in gunpowder warfare and especially better canons, European states greatly improved castle defense through designing short, star-shaped fortresses with bastions that jutted out from the corners of the fort. The rebuilding of castles in the sixteenth and early seventeenth centuries led to a stunning increase in the cost of warfare and also very lengthy battles, for cities guarded by new castles could only be taken through siege warfare. Armies besieging cities either had to sit down and starve the population out or very slowly advance their trenches until they could bombard the fortress at close range. These sieges could last for years and required larger armies – sometimes even double the number of troops – which raised the cost of war significantly in an era of European-wide conflicts.[54] Indeed, in the seventeenth century, there were only two entire years – 1670 and 1682 – without a war between the states of Europe, and the century witnessed more state breakdowns than any previous or subsequent period. Costly wars became the norm for resolving both domestic and international problems throughout most of the Northern Hemisphere.[55] In this violent context, it is no wonder that Thomas Hobbes argued in *Leviathan* in 1651 that "without a common Power to keep them all in awe," man's natural state was war; "such a war, as is of every man, against every man," and the "life of man, solitary, poore, nasty, brutish, and short."[56]

---

[54] For example, the siege of Oostende in the Netherlands last for almost three straight years, and in 1629 alone, the Dutch army almost doubled, from roughly 70,000 men in arms to 128,000. Geoffrey Parker, *The Military Revolution: Military Innovation and the Rise of the West,* 2nd ed. (Cambridge: Cambridge UP, 1996), 1-14.

[55] Parker, "States Make War But Wars Also Break States," *The Journal of Military History* 74 (January 2010): 11-34, esp. 14-16.

[56] Thomas Hobbes, *Leviathan,* ed. Richard Tuck (Cambridge: Cambridge UP, 1997), I.13, p. 88-89.

The "General Crisis" of war and state conflict, as historians like to call it, was in fact a global phenomenon in the seventeenth century, with near contemporaneous revolts in China, Morocco, and India as in Europe. In explanation, historians have partially blamed the weather, pointing especially to the Little Ice Age experienced in the north Atlantic region which entailed a series of major volcanic explosions and also a lull in the radiation coming from the sun, due in part to the disappearance of sun spots; these together produced global cooling and the expansion of mountain glaciers in several locations, which either caused or coincided with an unparalleled number of episodes of El Niño and prolonged droughts in some areas. John Winthrop, Governor of the Massachusetts Bay Colony, noted in his journal during the landmark winter of 1641-62 that "The frost was so great and continual this winter that all the Bay was frozen over, so much and so long, as the like, by the Indians' relation, had not been so these forty years….To the southward also the frost was as great and the snow as deep, and at Virginia itself the great [Chesapeake] bay was much of it frozen over."[57] In Japan in this same winter, "ice lay in the fields one foot deep" and "the corpses of those who had starved to death filled the streets while the peasants, artisans and merchants who begged for food were numerous." In the Alps in Europe, fields, farmsteads, and even whole villages disappeared as glaciers advanced to their maximum extent, while in Macedonia, "there was so much rain and snow that many workers died through the great cold."[58] Historians have tied these weather patterns to increasing warfare, starvation, poverty, and political insecurity, even the European witch craze.[59]

With military technology and global climate challenges, religious divisions forged through the reformations of the sixteenth century played a significant role in the growing

---

[57] Qtd. in Parker, "States Make Wars," 17-18.

[58] Ibid., 18.

[59] Wolfgang Behringer, "Weather, Hunger, and Fear: Origins of the European Witch Hunts in Climate, Society, and Mentality," *German History* 13.1 (Jan. 1995): 1-27.

centralization of states and their national identities. Historians have been divided as to whether religious disputes principally fueled the Wars of Religion and the Thirty Years War fought on the European continent in the sixteenth and seventeenth centuries, or whether these wars in fact served as a cover for political or economic disputes between those seeking power or between increasingly large nation-states jockeying for expansion.[60] Either way, states and monarchs frequently crafted their identities and waged wars in the name and protection of religion, whether at home or across the Atlantic. Through the Peace of Augsburg (1555), the new Protestant faith became recognized as having an equal status with the Catholic faith; its stated doctrine of *cuius regio, eius religio* (whoever rules chooses the religion) meant that each territorial prince and free city would decide which faith should be practiced by their subjects or citizens.[61]

Secular rulers gained new powers over local and national churches, and through a process that historians call confessionalization, rulers used religious differences to cement political identities. Protestantism became part of the English, Prussian, Dutch, and Swedish identities in the early modern period, and conversely Catholicism became part of what it meant to be Spanish, Portuguese, Austrian, or French. In 1534, for example, England's Act of Supremacy established a national church with Henry VIII as head; by the late sixteenth century, under Queen Elizabeth, John Aylmer would chide his fellow Englishmen "to thank God 7 times a day that they were born Englishmen and not Italians, Frenchmen, or Germans," for along with its abundance of goods, England was blessed because "God and his angels fought on her side against her foreign foes." In the marginal note, Aylmer

---

[60] Mack Holt, "Putting Religion Back into the Wars of Religion," *French Historical Studies* 18 no. 2 (1993): 524-551.

[61] *Encyclopedia of Nationalism,* vol. II (San Diego: Academic Press, 2001), 584.

summarized his position by declaring (very mistakenly) that "God is English."[62]

Whether Protestant or Catholic, however, secular rulers employed religion to help establish social discipline in areas in which neither church nor state had been competent to exercise authority before.[63] Inquisition courts tracked down bigamists (people who had married more than once) even more than heretics, and Protestant ecclesiastical church courts refereed familial disputes and adultery cases far more than doctrinal issues. This "disciplinary revolution," as one sociologist called it, included the creation of workhouses for the poor and forbade vagrancy and the begging of alms or daily bread on the streets.[64] In one Dutch Calvinist version, the ne'er-do-well was locked in a room that contained nothing but a faucet and a pump. The workhouse authorities pumped in water through the faucet and began filling the room until the poor man found the work ethic to start cranking the pump. The lesson was obvious: learn to work or learn to swim. By turns cruel and effective, government-run institutions, including orphanages, workhouses, hospitals, insane asylums, and prisons, became sites of social discipline organized by the state, and often funded through the paying of taxes.[65]

European governments significantly expanded their organization and bureaucracy to meet these expensive and disruptive challenges from natural crises, rebellion, warfare, and confessionalization. In France, for example, Louis XIV responded

---

[62] John Aylmer, *An Harborowe for Faithfull and Trewe Subjects* (London, 1559), P4v-Q1r.

[63] R. Po-Chia Hsia, *Social Disciplining in the Reformation: Central Europe, 1550-1750* (London: Routledge, 1989).

[64] Philip Gorski, *The Disciplinary Revolution: Calvinism and the Rise of the State in Early Modern Europe* (Chicago: University of Chicago Press, 2003).

[65] Thomas Max Safley, *Reformation of Charity: The Secular and the Religious in Early Modern Poor Relief* (Leiden: Brill, 2003); Robert Jütte, *Poverty and Deviance in Early Modern Europe* (Cambridge: Cambridge UP, 1994).

to these broader challenges and the specific rebellions and violence against his rule, by stripping nobles of their traditional powers and forging an absolutist regime wherein all power flowed through the monarchy. While nobles became ritually enmeshed in the elaborate politics of luxury at the Palace of Versailles, where they jostled for position and access to the king (including the high honor of helping the king at the toilet), appointed royal officials called *intendants* carried out the mechanisms of the centralized state in each of France's provinces. These bureaucrats supervised local officials, organized relief for crises such as crop failures, represented the crown in provincial assemblies, and informed Louis's central government about the economic situation and public opinion of their region.[66] At the same time, the vigorous expansion of national identity and centralized power in European states developed from and encouraged commercial, imperial, and religious expansion and competition overseas.

Defining Revolution and Liberty

When faced with so many crises which appeared new, extreme, or unprecedented, Europeans looked both forward and backward for political understanding. They turned to the "New Science" and new modes of discovery, quantification, empirical research, exploration, and ways of knowing to craft increasingly powerful states and bureaucracies. Simultaneously, they looked backward to past eras of natural and human history to understand their moment and to predict future developments. During and following the Renaissance, writers across Europe had recovered and translated ancient writings of the Greeks and Romans and sought to put their ideas and practices into use. Richard Greneway, an English translator of the Roman historian Tacitus, argued that history provided "the treasure of times past, and as well a guide, as image of man's present estate, a true and lively pattern of things

[66] Jeremy Popkin, *A Short History of the French Revolution*, 7th ed. (NY and London: Routledge, 2020), 2-7.

to come, and as some term it, the work-mistress of experience, which is the mother of prudence…."[67] Greneway and his contemporaries understood history as operating through patterns or cycles; the prudent person could and should locate themselves in such a cycle and learn from the experiences of others in the past who lived through a similar pattern.

This view of history was reflected in the very word that early modern people developed to describe political upheaval: revolution. In the late Middle Ages, the word "revolution" referred principally to the movement of the planets in a circular or elliptical course around a central mass; more broadly, it could mean a reversal or change of fortune. Beginning in the sixteenth century, revolution came also to mean the overthrow of a government by those previously subject to it or the forcible substitution of a new form of government.[68] How did this old definition of revolution relate to this new one? The answer lies in the ancient texts that early modern thinkers frequently read. From Plato, Aristotle, Polybius, and others, European political thinkers conceptualized political constitutions as cycling between good and corrupted forms. A country founded by a monarch would eventually find itself ruled by a tyrant, so this view generally held. The tyrant later on would be overthrown and an aristocracy formed, until eventually the few aristocrats in charge would degenerate into an oligarchy (rule by a corrupt few). The cycle would continue with the overthrow of oligarchy and formation of a democracy, until

---

[67] *The Annales of Corenlius Tacitus. The Description of Germanie,* trans. Richard Greneway (London, 1598), dedicatory epistle to Robert Devereux, second earl of Essex.

[68] Karl Marx and Frederich Engels in the *Communist Manifesto* (1850) would redefine the term even more precisely to mean "the violent overthrow of the ruling class and the seizure of power through control of the means of production by a class to whom such control was previously denied; the historically inevitable transition from one system of production to another and the political change which ensues, leading to the eventual triumph of Communism." See "revolution, n." *Oxford English Dictionary* Online. March 2023 (Oxford University Press). Accessed May 16, 2023.

that form corrupted into an anarchic mob. At the end of this cycle, the constitutional forms would begin again with the rise of a single ruler. Monarchy to tyranny, aristocracy to oligarchy, democracy to mob rule – it was a repeating pattern of evolution and degeneration, which spiraled through decades and centuries of political systems.

A revolution, thereby, would mark one of these changes in the cycling of governments. Political thinkers in the sixteenth through eighteenth centuries, confronted by many such rotations, debated passionately about which form of government would prove the most stable, which would create the most powerful, authoritative, or happiest regime, and if any constitution might break this cycle entirely and bring long-term stability. From this lens, the famous (and infamous) writings of Niccolò Machiavelli can be well appreciated. His advice manual *The Prince* (c. 1513-1519) cautioned individual rulers that they must fight fortune and prevent the overthrow of their government through adopting crafty designs in politics and doing at least some immoral things. Machiavelli's *Discourses on Livy* (c. 1513-1519), which provided reflections on Livy's histories from the late Roman republic, examined how republics might achieve lasting stability and imperial expansion through combining all three forms of government: the rule by one (monarchy), rule by a few (aristocracy), and rule by many (democracy).[69]

Several early modern political thinkers through the seventeenth and eighteenth centuries sought to create mixed models of governance which combined these three forms of government with separated powers and responsibilities; so, for example, in the English system they would promote a mixed constitutional monarchy with a king (the one) and a dual legislature of parliament, comprised of the house of lords (the few) and the house of commons (the many). Through providing "checks and balances" between these forms, political thinkers in this republican tradition hoped to prevent corruption and

---

[69] Niccolò Machiavelli, *Discourses on Livy,* trans. Julia Conaway Bondanella and Peter Bondanella (Oxford: Oxford UP, 2008), I.2, p. 22-28.

instability. Our own American constitutional system, with its "checks and balances" between the one, few, and many, was largely derived from this long European tradition. The English news editor Marchamont Nedham, who was greatly influenced by Machiavelli as well as ancient political writers, crafted a constitutional system of "checks and balances" in the wake of the English Revolution, and the French Enlightenment thinker, Baron de Montesquieu, mapped out such a notion in *The Spirit of the Laws* in 1748, based upon the English constitutional system.[70] These, in turn, informed people like James Madison and John Adams, as they sought to craft constitutions for United States on the federal or state level.

But forging and balancing constitutional systems in the wake of revolutions would not wholly solve the questions surrounding "liberty" in the early modern period (or today) nor would they guarantee the prevention of corruption or creation of stability. As the opening example of the English Revolution showed, early modern constitutional conflicts raised difficult questions about legitimacy, sovereignty, accountability, and freedom – who could or should be free, and what did this freedom entail? With the growing crises and centralization of early modern governments, a further question would be added – would powerful, large nation-states or even empires make individuals more or less free?

To answer these questions, thinkers in the liberty tradition developed multiple competing systems of thought, in some cases drawing upon older Greek and Roman notions of humans as "political animals" who formed communities naturally with each other, and in other cases drawing upon newer socio-scientific notions of humans as naturally unattached individuals in a "state of nature" who entered contractual societies. These competing ideas have sometimes been distinguished by calling them "ancient liberty" and "modern liberty"; since a lecture delivered in 1969 by

[70] Blair Worden, "Checks and Balances: The Cromwellian Origins of the Presidency," ; David Wootton, "Liberty, Metaphor, and Mechanism: 'Checks and Balances,'" in *Liberty and American Experience in the Eighteenth Century*, ed. David Womersley (Indianapolis: Liberty Fund, 2006), 209-74.

Isaiah Berlin on "Two Concepts of Liberty," many contemporary political philosophers have adopted the terms "positive liberty" and "negative liberty" to describe these competing definitions of liberty.[71] As we will see, both conceptions of liberty were highly operative in the early modern period, and both continue to shape our debates about liberty today.

Let us start with the more modern idea of negative liberty, as it may be more familiar. If one conceives of liberty in the "negative" sense, one understands liberty as an individual's freedom to make choices without interference; on this model, to be free is, more or less, to be left alone to do whatever one chooses, as long as that choosing does not harm or deprive another. In his *Leviathan,* Thomas Hobbes provided the analogy of the individual walking down a lane that is lined by tall hedges. Laws, like hedgerows, should be designed not to interfere with individuals traveling along the road or traveling in the manner or direction they wish; laws, like hedges, should only keep individuals within certain boundaries so they avoid harming others or damaging things that are not theirs (like the private property on the other side of the hedge).[72] Perhaps the best articulator of this view was John Stuart Mill, who argued that "the only freedom which deserves the name, is that of pursuing our own good in our own way, so long as we do not attempt to deprive others of theirs."[73]

---

[71] Frank Lovett, "Republicanism," *The Stanford Encyclopedia of Philosophy,* eds. Edward N. Zalta and Uri Nodelman (Fall 2022 Edition), For the older terminology of ancient and modern liberty, see Benjamin Constant, "The Liberty of the Ancients Compared with that of the Moderns," (1819).

[72] Hobbes, *Leviathan,* 239-40.

[73] John Stuart Mill, "On Liberty (1859)," in *On Liberty and Other Essays,* ed. John Gray (Oxford: Oxford University Press, 1991), 17. Hobbes and Mill disagree, however, on a number of issues, including whether the government can interfere when individuals might harm themselves. Hobbes, in the hedgerow passage, makes clear that governments can stop people from hurting themselves, whereas Mill objects to governmental interference to prevent one from harming oneself. He deems such interference paternalistic and problematic.

John Locke, in his late seventeenth-century *Second Treatise of Government*, crafted the formulation of negative liberty that likely had the greatest influence upon the American revolutionaries. Locke argued that the natural state for humans was one of perfect equality and perfect freedom, wherein each individual could "order their Actions, and dispose of their Possessions, and Persons as they think fit, within the bounds of the Law of Nature, without asking leave, or depending upon the Will of any other Man."[74] Although a state of perfect liberty, Locke cautioned that this "state of nature" was *not* a state of "license"; human beings did not rightfully have the liberty to destroy themselves or others, and they ought not to "harm another in his Life, Health, Liberty, or Possessions." Neither did human beings have an obligation to submit to the "unjust will of another."[75] However, Locke imagined that humans in the state of nature would eventually break these natural laws and enter conflict and warfare; in response, they would come together to forge a political society through a **social contract**, whereby they would voluntarily consent to "joyn and unite into a Community" for the purpose of preserving their rights of "life, liberty, and property."

Very importantly for Locke, the people who join together into society agree to obey the laws and executive power of a legislature, but they retain a right to resistance, "*a Supream Power* to remove or *alter*" their government should it become "contrary to the trust reposed in them" or violate the people's basic liberties.[76] On this model, the individual, who possesses basic and natural liberties, consents to be governed by the majority will while retaining the right of revolution. In the *Declaration of Independence* a century later, Thomas Jefferson would follow this formulation almost exactly:

> *We hold these truths to be self-evident, that all men are created equal, that they are endowed by their Creator with certain unalienable Rights, that among these are Life, Liberty and the pursuit*

---

[74] John Locke, *The Second Treatise*, 269.

[75] Ibid., 271, 276.

[76] Ibid., 331, 350-352, 367.

> *of Happiness.--That to secure these rights, Governments are instituted among Men, deriving their just powers from the consent of the governed, --That whenever any Form of Government becomes destructive of these ends, it is the Right of the People to alter or to abolish it, and to institute new Government, laying its foundation on such principles and organizing its powers in such form, as to them shall seem most likely to effect their Safety and Happiness.*[77]

The negative liberty tradition thereby emphasizes that governments (forged by the consent of the governed) form the "hedgerows" of laws, protecting the individual practice of basic liberties without interference. This system of thought, which is often called political liberalism, emphasized fundamental rights and governmental limits in an era of growing governmental power and reach.[78]

Whereas the negative liberty tradition emphasizes *freedom from* the interference of others in one's rights, the positive liberty tradition emphasizes the *freedom to* become an active participant in one's civic community, which is generally envisioned as a natural development of humans associating with each other. Crafted from models of the ancient city-states and empires such as Athens and Rome, the positive liberty tradition does not begin by describing a "state of nature," but usually begins by describing how humans historically have formed communities from families and increasingly large groupings of family units. Humans can fully develop their full potential, it is argued, through participating as citizens in a political system founded on virtue and liberty. This positive liberty happens not through private individuals practicing rights but through the public exercising of one's obligations to the community in collective decision-making (such as serving in

---

[77] "Declaration of Independence: A Transcription," *National Archives* (accessed June 5, 2023).

[78] Note that "political liberalism" here does not mean "Liberal" as in left-wing, democratic, or progressive. In fact, the modern-day American political movement that most closely follows this model is probably Libertarianism.

government or at least choosing one's governors) and through communal service (such as fighting in the military or teaching and upholding good morals and good laws). On this model, the purpose of the commonwealth and its shared concern for justice is the realization of human potential and flourishing, not the possibility of private endeavors or the private pursuit of gain.[79]

Thinkers in this tradition emphasize that the great enemy of positive liberty is political corruption, whereby individuals seek to gain power and make decisions for their private gain rather than, or at the expense of, the public or common good of the community. As the highly influential seventeenth-century poet and thinker, John Milton, described to his fellow countrymen in the 1650s, "your own character is a mighty factor in the acquisition or retention of liberty," requiring "true virtue" which is "sprung from piety, justice, temperance." For Milton, the history of ancient countries showed that "Liberty hath a sharp and double edge, fit only to be handled by Just and Vertuous Men...by them who have the happy skill to know what is grievance, and unjust to a People...; what good Laws are wanting [or needed], and how to frame them substantially, that good Men may enjoy the freedom which they merit, and the bad the Curb which they need."[80] This system of positive liberty holds that laws must be crafted by the virtuous, who would rule for the sake of all. Those corrupted by vices and selfish desires would not craft good or fair laws but immoral laws.

Civic humanists and "classical republican" writers who defended this tradition in the early modern period extensively debated who would be capable of such participation in governance, for on the positive liberty model, citizenship required the virtues necessary to serve the common good (virtues like

---

[79] Cary Nederman, "Civic Humanism," *The Stanford Encyclopedia of Philosophy*, eds. Edward N. Zalta and Uri Nodelman,

[80] Quotations from *The Second Defence of the English People* and *Digression from the History of Britain*, in *Complete Prose Works of John Milton*, 10 volumes, gen. ed. Don M. Wolfe (New Haven: Yale UP, 1953-82), esp. vol. IV.1, 680 and vol. V.1, 448.

justice, prudence, wisdom, and courage). Would only wealthy men or all men be capable of virtuous participation? Could women be considered capable of full liberty and virtue? And did some men – due to their natures or bodies or characters – merit slavery or "passive citizenship" rather than full citizenship? More broadly, if good government required virtue, how could people be made virtuous? Writers like Alexis de Tocqueville in the eighteenth century, and other Enlightenment writers, sought to solve these questions of citizenship, virtue, and equality by arguing for broadly understood civic education and varying levels of citizen engagement in local government, national government, and "intermediate" voluntary associations of public engagement.[81] As Tocqueville explained, "Town meetings are to liberty what primary schools are to science; they bring it within the people's reach, they teach men how to use and how to enjoy it."[82] Others, like Jean-Jacques Rousseau, crafted treatises on education to specify how citizens might become inculcated in freedom and the common good, making them fit to uphold the "general will" of the legislature.[83]

Central to most of these discussions about positive liberty and citizenship we find a prejudice inherited and developed from the classical tradition which envisioned men as the true bearers of virtue necessary to govern others, and women in their very biology as incapable of developing courage, prudence, wisdom, or justice. Indeed, the word virtue in English derived from the Latin word *virtus*, which means "manliness," and the highly influential

---

[81] Jeffrey C. Alexander, "Tocqueville's Two Forms of Association: Interpreting Tocqueville and Debates Over Civil Society Today," *The Tocqueville Review/La Revue Tocqueville* Vol. XXVII.2 (2006):

[82] Jack Crittenden and Peter Levine, "Civic Education", *The Stanford Encyclopedia of Philosophy* (Fall 2018 Edition), ed. Edward N. Zalta, https://plato.stanford.edu/archives/fall2018/entries/civic-education/. Accessed June 5, 2023.

[83] For competing articulations of civic education, see Gianoutsos, "Locke and Rousseau: Early Childhood Education," *The Pulse* 4.1 (Fall 2006): https://www.baylor.edu/Pulse/index.php?id=42091nb.

Roman philosopher Cicero repeatedly envisioned human excellence in reason, courage, and justice as male and never female qualities.[84] Mary Wollstonecraft in late eighteenth-century Britain argued forcefully in *A Vindication of the Rights of Woman* (1792) that women were fully capable of the virtues necessary for positive liberty, equality, and political citizenship historically reserved for males only. Girls and women only appeared less capable of virtue due to their lack of equal education and lack of opportunity to participate fully in public life, Wollstonecraft maintained; if you free women from "all restraint by allowing them to participate in the inherent rights of mankind," and educate girls alongside boys in public school classrooms, women "will quickly become wise and virtuous, as men become more so." Whereas writers in the positive liberty tradition – going all the way back to Aristotle – had emphasized the education of men and encouragement of their virtues to rule over the "weaker" and more "irrational" sex, Wollstonecraft contended that women were fully capable of virtue, and that the improvement of men and women in virtue and

[84] Aristotle used the word *aretê*, or "character excellence," when describing the concept of virtue, but his biological theories of the female as the privation of the male upheld that only men were capable of realizing the human potential of self-governance by reason, and by extension, the potential to rule others justly. Women, for Aristotle, are not fully rational animals nor fully capable of *aretê*; for much of the early modern liberty tradition, writers repeated and defended these gendered distinctions. In contexts where virtue is being discussed, Aristotle and those in his wake used the word "mankind" to mean men to the exclusion of women, not "human" more broadly. See Gianoutsos, "Tyranny, Manhood, and the Study of History," in *The Rule of Manhood: Tyranny, Gender, and Classical Republicanism in England, 1603-1660* (Cambridge: Cambridge UP, 2021), esp. 30-53; Christine Garside-Allen, "Can a Woman Be Good in the Same Way as a Man?", *Dialogue* 10 (1971), 534-44; Lynda Lange, "Woman Is not a Rational Animal: On Aristotle's Biology of Reproduction," in *Discovering Reality*, eds. Sandra Harding and Merrill B. Hintikka (Dordrecht: Kluwer, 2003), 1-15.

freedom must be mutual, for injustice for one group would be corrosive for the common good as a whole.[85]

Liberty, Equality, and Slavery

Both conceptions of liberty, whether negative or positive, have the possibility of articulating radical equality. Negative liberty accounts, for example, might emphasize equality and rights as natural to *all* human persons, for all were rational and equal in the state of nature, governed by a shared law of nature and created by the same divine being; positive liberty accounts might emphasize the necessity of political participation and civic education for all human persons in order to promote a truly "common good" and universal human flourishing. Historically, however, apart from questions of sexual and gender difference considered above, many writers supporting both systems of thought justified the growth and promulgation of colonialism, imperialism, and racial-based slavery in the early modern Atlantic world.[86] At the very least, if not promoting slavery outright, many promoting liberty and revolution decried their own "enslavement" under unjust regimes while ignoring the rights and equality of those actually born enslaved or forced into chattel slavery (slavery in which people are

---

[85] See Wollstonecraft in this text.

[86] "Both colonialism and imperialism were forms of conquest that were expected to benefit Europe economically and strategically. The term colonialism is frequently used to describe the settlement of North America, Australia, New Zealand, Algeria, and Brazil, places that were controlled by a large population of permanent European residents. The term imperialism often describes cases in which a foreign government administers a territory without significant settlement; typical examples includes the scramble for Africa in the late nineteenth century and the American domination of the Philippines and Puerto Rico." Margaret Kohn and Kavita Reddy, "Colonialism," *The Stanford Encyclopedia of Philosophy* (Spring2023),
https://plato.stanford.edu/archives/spr2023/entries/colonialism/.
Accessed June 21, 2023.

considered legal property and can be bought, sold, and owned forever). As Englishman Samuel Johnson flatly questioned in 1775: 'How is it that we hear the loudest *yelps* for liberty among the drivers of Negroes?'[87]

How indeed did liberty writers profess such clear hypocrisy? Very often, they made distinctions between people to undergird their systems of inequality and, very often, they sought to justify enslavement *after the fact* – after the exploitative and brutal Atlantic labor system had developed in contingent and piecemeal fashion through decades or centuries of Atlantic encounter. In other words, political thinkers often defended slavery or at least refused to decry it after their country's economies and their own pocketbooks reaped lucrative profits from this exploitative labor system. Defenses of inequality, colonialism, and racial slavery borrowed from a variety of old and new thought systems. These justifications can be grouped into several main types:

Arguments that certain people or types of people are intended for slavery "by nature" can come in a variety of forms, but most modern justifications of natural slavery in Europe and the Americas developed alongside an emerging concept of race, which came to mean the division of humanity into a small number of groups based ostensibly on biological foundations of difference between human groups, inherited from generation to generation. Race is usually tied to geographic origin, alongside claims that this inherited biology manifests itself physically (especially in skin color, but also eye shape, hair texture, bone structure) and perhaps also behaviorally (intelligence, creativity, etc.). This full-blown system of thought was not really present or neatly worked out in the sixteenth century; it was not fully developed until the nineteenth century. Even differentiating people by clear color categories (black, white, red, yellow, brown) was not usual in the earlier period.

As we will see, however, racism existed in a form prior to the modern, fully articulated theory of race; it is the belief that

---

[87] Gary B. Nash, *The Unknown American Revolution: The Unruly Birth of Democracy and the Struggle to Create America* (NY: Penguin, 2005), 212.

members of a particular racial group indeed possess innate characteristics or qualities, and usually also asserts that these qualities make groups superior or inferior to others. In the early modern Atlantic world, arguments justifying slavery as a natural human system increasingly relied upon particular understandings of racial difference, but on the whole, defenses of slavery as "natural" for certain humans or groups of humans in this period also included claims that were very old alongside those that were new – and contemporary scholars have shed a lot of ink debating and teasing out which strands are which.

In ancient and medieval sources, writers could find arguments in support of a "natural hierarchy" between humans and potential explanations for the ways that the natural world could cause humans to possess certain attributes that made them more fit to rule or be ruled. In the *Politics*, for example, Aristotle had asserted that "all things rule and are ruled according to nature." Describing a series of hierarchies that existed – freeman over slave, male over female, adult over child – Aristotle argued that the freeman ruled because slaves have "no deliberative faculty [ability to reason] at all," and slaves are deficient in virtue.[88] Tying this hierarchy to a biological basis, Aristotle described the "natural slave" as a "tool that breathes," a kind of "thing" to be owned, whose body is like an animal or beast of burden. As Aristotle spelled out: "The intention of nature therefore is to make the bodies of the freemen and of slaves different – the latter brawny for necessary service, the former erect and unserviceable for such occupations, but serviceable for a life of citizenship."[89]

[88] Women, in contrast, have a limited amount of rationality but "without authority," and children immature rationality. See Aristotle, *Politics* I.3

[89] Aristotle, *Politics* I.2.14-15. See J. Albert Harrill, "Invective against Paul (2 Cor. 10:10), the Physiognomics of the Ancient Slave Body, and the Greco-Roman Rhetoric of Manhood," in *Antiquity and Humanity: Essays on Ancient Religion and Philosophy* (Tübingen: Mohr Siebeck, 2001), 189-213, esp. 193-94.

While most scholars hold that the fully-fledged concept of race, based on pseudo-scientific biological claims of difference (such as skin color), is modern, many do debate the extent to which racism, even absent a developed race concept, may have existed very early in history, going back to the ancient Greek and Roman worlds. Some hold that the ancient and medieval world exhibited *proto-racism*, which lacked ideas of deterministic biology yet attributed to groups of people collective traits and common characteristics considered to be unalterable.[90] In ancient Greece and, with variations, in ancient Rome, writers widely supported a type of environmental determinism which held that groups of people are permanently determined in their body and mind by climate and geography, and that these characteristics, in turn, shaped their political development and, over time, their inheritable traits.[91] The ancient medical treatise by Hippocrates, *On Airs, Waters, and Places*, described how peoples in varying climates of the world develop distinctive bodily constitutions and temperaments, with significant moral, cultural, and political effects. "The inhabitants of Europe," he claimed, are "more courageous than those of Asia; for a climate which is always the same induces indolence, but a changeable climate [induces] laborious exertions both of body and mind." The strongest of the "natural causes of difference," Hippocrates claimed, was whether a climate changed seasons or

---

[90] Benjamin Isaac, "Proto-Racism in Graeco-Roman Antiquity," *World Archaeology* 38.1 (Mar. 2006): 32-47, esp. 34.

[91] With Rome, the claim of "natural slavery" gets a little tricky, because Roman law held that slavery was "contrary to the natural right" of men and a man-made institution, part of the law of nations (*jus gentium*). Put simply, people became enslaved because of conquest or force not because of nature. However, Roman law did say that slavery could be passed by birth from an enslaved mother, and in describing how it was that the Romans defeated and enslaved others through conquest, many Roman authors claimed a type of natural superiority based on climatic theory.

not, and those who lived in more extreme climates with fewer changes usually had less desirable traits to show for it.[92]

Decrying others as lesser based upon climate and geography became a fairly standard feature of Greek and Roman writings in the ancient period, especially for those desiring to justify the conquest or enslavement of foreign peoples to build their empire. Many in the medieval and early modern world repeated and developed these threads of thought (and, very often, developed them to support the supposed superiority of their own climate and interests). For example, in the eleventh century, Toledo historian Sā'id al-Andalusi employed climatic theory to disparage "dark" slaves in the Muslim world. He argued that because those peoples who inhabit Africa "near and beyond the equinoctial line" live where the "presence of the sun…makes the air hot and the atmosphere thin," their human "temperaments become hot and their humors fiery, their color black and their hair woolly. Thus, they lack self-control and steadiness of mind and are overcome by fickleness, foolishness, and ignorance. Such are the blacks, who live at the extremity of the land of Ethiopia, the Nubians, the Zanj and the like."[93] Scholars have argued that racism such as this not only preceded modern, biological categories of race in the modern world, but made possible the system of human bondage that developed in the Americas in the fifteenth and sixteenth centuries.

The later rise of modern natural philosophy and new scientific concerns with taxonomy, however, more closely linked the concept of race and especially skin color with ideas of determ-inistic biology and the supposedly natural enslavement of certain peoples. In "A New Division of the Earth" (1684), Francois Bernier seems to have first presented a division of humanity into "four or five species or races of men in particular whose difference is so remarkable that it may be properly made use of as the foundation

---

[92] Hippocrates, *On Airs, Waters, and Places.* Trans. by Francis Adams. (The Internet Classics Archive by Daniel C. Stevenson), Part 24. http://classics.mit.edu//Hippocrates/airwatpl.html.

[93] James H. Sweet, "The Iberian Roots of American Racist Thought," *The William and Mary Quarterly* 54.1 (Jan. 1997): 143-66, esp. 146.

for a new division of the earth." Questions about whether the human species could *really* be divided on racial lines would increasingly be taken up with vigor in the Enlightenment, and particularly, the question about whether all humans originated from the same common ancestor, as was described in the Biblical account of Genesis, or whether different human races descended from different ancestral roots.[94] The "science" of race built especially on skin-color prejudice and classification would develop most notably through these debates into the nineteenth century, and would be propped up by pseudo-scientific studies of differences between humans thought to be measurable (such as the size of craniums).[95] By the height of the Atlantic slave trade, chattel slavery, and colonial plantation systems, scientific and taxonomic classifications made it possible for racism to be fully "racial" as we understand it today.

Another unfortunate example of the ways that ancient sources could be used in the early modern period to justify slavery as inheritable or as natural for certain groups was the Bible. The story of the Curse of Ham from Genesis 9 played a role in shaping conceptions of enslavement as passing down to descendants of Noah's son, Ham, which by the early modern period, would mean sub-Saharan African peoples.

In Genesis 9, after Noah obeys God in building the ark for his family and numerous animals, and God sends the ruinous flood to destroy all other humans and creatures, God renews his covenant

---

[94] The position for one common ancestry is called monogenesis and multiple ancestries, polygenesis. Eventually, ideas of polygenesis declined in popularity through the intellectual success of Charles Darwin's theory of evolution in the late nineteenth century. Later race thinkers would replace polygenesis with natural selection and sexual selection as scientific mechanisms whereby racial differentiation could slowly, unintentionally, but nevertheless inevitably proceed. See I. Hannaford, *Race: The History of an Idea in the West* (Baltimore: The Johns Hopkins University Press, 1996), 273.

[95] Michael James and Adam Burgos, "Race", *The Stanford Encyclopedia of Philosophy* (Summer 2023 Edition), Edward N. Zalta & Uri Nodelman (eds.).

with Noah and creation, and blesses them to be fruitful and multiply. From Noah's three sons, Shem and Ham and Japheth, "the whole earth was peopled," Genesis says. Noah cultivates the land that God restored, and in doing so, ends up being the first to plant a vineyard and become drunk from it, which caused Noah to pass out uncovered in his tent. Genesis then recounts that Ham, Noah's youngest son, not only saw his father's nakedness but even blabbed about it to his brothers, Shem, and Japheth. They, in turn, responded to the event much more honorably by walking into the tent backwards with a garment to cover their father's nakedness, keeping their faces turned to prevent seeing his shame. When Noah learns what happened, he proclaims a curse on Canaan, who is Ham's son: "Cursed be Canaan; lowest of slaves shall he be to his brothers.... Blessed by the Lord my God be Shem; and let Canaan be his slave. May God make space for Japheth, and let him live in the tents of Shem; and let Canaan be his slave."[96] The next chapter of Genesis then details some of the descendants of each son.

There are several parts of this story we need to notice. First, Ham's particular crime was an offense against his father's patriarchal dignity; notice then that the punishment, by this logic, is the degradation of Ham's *son* and, by extension, his descendants thereafter. Ham shamed his father; now Ham's son, Canaan, will shame Ham (and so on). Second, the biblical account is quick to note that Ham's son was Canaan, and with the listing of his further descendants later, we find out that Canaan's descendants would include the settlers of Sodom and Gomorrah. Anyone who has read much of the Hebrew Bible / Old Testament will know that the Canaanites became the foreign enemies of God's people, the Hebrews and Israelites. The Canaanites are frequently condemned in the Bible for their wickedness and idolatry, and in later generations, they will be cast out of the Promised Land by Hebrew armies after Moses leads the Hebrews out of Egyptian captivity. Third, notice in the blessing and cursing delivered by Noah and in

[96] Genesis 9:25-27 (NRSVCE)

the listing of descendants that enslavement here is envisioned as both caused by a sin *and also* able to taint future generations of a family, who themselves will continue to act in a sinful manner (again, think Sodom and Gomorrah and the Canaanite idolatry); the Canaanites, in their wickedness, will be conquered by the Hebrews. Finally, we should notice that within the biblical story, Ham and Canaan are *not* described as "black" or dark-skinned, and skin color is never mentioned in biblical descriptions of the Kushites, their descendants.[97] The geographical region provided is also rather tenuous. Many of Canaan's descendants would live in North Africa and the land of Cush, or Ethiopia, just bordering what we call the Middle East, but Cush's son, Nimrod, was usually linked to an Asiatic location in Mesopotamia.[98]

What seems clear from all of this "noticing" is that the biblical account provides an idea of slavery as a punishment for sin and as enacted on a man's son and his descendants due to the crime's patriarchal nature. However, while the curse is passed down to a group of people who will be enemies of the Hebrews, the account does *not* provide a restrictive geography, a racialized view of enslavement, nor a clear indication that this slavery would be inheritable in all cases. Moses, in fact, married a Kushite woman, and another biblical Kushite, Ebed-melech, is highly praised in biblical and postbiblical accounts, as is the "Kushi" prophet Zephaniah.[99]

How then did ideas of the "Curse of Ham" become a dominant justification for the racialized enslavement of "black" people in the Atlantic world? For one thing, long before Atlantic slavery, interpreters of this passage in the Judeo-Christian tradition began associating "blackness" with Ham. This idea of "blackness" was

---

[97] David Goldenberg, *The Curse of Ham: Race and Slavery in Early Judaism, Christianity, and Islam* (Princeton: Princeton UP, 2003), 195.

[98] Benjamin Braude, "The Sons of Noah and the Construction of Ethnic and Geographical Identities in the Medieval and Early Modern Periods," *The William and Mary Quarterly* 54.1 (Jan. 1997): 103-42, esp. 108-9.

[99] Goldenberg, *The Curse of Ham,* 196.

symbolic and not physical, and especially not meant to map on to a person's coloring (skin, hair, or otherwise). A second century BC text, known as the "Animal Apocalypse," for example, described the genealogy of righteous and wicked peoples in the Bible by ascribing animal names and traits to them, with black animals representing wickedness and white ones representing righteousness;[100] this is not much different than the medieval Christian conceit of having a "white angel" and a "black demon" on one's shoulder, alluring a person to make a good or bad decision. By the early modern period, these associations of "blackness" with sin, evil, the devil, and cursing, however, would be wrongly ascribed to darker skinned peoples, and read back onto the Curse of Ham and other literature of "blackness." Indeed, some early modern writers defended Ham's "blackness" as physical because they likewise subscribed to a mistaken view about the biblical "Curse of Cain," which claimed that Cain physically turned black after killing his brother Abel.[101] The idea that these metaphors related to actual physical markers became far too easy in a pseudo-scientific racial landscape bent on justifying a profitable labor system.

Between the fourth and twelfth centuries, moreover, a number of Middle Eastern Christians, Jews, and Muslims began elaborating on the curse of blackness and enslavement by tying it to specific African peoples they viewed as enemies or whom they hoped to conquer, and in these writings, we do find markers of physicality identified. A tenth-century Persian historian, Tabarī, for example, identified his own people, "all who have beautiful faces and hair," as descendants of Shem, whereas "Ham begot all blacks and people with crinkly hair," those sub-Saharan Africans (not accidentally) with whom the Persians were in conflict.[102]

---

[100] Goldenberg, *The Curse of Ham*, 152.

[101] In 1883, for example, George W. Williams referred to the Curse of Cain as "the generally accepted theory" explaining black sin, in his *History of the Negro Race in America: From 1619-1880* (NY, 1883), I:19.

102 Qtd. in Sweet, "The Iberian Roots of American Racist Thought," 148-49. In art and images, however, Ham would still be drawn and

Geographically-speaking, though, the tie of Ham to the region Africa specifically became far more solidified through the late medieval work, *The Travels of Sir John Mandeville,* which was probably the most widely read travel book in the Atlantic world between 1350 and 1600, and one which shaped Columbus and probably every other early explorer.[103] A *racialized* theory of the Curse of Ham – one that directly connected Ham to "dark" people living in Africa – did not come together until Europeans had reason to justify the enslavement of Africans.[104]

In our chapter on Encounter, we saw that the Europeans who arrived on the shores of Africa and the Americas were not more sophisticated, powerful, or technologically advanced than other Atlantic peoples, nor does an easy retelling of their conflicts make sense of the reality "on the ground" or the choices they made. Yet many of the justifications for slavery and colonization that developed by Europeans during and after these encounters rested upon claims of civilizational superiority, including arguments that the Europeans conquered "savage" or "barbarian" peoples, and that colonization would benefit these peoples through introducing "civilization."

Both liberty traditions described in the previous section played a role in the development of these problematic justifications of colonization. In the same decades that writers in the negative liberty tradition described the creation of "social contracts" by people in the state of nature, European writers also began describing the peoples discovered across the Atlantic as people actually still *in* the "state of nature." Aphra Behn in her novella *Oroonoko* (1688), for example, portrays the indigenous people of Suriname (in the northeast corner of South America) as living in a state of innocence similar to that of Adam and Eve before the fall.

---

colored as light-skinned even up through the sixteenth century. See Braude, "Sons of Ham," 121-22.

[103] Braude, "Sons of Ham," 115-16.

[104] And later, to support anti-Semitic views, some authors in fact changed the story to say Shem mocked his father's nakedness, and from Shem came the Jewish people. See Braude, "Sons of Ham," 138-39.

In their shy nakedness "these people represented to me," Behn claims, "an absolute idea of the first state of innocence, before man knew how to sin."[105] While ideas of "natural innocence" might sound positive in some of these accounts – especially when writers used these descriptions to criticize their own greedy or fallen societies in comparison – very often these narratives of foreign peoples as undeveloped "innocents" became central discourses to undermine their autonomy and self-rule, and central ways to legitimize dispossessing others of land. Those in a more "primitive," "barbarous," or "wild" state of living, it was claimed, had not laws but "customs," defective governments (at best), and no commercial system of cultivation and exchange necessary to transform their soil into private property.[106] In *The Second Treatise of Government,* John Locke laid the groundwork for such claims when he argued that people in the state of nature who had not consented to political society and the use of money owned no property beyond the immediate fruits of their labor on the soil which provided for their own self-preservation. Locke thereby argued that *in his own time* (the late seventeenth century) "great Tracts of Ground" in America laid in "waste" and unclaimed due to the supposedly primitive governments and associations of peoples on the continent.[107]

---

[105] Aphra Behn, *Oroonoko,* xx.

[106] Bruce Buchan, "The Empire of Political Thought: Civilization, Savagery and Perceptions of Indigenous Government," *History of the Human Sciences* 18.2 (2005): 1-22, esp. 4-6.

[107] Locke, *Second Treatise,* 299. Locke's activities as an investor and political worker further underscore his support of Atlantic slavery and Britain's developing colonial system in the late seventeenth century. Locke held shares in the Royal African Company from 1672 to 1675, invested in the Bahamas Company of Adventurers in the 1670s, drew up a proposal for the *Fundamental Constitutions of the Carolinas* in 1669 which asserted that "every freeman of Carolina shall have absolute power and authority" over "negro slaves," and made policies through the Council of the Board of Trade that greatly expanded colonial slavery and simultaneously proposed "Poor Laws" to confine the English poor to workhouses to better encourage and manage their labor for the good of

Alongside claims drawn from the "state of nature" discourses, Europeans styled themselves as the rightful inheritors of empire. Like their Roman forebears who conquered barbarian tribes and brought them to the "civilization" of Roman law, European nations argued that they should continue the work of subduing "wild and barbarous" peoples. English colonizers, for instance, emphasized their particular fitness to "civilize" others because they themselves had been subdued and conquered under the Roman Empire by Julius Caesar over a millennium earlier. Now, fully "developed" as a civilized society with laws, sociable manners, good religion, and commercial society, the English had not only a right but a *duty* to conquer their neighbors and bring them along to "civilization." In his letter in 1572 to the English colonizers of Ireland, for example, Sir Thomas Smith explained that "histories of things past" uncovered "how this country of England, once as uncivil as Ireland now is, was by colonies of the Romans brought to understand the laws and orders of the ancient orders"; England now, centuries later, Smith continued, had " more straightly and truly kept the molds" of this Roman civilization brought by Caesar even than the Italians, making the English the true inheritors of this tradition.[108] Similarly, Richard Hakluyt encouraged the famed privateer and colonizer, Sir Walter Raleigh, to emulate the Roman conquerors of old: "Up then, go on as you have begun, leave to posterity an imperishable monument of your name and fame such as age will never obliterate. For to posterity no greater glory can be handed down than to conquer the

---

English society. See John Marshall, "London, Locke and 1690s Provisions for the Poor in Context: Beggars, Spinners and Slaves," in *Politics, Religion and Ideas in Seventeenth and Eighteenth-Century Britain* (Woodbridge, Boydell Press, 2019), 181-200.

[108] Qtd. in David Beers Quinn, "Sir Thomas Smith (1513-1577) and the Beginnings of English Colonial Theory," *Proceedings of the American Philosophical Society* 89.4 (1945): 543-560, esp. 546.

barbarians, to recall the savage and pagan to civility, to draw the ignorant within the orbit of reason."[109]

Enlightenment writers in the mid eighteenth-century, such as Adam Smith in Scotland and Anne-Robert-Jacques Turgot in France, formulated these theories of civilizational development into a fully articulated "stadial" theory, which claimed that people groups achieved civility by progressing through successive stages of commercial and political development. First came the most uncivil Age of the Hunters, "a way of life highly inimical to thought and reflection," and one requiring few laws or regulation because there was no conception of property; then the Age of the Shepherds, which brought with it property in livestock and therefore the introduction of laws against theft; then the Age of Agriculture, with which came fixed settlement, property in land, and therefore more laws and regulations; and finally, as the most advanced stage, the Age of Commerce, and with it even more laws, together with the "softening" of manners and the flourishing of literature, science, and the arts. Parallel to these phases of economic development went a corresponding enlargement of the intellectual powers of the human mind.[110]

Enlightenment writers debated whether all nations and peoples might be capable of this "development" through colonization efforts, or whether – due to racial or other differences – certain peoples might never develop fully on this scale, making them fit to labor for advanced peoples. These civilizational discourses were used to justify efforts of dispossession and slavery around the world through the early modern and modern period, and we could probably identify several ways these ideas are around today. Why is it, for example, that the arts and textiles of people from the Americas tend to be housed in "natural history" museums, and the arts and textiles of Europeans and European settlers tend to be housed in "fine arts" museums? When Amer-

---

[109] Qtd. in Keith Thomas, *In Pursuit of Civility: Manners and Civilization in Early Modern England* (New Haven: Yale UP, 2018), 182.

[110] Thomas, *In Pursuit of Civility*, 142.

icans "export democracy," are we continuing this civilizational tradition, or not?

The concepts described in this chapter, including revolution, checks and balances, liberty, racism, and slavery, clearly remain with us today and color our contemporary debates in fascinating and complex ways. Whether you consider yourself right, left, or center in politics, you will likely claim that in some areas of life the government should leave citizens alone and in other areas the government should indeed intervene for the sake of the common good. As we will see in the next chapters, the significant mixture of these old and new concepts of liberty and slavery shaped the distinctive character of Atlantic revolutions in the early modern period and the creation of universal rights discourses, which have become foundational for ideas of citizenship and equality in our contemporary world.

Two Atlantic Revolutions: France and Haiti

By Jamie Gianoutsos

On a cold day in January 1793, 144 years after the beheading of King Charles I in England, the anointed monarch of France, Louis XVI, mounted a scaffold for his execution. Like Charles, Louis would die from his head being severed from his body in front of a crowd, but this time, the king's final speech would be drowned out by the banging of drums and the executioner's blade would be dropped by a new technological invention, the guillotine, which made such work more efficient and concise. Louis met his ignoble fate after deputies in the newly formed French National Convention tried the king in their own court of justice and found him "guilty of attempts against liberty and of conspiracy against the general security of the state." Evidence of such conspiracy came largely from a cache of documents discovered in a secret safe in the Tuileries Palace, which showed that the king had asked repeatedly for foreign aid and assistance to overthrow the revolutionaries.[111]

Liberty in France

From these documents, and from accounts of the royal family's attempted flight out of the country in 1791, an overwhelming majority in the Convention adjudged the king guilty; far fewer, however, desired to see Louis executed. Claiming themselves more enlightened than those earlier English butchers, Thomas Paine and his more moderate allies desired to banish Louis to the United States, or to ask through national referendum for the citizens of

---

[111] David Jordan, *The King's Trial* (Berkeley: University of California Press, 1979), 172.

France to determine the king's punishment.[112] The twenty-five year old fiery orator Louis-Antoine Saint-Just retorted that "those who worry about whether it is fair to punish a king will never establish a republic."[113] In the end, the radicals won the trial and the sentencing.

As we saw in the chapter on Liberty, the many types of liberty discourses, rights discourses, and slavery discourses that developed across the early modern period could be packaged and utilized in numerous ways, both to support equality and citizenship and also to justify inequality and slavery. The French Revolution reflected this complex legacy in numerous ways. France's Revolution (with its many phases, constitutions, and upheavals) produced several of the most important articulations of liberty, equality, and citizenship for the modern world, and successfully fused together modern and ancient ideas of liberty into what some historians have called "liberal republicanism." In *The Declaration of the Rights of Man and Citizen* (August 1789), for example, the French National Assembly declared in the fourth article, in the vein of the negative liberty tradition, that "Liberty consists in being able to do all that does not harm others; thus, man is only limited in his natural rights when they infringe on the rights of other members of society." Yet in article six, more closely echoing the positive liberty tradition, the *Declaration of Rights* declared the law to be "the expression of the general will," for which "all citizens have the right to participate" either "personally

---

[112] Although initially a British citizen (who had become an American citizen during the American War of Independence), Thomas Paine was one of seventeen foreigners accorded honorary French citizenship in August 1792 after being run out of Britain for his radical views. The next month, he was elected as a deputy to the new National Convention, which afforded him the position to vote on the trial and sentence of Louis XVI. Like many who opposed the Jacobin party, Paine would be arrested later in 1793 under the orders of Maximilien Robespierre and the Committee of Public Safety, but he survived and was released later that year.

[113] Saint-Just, *Oeuvres choisies* (Paris: Gallimard, 1968), 76.

or by their representatives."[114] The *Declaration*'s delineation of basic rights, and its preamble proclaiming the "Rights of Man" as "natural, inalienable, and sacred," would become the foundation of bills of rights in multiple nations, and eventually the basis of the United Nations' Universal Declaration of Human Rights.

The origins and causes of the French Revolution were many, ranging from intellectual and cultural developments that made it possible for a range of people to criticize their king and express new ideas, to political and economic conflicts which left France totally broke from foreign wars and unable to raise sufficient revenue through their highly regressive tax system, whereby the poor (who could least afford to pay) contributed the most, while the nobility (who could most afford to pay) contributed very little.[115] In 1789, after years of unsuccessful attempts to solve the crisis, King Louis XVI called a meeting of the Estates General, a representative body of France's population, to reform the system before financial collapse. The Three Estates called to meet in the Estates General represented the three classes of people in French society: the First and Second Estate, the Catholic clergy and nobility, made up 3% of France's population; the Third Estate, filled with untitled nobility, commoners, and peasants, made up 97% of the population. Initially, it was declared that each Estate would get 300 representatives (despite the massively larger size and diversity of the Third Estate), and that the representative bodies would follow a voting system that was advantageous to the noble estates.[116]

---

[114] This, of course, was also pulled from Jean-Jacques Rousseau's Enlightenment treatise, *The Social Contract*, itself a fascinating mixture of the positive and negative liberty traditions.

[115] Sylvia Neely, *A Concise History of the French Revolution* (Lanham: Rowman and Littlefield, 2008), 7-12, 29-50.

[116]The advantage involved whether the estates would vote together or separately. The government eventually allowed 600 representatives from the Third Estate to be called, but the severe inequality between the estates would continue if the Three Estates met separately and voted in bloc, rather than meeting together and voting by individual

Representatives from across France's provinces were elected to represent each of the Three Estates, and in the *cahiers de doleances* (lists of grievances) that local men and sometimes women drew up for their representatives, French subjects expressed their profound frustration not only with taxes but also with the highly inequitable system of power and privilege which kept those who made the necessary contributions to the public welfare from making corporate decisions or reforms in government. The Abbé Sièyes would argue in his pamphlet, *What is the Third Estate?* that, as far as what was needed to form a "complete nation," the Third Estate was "Everything; but an everything shackled and oppressed." Without the other two estates, Sièyes claimed, the Third Estate would still be "everything" yet "free and flourishing" and "infinitely better." Due to their privileges and expenditures, the First and Second Estate challenged the very idea of a nation of associated people, for in a nation, people must live under a common law and be represented by the same legislature.[117]

The election of the Estates General transformed the notion of government according to the people from an abstract slogan into a living reality in France, and the rise of thousands of cheap newspapers, political clubs, rallies and marches in the years following would solidify the role of this public in forging matters of state. Indeed, early direct action by citizens, including violent protest at the Bastille prison and other locations, would help to propel the Estates General representatives into the formation of a true National Assembly in the spring of 1789 led by the Third Estate and joined by sympathetic progressives in the First and Second Estate (such as the Abbé Sièyes). Those who formed the National Assembly took the Tennis Court Oath not to disband until a new constitution had been drawn up for the French nation.

---

representative. Jeremy Popkin, *A Short History of the French Revolution*, 7th ed. (NY: Routledge, 2020), 29.

[117] Emmanuel Joseph (Abbé) Sieyès, "What Is the Third Estate?" (1789)," *Liberty, Equality, Fraternity: Exploring the French Revolution,* accessed June 9, 2023, https://revolution.chnm.org/d/280.

Following the night of 4 August 1789, when the newly formed National Assembly declared an end to the feudal privileges of the First and Second Estates and drew up *The Declaration of the Rights of Man and Citizen,* more and more French citizens took to the streets to demand the rights of representation and citizenship, as well as fair prices on goods and necessities. During the October Days of 1789, over 20,000 women marched to the king's palace in Versailles with canons and weapons, demanding the royal family return to Paris to support the revolution. Peasants in the countryside attacked (both symbolically and actually) the manors and estates of the titled nobility, burning historic documents of feudalism. As hunting rights had been a privilege only for the nobility, peasants hunted and slaughtered forest animals and left them on the lawns of country manors, often decorating the protest scene with liberty poles dressed in revolutionary colors.[118]

Yet, the moderate constitution drawn up in these early years of revolution (1789-1791) would not satisfy many. Conservatives, including church officials and faithful provincial peasants, protested and fought the National Assembly's decision to place the Catholic Church in France under control of the state. The Civil Constitution of the Clergy (1791) stripped the church of its private lands, banned monastic vows, required all priests and bishops to swear an oath to the nation and not the pope, and left many citizens feeling that the Revolution was waging war not against privilege but against religious belief itself. Some priests fled, like the twenty-six-year-old John Dubois, who landed in the Catholic haven of Maryland.[119] Devastating civil war broke out in several

---

[118] John Markoff, "Violence, Emancipation, and Democracy: The countryside and the French Revolution," in *The French Revolution: Recent Debates and New Controversies,* 2nd ed. (NY: Routledge, 2006): 165-197

[119] John Dubois (1764-1842) was the third Bishop of New York (1826-1842), and, to this date, the only Bishop of New York without Irish ancestry. In 1808, he also founded a beautiful little college and seminary in Emmitsburg, Maryland, named Mount St. Mary's, and assisted St. Elizabeth Ann Seton in founding St. Joseph's College for women the following year.

provinces where "counter-revolutionaries" strongly defended the church against newly formed revolutionary units of soldiers.

Progressives, meanwhile, including more radical workers and artisans in Paris (the *sans-culottes)* and the rising Jacobin Club, decried the moderate provisions of the new constitution which left King Louis XVI in government with a suspensive veto and distinguished between "active" and "passive" citizens.[120] Only "active" citizens – males who had enough wealth to pay taxes equal to three days of an unskilled laborer's wage – could vote or run for office, this constitution confirmed; all women and a third of the male population meanwhile would be excluded from the full rights of active citizenship. Internal politics in France became especially volatile following the Pillnitz Declaration, wherein Austrian and Prussian rulers demanded the restoration of King Louis XVI's full rights as monarch, when the Legislative Assembly declared war on Austria, Queen Marie Antoinette's home country. By the summer of 1792, the French legislature had to respond to internal violence from revolutionary mobs in Paris, counter-revolutionary protests flaring in the provinces, foreign armies marching at the borders, and as we will see below, the mass insurrection of slaves in the French Caribbean colony, Saint-Domingue (Haiti). Foreign war raised the stakes of the revolution, for those who opposed revolutionary reforms could now be accused of treason, and at the same time, distinctions between "active" and "passive" citizens became harder to justify, as members of the lower classes were increasingly mobilized to fight in French armies and police forces.

In this climate, *sans-culottes* militants from the lower classes, incensed from the deaths of protestors in Paris at the hands of the Paris National Guard, violently attacked the royal palace in August 1792. Through their violence, which continued with the massacre of counter-revolutionaries (including priests) in Paris prisons during the September Massacres, the *sans-culotte* militants forced

---

[120] The term *sans-culottes* refers to the fashionable knee-length breeches (*culottes*) that French nobles wore. Being without (*sans*) breeches, in contrast, was a sign of being working class.

the Legislative Assembly to suspend the monarchy and call for new elections for the National Convention. As they marched on conservative strongholds and local governments, these militants sang battle songs such as *Le Marseillaise* decrying enemies of the revolution at home and foreign enemies at France's borders. *Le Marseillaise* remains France's national anthem:

> Let us go, children of the fatherland
> Our day of Glory has arrived.
> Against us stands tyranny,
> The bloody flag is raised,
> The bloody flag is raised.
> Do you hear in the countryside
> The roar of these savage soldiers
> They come right into our arms
> To cut the throats of your sons,
> your country.
> To arms, citizens!
> Form up your battalions
> Let us march, Let us march!
> That their impure blood
> Should water our fields
> Sacred love of the fatherland
> Guide and support our vengeful arms.
> Liberty, beloved liberty,
> Fight with your defenders;
> Fight with your defenders.
> Under our flags, so that victory
> Will rush to your manly strains;
> That your dying enemies
> Should see your triumph and glory

The new National Convention declared France a republic, and increasingly, French radicals called the Jacobins moved from unofficially supporting violent protest and militias to creating and justifying official state-sponsored violence. The Jacobins argued that the Revolution could not be complete until all enemies to the common good had been expelled and all remaining French citizens transformed into virtuous supporters of the common good.[121]

Amidst this violence, and the overthrowing of the Legislative Assembly, the newly formed National Convention ushered in the radical phase of the Revolution (1792-1794). They executed the king (and later the queen), drafted thousands of young men into war, created the "Committee of Public Safety" and declared that violent "terror is the order of the day." In the Constitution of 1793, however, they also enacted a number of democratic provisions: the universal right to vote for all men (regardless of wealth); the right of subsistence for all either through employment or welfare benefits; the creation of universal free public education; and the abolition of slavery in all French colonies. Despite their limitations (such as ordering the closing of female political clubs and telling all women to go home), these reforms went much further in fulfilling the revolutionary pledge for "Liberty, Equality, Fraternity" than any prior legislation. But such liberty would require Terror, Maximilien Robespierre explained, until the revolution was complete, until all of France's enemies foreign and domestic – the enemies of progress, of the common good, of equality – had been eradicated, and all citizens filled with virtuous patriotism for this new regime of liberty.[122] Following the erection of guillotines in city squares and the mass executions of thousands of French citizens in the revolting Vendée region, the final "Great Terror" in the summer of 1794 would include the decapitation of 1,300 victims in Paris alone in six weeks. Overall, revolutionary tribunals condemned some 17,000 people to death in 1793 and 1794, and with the slaughter of victims in the Vendée, the total

---

[121] Dan Edelstein, "Do We Want a Revolution without Revolution? Reflections on Political Authority," *French Historical Studies* 35.2 (Spring 2012): 269-289.

[122] Maximilien Robespierre, "On Political Morality" (February 5, 1794), *Liberty, Equality, Fraternity: Exploring the French Revolution,* accessed June 9, 2023, https://revolution.chnm.org/d/413.

number of violent deaths during the Terror period probably added up to something between 250,000 and 300,000 people.[123]

The Terror marked a new definition of the very idea of revolution, as it enacted widespread state-enforced violence in the name of revolution. Unlike prior conflicts producing constitutional change, this "revolution" did not have a clear ending: Could any state ever eradicate *all* enemies? And who qualified as an enemy – anyone who challenged any governmental policy? Through making "revolution" a continuous principle, rather than a specific constitutional or regime-change event, the French government in the Terror exerted extreme violence and control over citizen populations. A number of modern governments in the twentieth century have followed this model of continuous "revolutionary government," gaining levels of power and enacting means of violence to an extraordinary degree, with no check or ending.[124]

Did Napoleon Bonaparte solve this crisis? Depends on whom you ask. The government by Terror collapsed in July 1794 with the arrest of Robespierre, and during what historians call the Thermidorian and Directory Periods (July 1794-November 1799), the French government stabilized somewhat into a more

---

[123] Popkin, *A Short History of the French Revolution*, 104.

[124] Historians compare ideas of revolutionary government from the Terror to fascist and communist violent states in the twentieth century. "Political regimes that continued to govern on the basis of revolutionary authority, by contrast, tended to postpone the creation of a constitutional order. Before the overthrow of Fulgencio Batista, for instance, the restoration of the 1940 Constitution had been "the rallying cry" of the Cuban opposition, including Fidel Castro's 26th of July Movement. Once victory had been achieved, however, this objective was abandoned in favor of transformative socioeconomic measures. It would be another sixteen years (in 1976) before the Cuban government adopted a constitution. Even then constitutions do not necessarily curtail revolutionary authority: the extraconstitutional power of the Chinese Communist Party, for instance, is enshrined in the Preamble of its 1982 Constitution; article 6 of the Soviet Union's 1977 Constitution similarly granted the Communist Party an unchecked executive role." Edelstein, "Do We Want a Revolution without Revolution?" 285.

conservative republican compromise, seeking the "politics of balance" by suppressing royalists on one side and neo-Jacobins on the other, and channeling energy into external conquest. Through military ventures, the French expanded their "liberty" system to "Sister Republics" from Europe to the Middle East, including Egypt.[125] Many citizens voted in Directory elections, but the government had a bad habit of "correcting" the voters' decisions, which led to a number of *coups*. In the aftermath of the Terror, the government stopped rounding up enemies for the guillotine, but created a new national police force, the *gendarmerie,* to maintain order and crush free expression.

The Directory continued to use authoritarian tactics to "keep the peace," and this – alongside France's extensive military campaigns – made it possible for the remarkably accomplished and genuinely popular military commander, Napoleon Bonaparte, to overthrow the Directory government in 1799 in the name of protecting the achievements of the Revolution. In 1796 and 1797, French armies had penetrated deep into Germany and Italy, where the young general Bonaparte achieved spectacular successes, occupying the peninsula as far south as Rome. The French looted Italian churches and palaces, shipping many of the country's artistic masterpieces back to Paris (where many still sit in the Louvre Museum). Napoleon and his army crossed the Alps and, without instructions from the Directory, negotiated the treaty of Campo-Formio. Napoleon then led the Egyptian expedition, his popularity in France rising even as the French military suffered significant defeats in Europe in the first half of 1799.

Especially for the first five years of his rule, following his overthrow of the government on 18 brumaire (November 9, 1799), Napoleon claimed to be running a republic with himself as "First

---

[125] Interestingly, during Napoleon's expedition to Egypt, French propagandists even crafted the first modern proposals for the creation of a Jewish national state in France's model. Popkin, *A Short History of the French Revolution,* 122-23.

Consul."[126] In 1804, he abandoned the republican façade and crowned himself Emperor, making his power hereditary and permanent. It is difficult to assess how popular Napoleon was with French citizens before or after 1804, because he was a master of controlling public expression. He forced citizens to vote publicly on the initial constitution in 1800, which still got fewer votes than the radical democratic constitution of 1793 had received by secret ballot. Napoleon muzzled the political press, used the new police force to harass political enemies, and sent in "flying columns" of troops to turn suspects over to special military courts for quick punishment. He strengthened the already centralized bureaucracy by creating prefects with extensive powers, who rotated from post to post every few years to remain unattached from local interests and committed to federal authority.[127] In many ways, Napoleon solidified and perfected the centralization efforts of French kings before him.

Through incredible military victories, and the eventual treaty at Amiens in March 1802, Napoleon extensively expanded France's empire, allies, and dependent states from the Kingdom of Spain across Germany, Prussia and Austria, up through Denmark and Norway and down through the Italian peninsula. He also instituted a bloody reversal of colonial policies in the French Caribbean, re-instituting slavery. Haiti would gain its independence in defiance of Napoleon in 1804, but formerly

---

[126] During the radical phase of the revolution, which had resulted in the Terror, the revolutionary government threw out the Christian calendar and replaced it with a new revolutionary one, with the year divided into twelve months, each given a poetic name based on its weather (*niwôse* was the month of snow, *floréal* the month whem flowers bloomed, etc.). Each month was divided into three ten-day weeks, or *decades,* and years were to be counted from the establishment of the French Republic on September 22, 1792. So the year of Napoleon's *coup* was year VIII, and the month *brumaire,* named after the fog that frequently occurred in France in that month.

[127] Popkin, *A Short History of the French Revolution*, 133-34.

enslaved people on other French islands in the Caribbean would be re-enslaved.

On many islands, the process of re-enslavement was possible because governors had pursued a process of gradual emancipation, arguing that enslaved persons deserved the universal principle of basic emancipation but could not be trusted with full political rights and citizenship until the moral reform of their souls had been accomplished. As one supporter of gradual emancipation had explained to the slave insurgents, "Your souls, long oppressed by the debasement of vigorous punishment, have been degraded; slavery has snuffed out the divine fire that produces and maintains the virtues that are indispensable for the state of sociability."[128] In Guadeloupe, the ex-slaves had achieved extensive military victories against British troops, even conquering Saint Lucia, but many had already been forced back to work on plantations as the "price of liberty," deemed necessary by colonial governors like Victor Hugues both for the economic viability of the nation and the "moral cleansing" of the formerly enslaved through self-sacrificial hard work.[129] In 1802, Napoleon sent an expedition to re-establish slavery in Guadeloupe, Saint-Domingue (Haiti), and other French colonies; in Guadeloupe, more than 10,000 died resisting the reinstitution of slavery, but the majority of ex-slaves who had not already been laboring in the fields were forced back on plantations. Napoleon was the only leader to *re-establish* slavery after its abolition; the French would not fully abolish the system until 1848.

Through a deal with Pope Pius VII, Napoleon also brokered a "Concordat" or treaty with the papacy which recognized Catholicism as the majority religion in France but allowed the state to keep confiscated church lands, pay clerics, and nominate bishops.[130] Napoleon mainly desired a religious settlement because he understood religion to be a useful instrument of social control.

---

[128] Julien Raimond qtd. in Laurent Dubois, "The Price of Liberty: Victor Hugues and the administration of freedom in Guadeloupe, 1794-1798," *William and Mary Quarterly* 56.2 (Apr. 1999): 363-93, esp. 372-73.

[129] Dubois, "The Price of Liberty," 366-67.

[130] Popkin, *A Short History of the French Revolution*, 137.

In his Imperial Catechism, issued in 1806, children learned they were bound to all their duties toward the Emperor because "God, who creates Empires and apportions them according to his will, has, by accumulating his gifts upon [Emperor Napoleon], set him up as our sovereign, and made him the agent of his power, and his image on earth. So to honor and serve our Emperor is to honor and serve God himself."[131]

Had divine-right kingship reached its full expression? Or did Napoleon's achievements in fact save a republican revolution? Scholars who say the latter argue that Napoleon accomplished a number of initiatives that the original French revolutionaries had sought. He solidified the state's control of religion, solved France's financial crises, and modernized and vastly reformed France's citizen army, making it a nationalistic force.[132] Napoleon expanded opportunities for education and office-holding, built a "liberty regime" across Europe, and most importantly, instituted the *Code Napoléon*. This new civil law code enshrined the right of property and eliminated the last vestiges of feudal privilege. But the *Code Napoléon* also enhanced male-dominated visions of the family whereby husbands had full control of their family's property and the fate of their children. Although its provisions about women's rights have been modified, Napoleon's Civil Code still remains the basis of French civil law today.[133]

In 1812, Napoleon overplayed his hand. When Tsar Alexander of Russia broke the anti-British military alliance that Napoleon had forced on him, Napoleon amassed more than half a million soldiers to march into Russia – an army so large it took eight days to pass a given spot. But most of these soldiers would die in Russia, due to the scorched earth campaign the Russians employed and the brutal Russian winter. Over the next three years, Napoleon lost several more battles, and was even exiled for a time in the

---

[131] J. M. Thompson, "Napoleon's Imperial Catechism," *Napoleon Bonaparte: His Rise and Fall* (Friedland, 2018). Excerpted https://www.vision.org/napoleons-imperial-catechism-821.

[132] Chris Tozzi, xx

[133] Popkin, *A Short History of the French Revolution*, 138-39.

Mediterranean island of Elba. He would fight his last battle at Waterloo in 1815, when he was beaten in the field and exiled to the small island of Saint Helena.[134] Even after his defeat, Napoleon insisted that his authoritarian policies were necessary for French freedom. "Had I been in America, I would willingly have been a Washington...," Napoleon maintained while confined on the island of Saint Helena, "But had Washington been in France, exposed to discord within, and invasion from without, I would have defied him to have been what he was in America.... For my own part, I could only have been a crowned Washington."[135]

Liberty in Haiti

The French claimed to be champions of universal liberty, equality, and fraternity in the 1790s, but in reality, the enslaved people of France's colony, Saint-Domingue, were the ones to enact universal ideals. In the Haitian Revolution (1790-1804), which achieved the emancipation of slavery and the independence of Saint-Domingue (renamed Haiti), a vision of republican citizenship found its marriage with universal principles of equality and a resounding critique of the racism of colonial slave systems. At the same time, and much like the French Revolution, the Haitian Revolution failed to establish political rights for women (even though it emancipated female slaves), and Haiti's story (like France's story) continues to raise questions about the troubling role of violence in political revolution and the difficulty of creating legal systems to sustain true liberty. As one historian summarized: "Liberation is not liberty; the former is merely the latter's condition of possibility. Liberty, in contrast to liberation, requires a legal framework for the exercise of rights and for the protection of rights in the breach, without which the word right and the word citizen

---

[134] Paul Johnson, *Napoleon: A Life* (NY: Penguin, 2002), 128-132 and 169-187.

[135] Qtd. in Popkin, *A Short History of the French Revolution*, 145.

denote unrealized potentialities."[136] The Haitian Revolution is one of the most important events in the history of democracy – even though Haiti has not sustained a fully democratic or stable legal system over time.

The French colony of Saint-Domingue was widely known as the "Pearl of the Antilles," as it was the strongest export economy of the Americas and the world's largest producer of sugar and coffee, along with significant amounts of cotton, indigo, and cacao.[137] Its territory of around 10,600 square miles occupies the western third of Hispaniola, first claimed by Christopher Columbus when he landed in the northwest of the island in December 1492.[138] The territory was ceded to France by the Spaniards in 1697, and due to the Northeast trade winds, its principal northern city, Le Cap Français, served as the first port of call for ships arriving from Europe and the Americas; it took around forty-five days to travel to Saint-Domingue from France, and twenty days from the eastern coast of the United States. The indigenous native inhabitants of Hispaniola, the Taino people, had called the island "Ayti," the land of high mountains. The Taino people had largely disappeared through war, colonizing, and intermarriage with the Spaniards in the sixteenth century, but their legacy, intermixed with Europeans and Africans, shaped the culture of the island's "creole" identity.[139]

The revolution in Saint-Domingue had significant ties to the French Revolution but also highly distinctive root causes. Even as

---

[136] This original observation comes from Hannah Arendt. Miranda Frances Spieler, "The Legal Structure of Colonial Rule during the French Revolution," *The William and Mary Quarterly* 66.2 (Apr. 2009): 365-408, esp.

[137] Sudhir Hazareesingh, *Black Spartacus: The Epic Life of Toussaint Louverture* (NY: Picador, 2020), 4.

[138] The island of Hispaniola is now shared between Haiti and the Dominican Republic.

[139] Hazareesingh, *Black Spartacus*, 3-4. Part of creole identity is the Haitian creole language, which is a French-based language that emerged primarily from contact between French and West African language speakers (especially Fongbe and Igbo), with influences from Spanish, English, Portuguese, Taino, and other West African languages.

the people of Saint-Domingue avidly consumed the news of revolution in France which arrived in print and rumor from the ports, the shape of the revolution in Saint-Domingue had as much to do with the broader colonial rivalry in the Caribbean between Britain, France, and Spain and the perennial struggle within Saint-Domingue between its three main social groups. Three distinctive groups of people inhabited the colony in the late eighteenth century: about 30,000-40,000 white planters, who could be divided between *grands blancs* (rich plantation owners) and *petit blancs* (small farmers, employees, artisans, soldiers, and sailors); about 28,000 *gens de couleur* (free people of color); and between 500,000 and 800,000 enslaved persons of color. With these main groups were small outposts of *marrons*, or individuals who had escaped slavery and retreated to the bush where they formed bands or hid in plain sight in one of Saint-Domingue's three major cities.[140]

In 1789, as France erupted into revolution, Saint-Domingue's inhabitants disagreed vehemently on what principle their own society should be organized. Who should have the full rights of citizenship, voting, property, and political office-holding on the island? White planters argued that race should be the organizing structure of Saint-Domingue: *grands blancs* emphasized their right for autonomy from aristocrats and French ministers in the motherland, while *petit blancs* argued most forcefully for a rigid, racial hierarchy of rights in order to keep themselves distinct from their main rivals, the free people of color. As one *petit blanc* described, his group had three main enemies: "the philanthropists who supported the free men of color and the slaves, the ministers who ruled the colony from Paris, and the aristocrats (*grands blancs*) who dominated colonial society."[141]

---

[140] The free people of color included "mulattoes," those of mixed racial background, but not all mulattoes were free, and not all slaves were black. Alan Forrest, "War and Revolution in the Caribbean," in *The Death of the French Atlantic: Trade, War, and Slavery in the Age of Revolution* (Oxford: Oxford UP, 2020), 167-69.

[141] Forrest, "War and Revolution in the Caribbean," 167.

The free people of color (or *gens de couleur*) however, argued that property should be the main qualifier of rights-holding citizenship in Saint-Domingue, although some also used racial justifications for their views. Despite holding a free status and enjoying some liberty, they had found themselves increasingly from the 1760s onward the victims of legal and social prejudice which chipped away their equality with free whites by restricting their right to hold public office, forbade entry into certain professions, and limited their property-ownership and political representation. This group then, on the whole, tended to be less concerned with abolishing privilege altogether and more concerned with fully joining the privileged ranks. An early pamphlet by a free man of color proposed a society where whites and mulattoes (those of mixed race) would be grouped together as a single class of free men and where mulatto slaves would be automatically freed at birth. The writer justified this distinction through a racial argument: mulattoes, he said, were a race belonging particularly to the Americas, where slavery was not native, but "the color of the blacks indicates their origin in Africa" and thereby condemns them to be slaves.[142] Writers such as this desired precisely *not* to extend freedom to the enslaved, even arguing that a white and mixed-race alliance would strengthen slavery.[143]

In initial debates in Saint-Domingue and France, many *gens de couleur* especially held fast to arguments for their own enhanced political rights based on merit and property. "The free men of color are land owners in the colonies, they pay their taxes," Julien Raimond explained to the French National Assembly in 1792, "These qualities give them the right to be heard at a moment when troubles are tearing apart the colony and threatening it with imminent ruin."[144] When white planters refused to adopt any new reforms for citizenship for the free colored population, a few hundred *gens de couleur* rose up in what became a short-lived

---

[142] Forrest, "War and Revolution in the Caribbean," 169.

[143] Hazareesingh, *Black Spartacus*, 45.

[144] Forrest, "War and Revolution in the Caribbean," 171.

rebellion under Vincent Ogé. Following their trial in Cap in 1790, Ogé and his principal collaborator, Jean-Baptist Chavannes (who had fought in the American War of Independence), were condemned to death and horribly tortured before being broken on the wheel in the public square; white militias lynched, mutilated, and murdered anyone believed to have supported the insurgency.[145]

Saint-Domingue's new Colonial Assembly, elected in 1791, was dominated by white supremacists who opposed any dilution of their exclusive rights, and their lobbyists in France in 1790-1791 ensured that the *Declaration of the Rights of Man* would not be extended to "non-free" inhabitants unless their own colonial assemblies allowed it. They even forbade the printing of the *Declaration of the Rights of Man* in Saint-Domingue, while ensuring in the Assembly in Paris that the *Declaration*'s final clause enumerating the right of "property" would be used to shore up the "properties" of the white settlers – including their slaves – under the protection of the nation.[146] In their refusal to allow mulattoes and free people of color equal rights, and in their brutal suppression of Ogé's revolt, the white planters of Saint-Domingue drove this intermediary group, the *gens de couleur*, into alliance with the enslaved population.

Whereas white planters emphasized race as the basis of their superiority, and free people of color mostly emphasized merit and property, the half a million or more people enslaved in Saint-Domingue in 1790 argued that liberty and equality should be the organizing principles of their society. Their view stood in stark contrast to the reality of brutal inequality in the Caribbean. The 1685 *Code Noir*, the rule book which governed the treatment of slaves in French colonies, sought to afford some protections to slaves through granting them judicial recourse in cases of mistreatment, introduction to the Catholic faith and baptism, and the right to marry with the permission of their master. Slaves

---

[145] Forrest, "War in the Caribbean," 170; Hazareesingh, *Black Spartacus*, 45.

[146] Hazareesingh, *Black Spartacus*, 44.

under this code could not carry weapons, and their masters could physically punish them with chains, whips, and rods. While the Code sough to regulate the treatment of slaves to provide sufficient food and "reasonable" treatment, planters often treated it as a dead letter on the islands, such as in their frequent tearing apart of slave families through selling and separating children, parents, brothers, sisters, and cousins.[147] Although the *Code Noir* technically banned the significant torture and abuse of slaves, some planters still practiced horrific atrocities, including throwing slaves into furnaces, burying them alive, blowing up their bodies with gunpowder and cutting off their limbs, and enacting various forms of public torture such as castration and genital mutilation. Slaves living in "better" conditions still experienced extraordinary violence against their bodies every day, with the slavedriver's whip demanding their grueling work. Only one in three enslaved children survived to adulthood on many plantations, and due to working and living conditions and diet, grim disease frequently plagued enslaved bodies. Many slaves, if they survived adolescence, did not live past the age of 37.[148]

Black communities survived, bonded, and shared knowledge in this system of slavery in part through practicing ***voodou***, which fused West African religious practices with some indigenous Taino religious practices. Focused on the worship of spirits (known as *loa*), who were believed to preside over different aspects of earthly existence and communicate with humans during religious rituals, *vodouism* could sustain enslaved communities and also offer physical healing through herbal medicine. The activities of Jesuit missionaries and Catholic churches also shaped the culture of enslaved persons in northern Saint-Domingue. Due to the efforts of Jesuit missionaries to teach slaves how to read and write, and due to their encouragement of slaves to marry, white planters

[147] Thomas Benjamin, *The Atlantic World: Europeans, Africans, Indians and Their Shared History, 1400-1900* (Cambridge: Cambridge UP, 2009), 393-94.

[148] Hazareesingh, *Black Spartacus*, 21-23, 27.

expelled the Jesuits in 1763.[149] In this context of violence, misery, and shared community, even across plantations and regions, the enslaved population of Saint-Domingue inhabited complex social networks and exchanged knowledge and news.

In August 1791, a year after Ogé's failed uprising, slave insurrection began when a few thousand rebels attacked a number of plantations in northern Saint-Domingue, and within a matter of days, the entire northern plain of Saint-Domingue's finest sugar plantations was ablaze in a "terrible spectacle." While some white planters and their families were saved, very often by their own slaves, hundreds of white men, women, and children were put to death, and others taken prisoner.[150] The black insurgency had been launched following two earlier August meetings. In the first, slave representatives from about 100 northern plantations gathered to make initial plans. About a week later, in a ceremony at Bois-Caïman with about 200 participants, the conspiracy was sealed through a religious ritual which brought together a variety of spiritual practices including *voudou*. The 1791 insurrection marked the coming together of slaves and free blacks, African-born and creole born (those born in Saint-Domingue), *marrons* and even clergymen, as a large majority of Catholic priests in the northern parishes of Saint-Domingue supported the slave rebellion.[151]

It is somewhat unclear as to whether the majority of revolutionaries in the initial insurrection sought the immediate abolition of slavery or gradualist arrangements that would allow them to earn their freedom within the context of the plantation system and a multiracial society. Those who supported the latter, for example, argued that slaves should receive three free days a week, during which they could work toward their manumission.[152] Yet in a letter dated July 1792, and published in the Parisian

---

[149] Hazareesingh, *Black Spartacus*, 23-26.

[150] Hazareesingh, *Black Spartacus*, 47.

[151] Hazareesingh, *Black Spartacus*, 49.

[152] Popkin, "A Haitian Revolutionary Manifesto? New Perspectives on the 'Letter of Jean-François, Biassou, and Belair," *Slavery & Abolition* 43.1 (2022): 3-19, esp. 3-4.

newspaper *Le Créole Patriote* the next year, the leaders of the slave insurrection made the philosophical case for general abolition by highlighting the absolute contradiction between the *Declaration of the Rights of Man* and the maintenance of slavery in French colonies. How could "freedom, property, security, and resistance to oppression" be deemed as "universal natural rights" and emblazoned in France, when these very rights were denied to the half-million black inhabitants of the French colonies? While identifying this hypocrisy, the letter profoundly denounced justifications of slavery through racial difference and portrayed those who enslaved others as truly "barbarous" and uncivilized, driven by avarice and ignorance. "We are black, it is true," the letter reads, "but tell us, Gentlemen, you who are so judicious, what is the law that says that the black man must belong to and be the property of the white man?.... We are your equals then, by natural right, and if nature pleases itself to diversify colors within the human race, it is not a crime to be born black nor an advantage to be white." Being "children of the same father created in the same image," black persons were as free as any white person.[153]

The first two purported signatories of the *Lettre originale des chefs nègres révoltès* were the recognized leaders of the black insurrection, Jean-François Papillon and Georges Biassou.[154] Beginning in the fall of 1792, these two leaders would form an alliance with the Spanish across the Dominican border of the island, hoping to gain freedom at least for the slave leaders in return for fighting with Spanish forces. Both Spain and Britain openly declared war on revolutionary France in this period,

---

[153] *The Letter of Jean-François, Biassou, and Belair* in Celucien L. Joseph, *Revolutionary Change and Democratic Religion: Christianity, Vodou, and Secularism* (Wipf and Stock, 2020), 46-56.

[154] The third signatory, Belair, cannot be positively identified, but may be Charles Belair, who would be executed by the French with his wife, Sanite, in 1802. Sadhir Hazareesingh has argued that Toussaint Louverture in fact penned the letter, but this is still debated by scholars. See Popkin, "A Haitian Revolutionary Manifesto?", 4; Hazareesingh, *Black Spartacus*, 54-55.

hoping to seize the highly profitable Saint-Domingue in the process. Spain continued to make overtures to black insurrectionists while the British wooed white planters, promising to re-secure their "natural rights" to property, which included land and slaves.

In the midst of these shifting global alliances, one of the most talented of the black insurgents and military leaders, Toussaint Louverture, issued a series of proclamations decrying the French republicans for failing in their own revolution in France to support the poor, for beheading their king, and for shedding the "innocent blood" of religious believers in the French provinces, while sending "scoundrels" to Saint-Domingue to put the black people "in chains" and to wage a war of extermination against the insurgents, pursuing them "like wild beasts."[155] In private and then public battles with Papillon and Biassou, Toussaint also called out with indignation his fellow black insurgent leaders for becoming actively involved in the buying and selling of slaves, and for striking deals with the Spanish for their own liberation at the expense of others. The fall of 1793 and winter of 1794 marked a significant turning-point in the Saint-Domingue insurrection. Forced to side unequivocally either with the white planters or black slaves, the French National Convention in Paris abolished slavery in all French colonies.[156] In the same period, Toussaint Louverture defied other insurrection leaders and rejoined the French cause. Leading a 6,000-strong revolutionary army of slaves, *marrons,* and *gens de couleur,* Toussaint envisioned a new project of creating a true community of equals, in which black, white, and mixed-race people could coexist peacefully on the island.

Over the next five years, Toussaint's revolutionary army would retake the island for France, first defeating the Spaniards and then driving the British and their French royalist allies off the colony, and in the process creating a disciplined black army of "brave republican warriors." Toussaint's defeat of the British would be aided by bouts of yellow fever plaguing the British

---

[155] Hazareesingh, *Black Spartacus,* 59-60.

[156] "War and Revolution in the Caribbean," 179-80.

troops, and by aid from John Adams in the United States, who helped with ships and supplies.[157] While France, Spain, and Britain entered the fray for multiple reasons, Toussaint argued repeatedly that the elimination of human bondage lay at the heart of his campaign. He sought to achieve this aim through liberating royalist strongholds and through demonstrating, in honorable acts of war, that those who had gone from servitude to dignity were worthy of enjoying the benefits of freedom.[158] Toussaint's armies declared themselves champions of France's revolution; one regiment named itself after the *sans-culottes*, and among their marching songs, his battalions chanted *Le Marseillaise*.

But military accomplishments and emancipation did not solve all problems of rule. Increasingly during the Directory period, Toussaint began acting more and more as an independent ruler of an island under the supervision, but not the direct rule, of France. By 1801, Saint-Domingue had a new constitution, confirming its loyalty to the French empire but declaring Toussaint as governor for life (and, secretly, with the power to appoint his own successor). The document forbade all forms of racial discrimination and deemed slavery abolished forever; successive governors would have five-year terms for rule, as the island would then be fully settled into the new constitution. To ensure the economic vitality of the island, Toussaint had ordered former slaves to return to their plantations as free laborers, to be paid wages for cultivation work. Many workers who did return worked small plots of land primarily for their family's subsistence, which

---

[157] Benjamin, *The Atlantic World*, 510. Adams was partly motivated to help Toussaint because he wanted to put pressure on the French during the "Quasi-War" between France and the United States that resulted from French aggression in Europe in the 1790s and the "XYZ affair." Helping Toussaint would distress the French because Toussaint increasingly pulled Saint-Domingue from French control. See Popkin, *A Short History of the French Revolution*, 121.

[158] Hazareesingh, *Black Spartacus*, 68-69.

allowed the island to survive economically but greatly reduced its global commercial value.[159]

Napoleon sought to re-take political control of Saint-Domingue both to regain France's power over the colony and to again turn it into an economic powerhouse for France, which would require recreating the lucrative plantation system and – he believed – the re-enslavement of black labor. Napoleon tried to send General Victor-Emmanuel Leclerc in secret to capture the island and declare a new decree of slavery, but the news of his campaign leaked and spread like wildfire among the blacks of Saint-Domingue. When Leclerc arrived, his 20,000 troops encountered tropical disease and fierce armed resistance; in the countryside, white planters and black laborers fought with savage ferocity in a war characterized by tit-for-tat killing and intermittent racial massacres.[160] Toussaint himself was captured, taken as a prisoner to France, and left to die in prison in the Jura. His successor, Jean-Jacques Dessalines, took over the resistance and ordered its extreme: the extermination of all whites on the island. On January 1, 1804, Haiti declared its independence from France. The *Haitian Declaration of Independence,* written in French, issued a call to arms, a rejection of the colonial order, and severe vengeance for the bloody enslavement of the island. It renamed the island Haiti, to honor its indigenous roots before the conquest of white settlers.

Haiti's revolution shocked and inspired the Atlantic world. In 1799, Thomas Jefferson denounced Toussaint and his revolutionary comrades as "cannibals of the terrible Republic," warning that their "missionaries" could provoke a "combustion" in America among the enslaved. The British War Secretary Lord Hobart in 1801 denounced the idea of the "power of a Black Empire under Toussaint," and other planters and merchants across the Atlantic world echoed these alarms and defamed Toussaint as the "Robespierre of Saint-Domingue." But simultaneously, Toussaint and his fellow revolutionaries encouraged other Atlantic rebels,

---

159 "War and Revolution in the Caribbean," 182.

160 "War and Revolution in the Caribbean," 184.

revolutionaries, and abolitionists, from Nat Turner and Denmark Vesey to Frederick Douglass.[161] Toussaint had predicted the universal reach of their revolution: "Reason and education will spread across our regenerated soil; once crushed under a yoke of enslavement which was as odious as it was degrading, man will elevate himself on the wings of liberty."[162] Fifty years later, Frederick Douglass lauded Toussaint for "demonstrating that, even with the worst odds against them, this race is entirely capable of achieving liberty, and of self-government.... [B]y abolishing caste, [Toussaint] proved the artificial nature of such distinctions, and further demonstrated that even slavery cannot unfit men for the full exercise of all the functions which belong to free citizens."[163]

But the French, in the end, would succeed in hindering Haiti from realizing its full potential as a free republic. Trading and export economies are only as good as their global trading partners, and the newly independent Haiti would often be denied recognition and economic rights in the global order.[164] On July 3, 1825, French warships sent by Charles X, the newly installed king of France, sailed into the port of Port-au-Prince, Haiti's capital. The ships had been sent to enforce an ordinance: "in exchange for 150 million francs, and an enormous reduction in custom taxes on French goods, France would recognize its former colony's independence." If the Haitian government did not accept the ordinance, the French would declare Haiti "an enemy of France" and blockade its port. France justified its violence due to its economic losses, emphasizing that French planters had wrongfully lost their lands. Now, those who had been in chains would need to pay their former masters.

---

[161] Hazareesingh, *Black Spartacus,* 3.

[162] Hazareesingh, *Black Spartacus,* 1-2.

[163] Frederick Douglass, *A lecture on the Haytien revolutions: with a sketch of the character of Toussaint L'Ouverture* (NY: D. Fanshaw, 1841), 24-25.

[164] The United States, for example, did not acknowledge Haiti until 1862 under the leadership of Abraham Lincoln.

With their hands tied, and without the money to pay such an exorbitant fee, the Haitians agreed to pay the French through a French loan. This "double debt," the cost of payment with interest, would be necessary for independence and freedom. For generations, and well into the twentieth century, the Haitians were forced to pay the descendants of their former slave masters. These included the Empress of Brazil; the son-in-law of the Russian Emperor Nicholas I; Germany's last imperial chancellor; and Gaston de Galliffet, the French general known as the "butcher of the Commune" for crushing an insurrection in Paris in 1871. French banks, meanwhile, earned wild profits from the loans, which helped to finance (among other things) the Eiffel Tower. Banks in the United States also sought and gained these profits, including one Wall Street institution which would become Citigroup.[165] With its economy crippled from external exploitation, and a fully democratic constitution rarely upheld in its internal politics, the story of Haiti both inspires and warns. It demonstrates the possibility of universal equality and reveals the stark limitations of liberation without liberty. Both France and Haiti show us that liberty requires laws and citizenship, economic viability, and a global system of justice.

---

[165] Catherine Porter, Constant Méheut; Matt Apuzo, and Selam Gebrekidan, "The Root of Haiti's Misery: Reparations to Enslavers," *The New York Times*, May 20, 2022.

Atlantic Encounters and the Question of Slavery in the United States

By Timothy Fritz

As previous chapters demonstrate, people and the cultures they create do not exist in isolation. Instead, they are often defined in contrast, opposition, comparison, and through competition with each other. In North America, these factors are seen through the lingering impact of the encounters between Iberians and Native North Americans. While Dr. Murry focused on the complexities of those interactions earlier, the legacy of those relations significantly influenced the formation of all American societies, including the eventual United States. The Columbian Exchange shaped the expectations and participants in an Atlantic world, which historian J.H. Elliot describes as "the creation, destruction, and re-creation of communities as a result of the movement, across and around the Atlantic basin, of people, commodities, cultural practices, and ideas."[166] In this chapter, we are most concerned with the economic exchange of people across and within the Atlantic world. Specifically, we will trace how exchange and migration shaped conceptions of liberty and freedom in the imaginations of both the oppressed and the oppressor through the 1850s.

As context, this chapter will discuss the development of North America and the United States through its connection to – and competition within – the Atlantic world. We will use the lens of slavery and migration to examine how Atlantic encounters shaped evolving notions of personal liberty while also considering how enslaved people shaped and participated in American culture, economics, and faith in ways that often conflicted with European ideas of freedom. Since North America's Chesapeake and Low-

---

[166] John Elliot, "Atlantic History, A circumnavigation," in *The British Atlantic World, 1800-1800,* David Armitage and Michael Braddick eds. (New York: Palgrave Macmillan, 2009), 254.

country regions grew into the areas where slavery was most influential, our discussion will mostly center on the development of Maryland, Virginia, and the Carolinas for its geographic focus. We will first trace the ideas of encounter, introduced in the first chapter of this text, as it gave way to an established system of slavery. Secondly, examining slavery's role in the physical and political landscape of the United States is necessary to understand America's ongoing connection to the Atlantic world through the mid-nineteenth century.

Native American Migration and Captivity

European encounters with indigenous Americans did not introduce the concept of exchange. Though the Atlantic crossing initiated by the Spanish created new paths and markets through the Columbian Exchange, trading networks that crossed the continent were foundational to Native North American societies before 1490. North America boasted a population of four million, similar to England at that time, while Central Mexico had three times as many people as Spain and Portugal combined in 1492. A fifth of these people lived in the resource-rich Pacific Northwest, while the Great Plains, Great Basin, and the Arctic held a quarter of the population. Another quarter of the population lived in what we now call the American Southwest, thanks to extensive irrigation canals whose legacies remain in modern-day Arizona, Nevada, and California.

The Native groups who most frequently interacted with European colonists, however, were one-third of the population living in the woods of the east in 1490. Consisting of three major language groups Algonquian, Iroquoian, and Muskogean – these people were politically organized into **chiefdoms**, defined by historians as societies ruled by hereditary elites who created and exercised power through collecting tribute from subordinates and negotiating the supernatural realm to improve their societies.[167] From 800 CE to 1600 CE, specific chiefdoms from the Midwest to the Southeast were known for constructing large earthen mounds notable for their tiered platforms. These mounds were at the center of Mississippian cities, the largest of which was Cahokia. Named Monks Mound and recognized as the largest prehistoric earthwork in the Americas, Cahokia's cultural and economic center still stands almost 100 feet high outside of modern-day St. Louis, Missouri. Visible for many miles, the tiered rectangular mounds represented the strictly ordered Mississippian society. In addition to serving as burial sites of the elite, the tiers themselves supported buildings of related importance, with the most important ceremonies involving the chief taking place on the uppermost tier. As physical representations of societal power and influence, these earthworks were the signature of the Mississippian culture that dominated the eastern seaboard at the time of Hernando De Soto's arrival in North America. With some Mississippian cities estimated at nearly 20,000 residents, mounds were surrounded by urban centers with dense populations higher than many European cities. Such indigenous sophistication must have been a marvel to Spanish conquistadores. Spanish contact, however, brought diseases and introduced new resources that slowly destabilized Mississippian cultures and economies over time. Mississippian decline gave way to smaller, more militaristic indigenous groups who competed to control the economic trade with Spanish, French, Dutch, and English colonists. But what began as a trade in beaver pelts and deerskin, ended in the trafficking of Native Americans and eventually enslaved Africans.

---

[167] Joseph Hall, "Between Old and New," in *The Atlantic World and Virginia 1550-1624,* Peter Mancall and Omohundro Institute of Early American History & Culture eds. (Chapel Hill: Published for the Omohundro Institute of Early American History and Culture Williamsburg Virginia by the University of North Carolina Press, 2007), 31.

Native American Slavery

Europeans and Native Americans did not have a shared definition of slavery. The chattel slavery discussed in Chapter One was a European invention of the sixteenth century. In Native societies, warfare resulted in taking captives. While the fate and status of the captives varied among indigenous cultures, the fact that captives could be adopted into family units, and that captive status did not pass to offspring remained consistent. European and Native North American approaches to "slavery" were determined by their respective long-term goals. Catholic missionaries from New France down to Spanish Florida determined that indigenous captives were ideal candidates for conversion. The distinctive and inconsistent ways that Catholic missionaries documented their experiences with indigenous captives shaped European expectations of Native American cultures for centuries thereafter. For example, in the 1640s, French Jesuit missionary documents written by Father Lalemant in the Great Lakes region, labeled a young captive Huron female living among the Iroquois as a "servant," since she was assigned to assist some hunters. Later, in the 1660s, Fr. Lalemant also deems children helping an Iroquois leader as "slaves." These observations had more to do with the European view of manual labor as "slave work" and less to do with any sort of task-based slave system in Native American society. In fact, ethnohistorians argue that prisoners of war not immediately executed could potentially be adopted into an Iroquois family as a "burdener," or someone assisting in physical labor tasks, with the chance to gain social prominence within the society.[168] In a way, this system was designed to effectively replace original family members who either perished in war or became victims of captivity by ensuring that all cultural roles remained occupied.

---

[168] William Fox, "Events as Seen from the North: The Iroquois and Colonial Slavery," in *Mapping the Mississippian Shatter Zone: The Colonial Indian Slave Trade and Regional Instability in the American South*, Robbie Ethridge and Sheri M. Shuck-Hall eds. (Lincoln: University of Nebraska Press, 2009), 72-73.

Captive taking and adoption sometimes became the sole purpose of warfare; a phenomenon historians call mourning wars.

The Virginia Company's 1607 expedition placed European colonists in the middle of the turbulent decline of Mississippian culture and along the Chesapeake Bay, where many Native American groups relocated to escape the same little ice age described in earlier in this text. One such group was the Powhatan chiefdom, which was still growing and in need of allies. Virginian colonists represented a new potential European partnership but not the first European contact, as the Spanish and French battled in the area in decades prior, and the English had attempted a colony at nearby Roanoke. However, Spanish missions proved unsuccessful, leaving the Powhatan and other migrant indigenous groups available as trade partners for food, skins, and indigenous produced goods. The oversimplified story that follows is familiar to most American history students. Colonists like John Smith negotiated an alliance with Powhatans through the chief's daughter Pocahontas after a period of warfare. Popular culture tends to end the story with Pocahontas' marriage to John Rolfe, ignoring Pocahontas' prior marriage, son, and likely murder of her husband by Virginians.[169] The story continues in a grim direction. After paramount Chief Powhatan's death, his brother, having always been a skeptic of the English alliance, used his inherited power to attack Jamestown.

The peace brokered with Virginians in 1614 abruptly ceased in 1622, when Powhatan's brother, Opechancanough, led an attack killing 300 out of around 1200 colonists in the Uprising of 1622. Though shaken, the English prevailed in their military response. According to Governor Francis Wyatt, the Virginians concluded that this attack proved that Native Americans could not be trusted and that previous agreements on the boundaries of English settlement were no longer valid. Furthermore, the breach of trust led Virginia's leadership to enslave many Powhatans, thus ushering in an acceptance of using Native Americans as chattel

[169] Phoebe Mills Farris, "Pocahontas' First Marriage: The Powhatan Side of the Story," *American Indian* 15, No. 1, (Spring 2014).

slaves. After one last attempt by Opechancanough to dislodge the English in 1644, the colonists forced the few remaining Powhatans to vacate the area, opening additional land for tobacco cultivation.

Migration brought both the Powhatans and Virginians to the Chesapeake in search of natural resources. The collapse of the Mississippian culture that spurred Powhatan relocation to a place also attractive for European settlement shows, how closely migration and exchange are related. Indigenous movement across North America intersected with European transatlantic migration. The ensuing shift from the indigenous captivity practices of Mississippian cultures to the chattel economic slavery of the Europeans, however, is best viewed through a particular migratory group that played a crucial role in both the Virginia and Carolina colonies. Originally part of the Erie Nation of the Great Lakes region and known to the other Native groups as *Riquehronnons*, this group was known to the Carolina colony as the Westo.[170] Their integration within the culture of the English Atlantic world is critical to understanding the development of North American European societies through the proliferation of chattel slavery in the region.

Human Consequences of Encounter

In response to European technology, like muskets, Native groups joined together for defensive purposes, which enhanced the effectiveness of Native American warfare. Similarly, political maneuvering to avoid war sometimes resulted in one large group integrating with another. Both circumstances describe the formation of the Five Nation Iroquois, a confederacy of indigenous groups loosely allied for warfare purposes who resided near the eastern Great Lakes. Iroquois political and martial intimidation led many groups to relocate if unable to defeat or join the Iroquois themselves, and during a period known as the Beaver Wars, many

---

[170] Eric Bowne, *The Westo Indians: Slave Traders of the Early Colonial South* (Tuscaloosa: University of Alabama Press, 2005), 38.

Native groups migrated south due to losing geographical access to the beaver hunting lands necessary for both indigenous and European trade. One such group was the Westo, who also relocated to the mid-Atlantic along the James River near the Virginian colonists in 1656, as the Powhatan did before them.

The Westos are of great significance to the dynamics of the American Southeast. Beginning in the 1640s, this tribe became involved in the fur trade as intermediaries between another Native group, the Susquehannocks, and the Virginians through Abraham Wood, the commander of Fort Henry.[171] Quickly negotiating a deal of their own, Westos allied with Virginian traders to secure "captives" for the colonists to use as chattel slaves, all in exchange for more weapons.[172] While this may appear as a straightforward, local agreement on the surface, Westo slave raids across the American Southeast reshaped Native-European alliances in the region, creating new paths of exchange resulting in the regular use of indigenous and eventually African slavery in the tobacco and rice fields, which soon became to cash crops of choice for English colonists. Westo kidnapping raids tormented Native Americans along the Atlantic coast as far south as Spanish Florida for forty years, and their targeting of Spanish-allied Indians made them a source of animosity between the English and Spanish. The Westos received firearms in return for beaver pelts, making them one of the most technologically advanced groups in the region. In 1674, South Carolinian diplomat and explorer Dr. Henry Woodward described the Westos as "well provided with arms, ammunition, tradeing cloath and other trade from the northward for which at set times of the year they truck drest deare skins furrs and young Indian slaves."[173] As the slave-operated Virginia tobacco industry became more profitable, the demand for enslaved people increased, along with business for the Westos.

---

[171] Bowne, *The Westo Indians,* 2.

[172] Bowne, *The Westo Indians*. 2.

[173] Henry Woodward, "A Faithful Relation of my Westoe Voyage," in *Narratives of Early Carolina, 1650-1708,* Alexander Samuel Salley, ed. (New York: Barnes & Noble, 1967), 132.

The decline in Spanish presence in the land that became South Carolina in 1670 and eventually Georgia in 1733, was directly related to the scattering of their Native allies in the face of English-sponsored Westo aggression, first by Virginia in the 1660s and later by Carolina in the 1680s.[174] The associated depopulation eased the settlement of the Carolina interior while simultaneously supplying Carolinians with enslaved Native Americans. In turn, demand for enslaved people also supported higher English demand for land to cultivate, and the depopulation caused by the Westo slaving wars made that land easier to acquire. Enslaved Native Americans were dispersed into the English Atlantic world, often sent to Caribbean islands toil in the sugar cane fields. Enslaved Native Americans could be found in all English colonies until the mid-eighteenth century. The influence of the Atlantic world systems of exchange, which increased the importation of enslaved Africans to the Carolina colony, intensified and eventually altered this cycle. The waning of the slaving wars and the resulting rise in enslaved African labor made the Spanish-allied Indians significantly less affected by English imperial expansion. Instead of leading to improved relations between English and Spanish colonists, however, the growing population of enslaved African labor in increasingly remote areas by the 1730s backfired on the English, leading to local animosity flaring up in the War of Jenkins Ear.

Slavery, Migration, and Religion in the English Atlantic – 2000

With an understanding of how the Native American world integrated European newcomers into their existing trade networks, we now turn to the migration patterns of the multiethnic members of the Atlantic World who found the Western

[174] The Westo devastated the Guale and Mocama people, who made up significant chiefdoms on what became the Georgia coast during the mid-seventeenth century. John Worth, *Struggle for the Georgia Coast* (University of Alabama Press: Tuscaloosa, 2007), 9-55.

Hemisphere their destination. Various African and European travelers found themselves part of colonial expeditions organized by the Spanish, Dutch, French, and English, whether by choice, force, or necessity. Such diverse populations differed in language, religion, and wealth, but no one group played a more significant role than the other in building a network of exchange, family, and ideas. To grasp these complexities, we will examine European migration paths before discussing the multifaceted experience of Atlantic world Africans.

Factors driving transatlantic migration for Europeans ranged from poverty to new business opportunities, striking it rich, military fame, and even religion. Some Europeans came over as indentured servants who, ideally, worked for a specified amount of time before being released into American society, expecting that the time spent working would have yielded social and business connections. This system was often abused, but still offered a path for migration for those who could not afford it. Other colonists migrated to broaden the family trade business, own property where they otherwise could not, or in search of religious freedom from rampant religious persecution in various parts of Europe. Many migrated as individuals, while some traveled in community or family groups. Regardless of the mode of travel, the journey was complex and uncertain. However, those who made it past the hurricanes, mutinies, and diseases, found themselves with many lifestyle options unavailable in Europe.

Iberian success in New Spain and South America motivated many English colonists. Stories of gold driven Spanish conquest, like Peter Martyr's *Decades of the New World,* had circulated through Europe since 1511.[175] Inspired by these accounts, English settlers hoped to uncover similar riches in the Caribbean. The islands of the Caribbean were not only closer to Europe, but generally free of indigenous people to challenge any European colonization after the Spanish-transmitted diseases took their toll in the first wave of settlement. Additionally, the agricultural soil of the islands proved

---

[175] Translated to English in 1555.

more productive, and export logistics were simpler than in the mainland Americas. As a result, many of the English colonists who inhabited the Chesapeake and Lowcountry in its developing years were second-time colonists, having often first tried their luck in the English islands of the Caribbean. They were quite aware that they participated in a growing English empire, having experienced and built the networks of empire themselves.

Atlantic encounters heavily impacted Virginia and Carolina. Lord Baltimore moved to Virginia from Newfoundland because he found it was too cold, before moving on to start the Maryland colony. In the seventeenth century, nine percent of Virginia's Eastern shore residents had family in other colonies.[176] Intercolonial migration usually came from places like the island colony of Barbados, which ended up being one of the wealthiest English colonies and the site of brutal slavery employed in sugar production. The sugar boom pushed out tobacco planters, many of whom moved to Virginia for better soil. Sugar profits also made land in Barbados very expensive, forcing unsuccessful planters of all types to relocate to Virginia to try again. In both cases, intercolonial migrants often brought their enslaved African labor with them.

The intercolonial paths are also very visible in places like Carolina, where rice became the major cash crop after lackluster experiments in cattle and indigo. As with Virginia, second-time colonists from Barbados significantly contributed to the population and culture. South Carolina was the first mainland English colony to rely on African slavery for its early labor needs. A transatlantic and intercolonial English family, the Colletons, moved from Barbados to Carolina in 1690 when rice cultivation became profitable.[177] Their social and economic networks are a

---

[176] April Lee Hatfield, *Atlantic Virginia: Intercolonial Relations in the Seventeenth Century* (Philadelphia: University of Pennsylvania, 2007), 88.

[177] Jack P. Greene, "Colonial South Carolina and the Caribbean Connection," *The South Carolina Historical Magazine* 88, no. 4 (October 1987): 152; Edward Rugemer, "The Development of Mastery and Race in the Comprehensive Slave Codes of the Greater Caribbean during the

great example of Atlantic connections. Barbadian Sir John Colleton was one of the Lords Proprietors of Carolina, a group of Englishmen who received permission from Charles II to start a colony as a gift of loyalty to his father, Charles I. In addition to these political connections, John Colleton worked on the Council for Foreign Plantations and the Royal African Company, directly tying him to the Atlantic slave trade; he wrote letters to John Locke advising Locke on how to make profit on his related investments in the Bahamas and Carolina.[178] John's son Peter followed his father as a proprietor, while another son, James, inherited John's Barbados and Carolina plantations, using that wealth and influence to become governor of Carolina from 1686 to 1690. The success of English colonization thus relied on two distinct networks that were not populated by English people at all, Native American trade and the African slave trade.

Slavery does not define the African experience in the Atlantic, though it is undoubtedly common among those who fell victim to the middle passage described by Alexander Falconbridge in "An Account of the Slave Trade on the Coast of Africa." All Africans were not subject to an enslaved condition, and even those in bondage consistently fought for autonomy in their everyday lives. In the sixteenth century, people from all over Africa and Europe imagined that the Americas held some economic promise. Africans looking to enlarge their networks of influence were present in the earliest days of European colonization, working as interpreters and laborers from the initial Spanish expeditions described in Chapter One, to the early days of the Virginia and Maryland colonies. Compared to Europeans, Africans in the Americas hailed from a larger geographic area and represented a wider variety of languages, experiences, and beliefs. Combined with European

---

Seventeenth Century," *The William and Mary Quarterly* 70, no. 3 (July 2013), 452.

[178] "John Colleton" in Walter Edgar, *The South Carolina Encyclopedia* (Columbia, S.C.: University of South Carolina Press), 2006. Barbara Armeil, *John Locke and America: The Defence of English Colonialism* (Oxford: Clarendon, 1998), 68-69.

ideas, African expressions of everyday life helped create a distinctly American culture based on sustained Atlantic encounters.

Historian Ira Berlin proposed that Africans' distinct motivations and experiences across the Atlantic World are best understood by dividing them into three generations: charter, plantation, and revolutionary. Our focus, for now, is on the charter generation, free and enslaved people of African descent who arrived in colonial America before plantation agriculture took hold, and whose experiences differed vastly. In French colonies like Martinique, and even St. Domingue, places that grew to host some of the most oppressive slave regimes in the Atlantic, the lines between black, white, enslaved, and free, were quite blurry. Here, before the advent of sugar plantations in the 1640s, marriage between French nationals and Africans was commonplace.[179] Similar social situations could be found in Virginia, where enslaved people built kinship and friendship networks by traveling the countryside and earning money for their owners. In New York, before American dependence on slave labor across the colonies, enslaved Africans briefly held the right to own property.[180] The multilingual and multicultural mastery these people possessed made them **Atlantic creoles**, a term historians use to define those of African origin who used connections outside of Africa to make a living within European colonization. Of paramount concern to the charter generation was membership in colonial society. Berlin may have said it best in his observation that, "Atlantic creoles labored to incorporate themselves into the larger life of the Chesapeake in the hopes that participation would lead to recognition, and recognition would eliminate the threat of racial ostracism. Being defined outside of respectable society -not subordination -was what black people of the charter generations feared most."[181]

---

[179] Ira Berlin, *Many Thousands Gone: The First Two Centuries of Slavery in North America* (Cambridge: Harvard University Press, 2009), 27.

[180] Berlin, *Many Thousands Gone*, 52.

[181] Berlin, *Many Thousands Gone*, 45.

In 1619, the *White Lion's* arrival on the shores of Hampton, Virginia, represented a series of events limiting the social mobility of Atlantic Creoles over the next century. Primarily used as an English privateer vessel, the *White Lion* landed for provisions. In exchange, they were willing to sell some enslaved Africans they had confiscated from the Spanish in their previous travels and thus conducted the first English slave sale on the American mainland. However, this was not the beginning of American slavery, nor was it the first time enslaved Africans set foot on the land that is now the United States. Historians believe the first Africans arrived in 1526 with Spanish explorer Lucas Vázquez de Ayllón during his failed attempt to establish the San Miguel de Gualdape colony near the Pee Dee River in what became South Carolina. Local Native groups quickly attacked this settlement, and the enslaved either escaped to the interior or were killed during the battle. One year later, the "Narratives of Estevanico el Negro in the Southwest" tell us of an Arabian-born African named Estevanico, who worked as an interpreter for Spanish expeditions in the Gulf of Mexico and beyond.[182] More Africans, free creole and enslaved, arrived around the founding of Spanish Florida at St. Augustine, recognized today as the oldest continuously inhabited European city in the United States. As previous chapters mention, African slavery was a global issue, integrated and entangled within the plans of every colonizing nation. The importance of 1619 is its role in ushering in a specific slavery system unique to English America, which spread among Spanish, French, and Dutch colonial projects as they were incorporated into the United States over the next 250 years.

While colonists always considered African slavery useful, it did not become integral to imperial economics beyond Iberian colonization until the 1640s Caribbean sugar boom that made producing that luxury good extraordinarily profitable and the sole

---

[182] This was an influential travel narrative published in the 1540s, notable for containing some of the first written descriptions of Native American people and culture intended for Western European audiences.

agricultural focus of the regions where it grew.[183] As more ships arrived on American shores, free and enslaved Africans feared the creation of systems to ensure perpetual chattel slavery. These horrors materialized in the mid-seventeenth century in conjunction with a rapid increase in English colonists fleeing the English Civil Wars or the religious persecution that followed, and additional land became available for agriculture as a result of continued Mississippian migration and reorganization.[184] Securing a long-term labor force to supplement indentured servitude made its way through various colonial legislatures, followed by legal codes requiring inhumane practices to manage enslaved Africans.

Though uniquely American, the contours of the English slave system held distinct origins in the Atlantic encounter. First and foremost, the *White Lion's* complement of enslaved people for sale were products of Spanish colonization. There was no English precedent for chattel slavery in English society, and the desire to emulate slave-driven profits from Iberian colonial enterprise is partially to blame for the French, Dutch, and English colonial experience in the first place. Those who enslaved people sold off the *White Lion* were listed with Spanish names (though likely not their real names), and in the coming years, Spanish words like *negro* and *mulatto* entered English parlance.[185] Virginians specifically sought Africans experienced in tobacco cultivation from non-English colonies throughout the Atlantic. The Chesapeake and Carolina colonies grew as colonists looked to the mainland to supplement business activities in islands like Barbados. They, too, brought their experienced slaves along with them, eager to replicate prior Atlantic success. By the 1630s, enslaved Africans outnumbered Europeans on Providence Island,

---

[183] Spain and Portugal both profited from sugar but had other major exports, like silver and gold.

[184] Between 1640 and 1670, the European population of Virginia expanded from 8,000 to 30,000. April Lee Hatfield, *Atlantic Virginia*, 111.

[185] Early Virginia censuses show that Iberian first names among enslaved Africans were more common than English ones. Hatfield, *Atlantic Virginia*, 137-139.

a Puritan colony in the Caribbean. When those enslaved rebelled in 1638, many survivors moved to Virginia with their human property. In 1602, the Dutch formed a joint-stock company that supplied enslaved people throughout the Atlantic, only for the English to replicate this model with a government-backed slave trading corporation of their own, the Royal African Company, in 1660. The proliferation of slavery became a key indicator of Atlantic colonial success.

As the tide of slave-driven profits rose throughout the Atlantic, Maryland, and Virginia took legal action to keep people enslaved. Virginia's Act XII stated, "that all children borne in this country shalbe held bond or free only according to the condition of the mother, And that if any christian shall committ ffornication with a negro man or woman, hee or shee soe offending shall pay double the ffines imposed by the former act."[186] Likewise, Maryland moved to force all black people in the colony to serve as slaves for life, regardless of prior enslavement. Clarified in 1692's "An Act Concerning Negro Slaves" to address children of mixed ancestry and their parents, Maryland added a penalty of servitude for white parents of biracial children, forcing them to become servants at the church for a specified time.[187] Both colonies sought the firm separation of African life from English society and the creation of a laboring class that would continue to reproduce itself.[188]

The involvement of churches in Maryland's punishment for parenting biracial children indicates that, on some level, churches in early America endorsed slavery. While Christianity was generally considered to encourage obedience among slaves, both colonies clearly indicated that religious belief was irrelevant to

---

[186] William Waller Hening, ed., *The Statutes at Large; Being a Collection of All the Laws of Virginia from the First Session of the Legislature, in the Year 1619* (New York: R. & W. & G. Bartow, 1823), 2:170.

[187] "An Act concerning Negro Slaves," *Maryland Assembly Proceedings*, May 10June 9, 1692, 546549.

[188] Dan Royles, *The Schlager Anthology of Black America : A Student's Guide to Essential Primary Sources*, (Dallas TX: Schlager Group Incorporated, 2021), 3.

slave status. For example, "Virginia's Act III" stated that neither conversion nor Christian baptism was a reason for freedom. This may not have even mattered since, as in Maryland, no method existed to certify religion. The divide between African and European lives grew wider with "Virginia's Act Concerning Servants and Slaves XXXIV" in 1705. This act consolidated laws from prior years regulating slavery and property rights for those owning slaves, and provided details needed to exclude people of African descent from public life. Even laws from the Chesapeake colonies, however, were part of a larger Atlantic conversation in the Church of England. Some Anglican missionaries were given enslaved people to help with the operation of colonial churches, and church's endorsement of slaveholding is seen in a 1711 sermon by William Fleetwood, Bishop of St. Asaph.[189] Fleetwood hoped for a "Blessed Medium," a society where "Slaves, tho' Christians, might be Bought and Sold, and used like Slaves" so long as people did not behave in a cruel manner.[190] Even going so far as operating their own plantation in Barbados, the Church of England did not free their enslaved until 1833.

Churches that allowed slavery made colonies like Carolina more attractive to those dedicated to enslaving people. In the case of the Lowcountry, Protestant endorsement of slavery made for a relatively tolerant society bolstered by the suspension of denominational requirements used in other colonies.[191] *The Fundamental Constitutions of Carolina*, adopted in 1669 and written

---

[189] Thomas J. Little, "The Origins of Southern Evangelicalism: Revivalism in South Carolina, 1700-1740," *Church History* 75, no. 4 (2006): 768-808, 780.

[190] William Fleetwood, "A Sermon Preached before the Society for the Propagation of the Gospel in Foreign Parts, at the Parish Church of St. Mary-le-Bow, on Friday the 16th of February, 1710/11" (London: Joseph Downing, 1711), reprinted in Frank J. Klingenberg, *Anglican Humanitarianism in Colonial New York* (Philadelphia: Church Historical Society, 1940), 195 – 212. Little, "Origins of Southern Evangelicalism," 781.

[191] Marion Eugene Sirmans, *Colonial South Carolina: A Political History, 1663–1763* (Chapel Hill, NC, 1966), 5.

with the help of noted philosopher John Locke from our chapter on liberty, attracted people who were primarily dissenters, defined as those who did not follow the Church of England's practices.[192] Locke wrote that any acknowledging of a God deserving of solemn worship, and any who made their doctrines public could form their own congregations, creating one of the most religiously English tolerant colonies on the continent outside of Rhode Island.[193]

In the cases of migration, religion, and slavery, Africans and Europeans followed economic paths. Prominent families, servants, and enslaved people expanded from England to the Caribbean and the American mainland to increase family influence. These movements started colonial communities needing churches and clergy, many of whom responded to their parishioners by endorsing race-based permanent human servitude to help keep colonists conformed to European society. Historian Henry F. May explained the process by noting that the well-connected slaveowners with political influence wanted "a decent, orderly religion which would remind everybody of his position, his duties, and his limitations."[194] Such an idea propped up their power while still providing some freedom for dissent. Together, these factors reminded participants of their European connections while at the same time emphasizing local kinship and business ties. Building community reflected the lived experience of these Atlantic citizens.

Slavery and Atlantic World Rivalries

The communities created in the eighteenth-century Atlantic World were often in conflict with each other. As mentioned previously, Peter Martyr's depictions of Spanish success spurred

---

[192] Sirmans, *Colonial South Carolina*, 10.

[193] Timothy David Fritz, "To Abjure Popish Heresys": Crafting a Borderlands Gospel during Queen Anne's War at St. James Parish, South Carolina, 1701–20, *Journal of Social History* 55, no. 3 (Spring 2022): 7.

[194] Henry F. May, *The Enlightenment in America* (New York: Oxford University Press, 1976), 66–75.

not just English curiosity but also Protestant jealousy of Catholicism's prominent influence in the initial phase of European colonization. In North America, the Spanish crown viewed English settlements in the Chesapeake and Lowcountry as an intrusion of lands to which they believed they had title by virtue of exploration and Catholic missionization. Protestant missionary work among local Native Americans under the Society of the Propagation of the Gospel (SPG) directly conflicted with earlier attempts by Jesuits and Franciscans to missionize indigenous villages along the Atlantic coast. In response, Spanish forces in Florida began regular attacks on English settlements in the Southeast in 1686, culminating in a joint Spanish and French invasion attempt at Port Royal, South Carolina, in 1706 as part of Queen Anne's War.

The Spanish and French had good reason to be upset, as Port Royal's exact location was once the French settlement, Charlesfort, in 1562, and even Spanish Florida's capital, Santa Elena, from 1566 to 1587. Repeated European attempts to occupy and integrate indigenous spaces demonstrate just how contested and fragile European colonization indeed was, and as a result, European rivalries were common in the Americas. In the colonial period, several wars were fought independently among North American colonists or as localized theatres of more international conflicts, such as the French and Indian War being a part of the much bigger Seven Years' War. Some of these conflicts, however, were more important to the development of slavery in the United States than others. The aforementioned War of Jenkins' Ear, itself part of the War of Austrian Succession, solidified the role of slavery in the British American colonies and sparked a debate over the full nature of freedom which lasted until the American Civil War.

European rivalries often led to war in the Americas, but the local entanglements of Atlantic communities made these battles more devastating to those involved. As new waves of English colonists brought more interpretations of Christianity, questions began to arise regarding what the "good" treatment of enslaved Africans might entail. By the eighteenth century, slavery was firmly enshrined in both Protestant and Catholic teachings, with a few notable exceptions, like Quakers. Colonists differed significantly, however, on the desired role of religion in the everyday life of enslaved Africans. The denominational nature of the Protestant church meant that each group interpreted Christian slave management differently. As European society multiplied, people of African descent were forced to sit outside the church during services or completely barred from attendance.

One SPG missionary, Francis LeJau, noticed that Christian education was an excellent way to teach English to the enslaved and ensure their loyalty. Accordingly, he believed enslaved people should be included in more communities' religious life. As for the issue of enslaved loyalty, LeJau worked as the rector of St. James Parish in South Carolina during Queen Anne's War and understood the many dimensions of European rivalry. He argued for more access to enslaved people as a move to protect the colony from the Spanish, while enslavers opposed their slaves having time away from the rice plantations when they could be working. Although not confirmed in his lifetime, history proved LeJau's stance on loyalty correct. One goal of those Spanish attacks that began in 1686 was to kidnap enslaved Africans. Upon their arrival in Florida, they were valued for their knowledge of English settlements and often joined Spanish and allied Native American soldiers in subsequent raids on the English in South Carolina to free friends and family members. This plan worked so well that the Spanish offered freedom to any enslaved Africans from South Carolina who escaped to Florida on their own and agreed to convert to Catholicism.[195]

LeJau's story demonstrates that Atlantic rivalries were also crucial to enslaved Africans. Their bondage did not mean they were any less informed of the geopolitical currents of the Atlantic world. Enslaved literacy and engineering expertise were critical to

---

[195] Governor Benavides to the Crown, November 2, 1725 (58-1-29, Doc. No. 84, duplicated in 58-1-31, Doc. No. 3), AGI. Irene Wright, "Dispatches of Spanish Officials Bearing on the Free Negro Settlement of Gracia Real De Santa Teresa De Mose, Florida," *The Journal of Negro History* 9, no. 2 (Apr. 1924): 145.

European colonies, and on many levels, their monetary value fluctuated with their ability to use this knowledge to work independently. Transporting goods by water and land was considered mainly a task for enslaved people, and they gained information through gossip and overhearing privileged information just like everyone else traveling throughout and between communities. This is how the Anglo-Spanish rivalry in South Carolina directly impacted the Stono Rebellion, considered among the bloodiest slave uprisings in American history. Enslaved people who heard about the Spanish freedom policy for escaped Africans and were motivated by the goal to travel to "St. Augustine for a reception afterward," carefully planned an operation that took place on Sunday, September 9, 1739, "not twenty miles from Charles Town, in which they massacred twenty-three whites after the most cruel and barbarous Manner to be conceived."[196] After securing guns and other weapons from a store, the rebels headed south toward the newly established Fort Mose, a Spanish fortification in Florida built to house escaped enslaved people from English colonies. On the road south from Charleston, the rebels killed many enslavers and liberated other enslaved people to join their ranks. Unfortunately, South Carolina's lieutenant governor, William Bull, encountered them along the road, raised the alarm, and sent a militia force to track down and destroy the rebels.[197] Over thirty Africans escaped, but many were hunted down in the following weeks.[198]

---

[196] "Report of the Committee Appointed to Enquire into the Causes of the Disappointment of Success in the Late Expedition against St. Augustine," in South Carolina, J. H. Easterby, R. Nicholas Olsberg, and Terry W. Lipscomb, *The Journal of the Commons House of Assembly* (Columbia: Historical Commission of South Carolina, 1951), 83-84.

[197] "Report of the Committee Appointed to Enquire into the Causes of the Disappointment of Success in the Late Expedition against St. Augustine,", 84.

[198] "Stono Rebellion," *The South Carolina Encyclopedia*, 933.

The War of Jenkins' Ear in the aftermath of the Stono Rebellion had lasting effects on American slavery. First, South Carolina passed the Slave Act of 1740, which among other things, restricted literacy in enslaved populations. Colonists were willing to have less productive enslaved Africans in return for limiting their knowledge. Many other colonies copied prohibitions on Black literacy, and became the status quo for the southern United States. Second, most mainland British North American colonies were swayed in favor of retaliation against Spanish Florida when the war allowed it in 1740, based on the argument that the mere existence of Florida was a threat against English desires from private property in the form of enslaved humans.

Member of Parliament, and veteran of the English Civil Wars, General James Oglethorpe, used his position as governor of the new Georgia colony established in 1733 to seek the use of Africans from South Carolina to implement his extensive battle plans to take St. Augustine in 1740. Not only did he arm 800 Black soldiers, but he also referred to enslaved Africans from South Carolina as pioneers in the aftermath of Stono; justifying his incursion into Florida as revenge against Spaniards who "favor the revolting of the Negroes."[199] Oglethorpe promised South Carolina Lieutenant Governor William Bull that he was "willing myself to do all that I possibly can for annoying the Enemy, as his Majesty has ordered, and shall spare no personal Labour nor Danger towards freeing Carolina of a Place from whence their Negroes are encouraged to massacre their Masters."[200] Bull, who discovered the Stono Rebellion in progress and mustered militia forces to put it down only weeks earlier, agreed with Oglethorpe's assessment of the complications and disorder encouraged by the mere existence of St. Augustine and Fort Mose. Oglethorpe requested help from as far away as New York, citing lingering concerns from that colony's

---

[199] "Oglethorpe to the Duke of Newcastle," in James Oglethorpe, *General Oglethorpe's Georgia: Colonial Letters, 1733–1743*, ed. Mills Lane (Savannah: Beehive Press, 1975), 441.

[200] "1740," South Carolina et al., *Journal of the Commons House of Assembly, Vol. 2.*, 160.

slave revolt in 1712 as the primary motivation for assistance. By presenting himself as an advocate for slave control and order, he requested soldiers to protect the economic security provided by systems of enslavement.[201] Ensuring slavery was worth war to English colonists in the Atlantic world.

Slavery and the American Revolution

On the eve of the American Revolution, South Carolina became the most prosperous English colony on the mainland, built on the backs of its rice-cultivating black demographic majority, while the average wealth of white Charlestonians reached as much as five times greater than that of their counterparts in Boston and Philadelphia. As such, discussions of the role of slavery in our new nation were central to compromises in the editing of the Declaration of Independence. Certain historians suggest that the Southern American brand of patriotism was built on fears that the British colonial authorities would outlaw the slave trade, presenting a severe problem for those colonies' bottom line. Others have argued that much of the patriot rhetoric was based on a slave and master relationship.

As the mainland British North American colonies matured, the number of colonists opposed to slavery increased. Those with close ties to England and the Anglican church were most likely to move to the Americas before the eighteenth century. Still, by 1750, many settlements and faith communities were against human bondage. Despite Oglethorpe's role in defending slavery in the War of Jenkins' Ear, slavery was outlawed in the Georgia colony's charter and prohibited until 1750. This unique labor structure attracted a German-speaking Protestant group called the Georgia Salzburgers. John Martin Boltzius, the leader and minister of the group's settlement Ebeneezer, wrote one of the earliest antislavery tracts to come out the British North America. Expressing

---

[201] "Oglethorpe to the Duke of Newcastle" in Oglethorpe, *General Oglethorpe's Georgia*, Vol 1, 457.

disappointment at Georgia's legalization of slavery, Boltzius claimed that his group would not have come if they knew slavery would be introduced in the colony, identifying it as a threat to hard work but not an issue of racial equality.

Around the same time, Quakers began to turn away from slavery as well. Though they famously protested against slavery in Germantown (now Philadelphia) in 1688 based on the fact that stealing people and separating families was prohibited by the Bible, Quakers at large were not outwardly opposed to slavery until the writings of John Woolman in 1753.[202] Woolman's tract argued that it was wrong to enslave other members of the same species and that if God had granted Europeans a privileged position, it should be used to uplift those not fortunate enough to be European. In response, Pennsylvania, New Jersey, and Delaware Quakers condemned slave buying and selling in 1754, and by 1774 Pennsylvania and New Jersey Quakers even condemned slave ownership as inconsistent with Christianity.[203] Quakers were some of the first to recognize the inconsistency between the rhetoric of the Revolution and the reality of slavery in America.

As the rhetoric of colonial enslavement to the passions of the mother country became more widespread, enslaved Africans in the colonies seized an opportunity to make their own argument against slavery by highlighting the contradictions that American colonists sought "freedom" from the British in a society which itself embraced a human lack of freedom. Now with White support, discussions around patriotism were forced to address slavery.[204] Despite this multiracial alliance, however, manumissions in Revolutionary America never topped 1000 and the importation of

---

[202] Friends Society of Germantown, Pa., *Germantown Friends' ProtestAgainst Slavery,* Facsimile, Pdf., https://www.loc.gov/item/2020772635/.

[203] Gary Nash, *Unknown American Revolution: The Unruly Birth of Democracy and the Struggle to Create America* (New York: Penguin Books, 2006), 41-42.

[204] Nash, *Unknown American Revolution,* 114

slaves increased at a greater rate than manumissions, so even though there was growing abolitionist sentiment, there was a corresponding entrenchment of slavery as well.[205]

Dunmore's Proclamation in 1775 pushed slavery to the forefront of colonial concern. John Murray, the Earl of Dunmore and the royal governor of Virginia, offered freedom to all enslaved people and indentured servants able and willing to join the British Army. Though only applying to Virginia and yielding only 800 men for this particular regiment, many colonists interpreted this action against slavery as at least a final signal that reconciliation with Britain was not possible, if not a reason to consider armed resistance.[206] Meanwhile, that same year in Philadelphia, the world's first abolition society, the Society for the Relief of Free Negroes Unlawfully Held in Bondage, held their first meeting right before the battles of Lexington and Concord that marked the start of the Revolutionary War. In late 1775, pro-slavery and anti-slavery ideas were closely connected to concepts of how the Atlantic world should continue to operate. The coming war presented opportunities for tens of thousands of enslaved people to escape slavery by fighting in either the British or Continental armies or using the cover of chaos to exit enslavement in some other way.

In the political realm, the elite colonists involved in the Continental Congress also struggled with slavery in drafting the Declaration of Independence. In addition to accusing England of trying to incite rebellion and violence against colonists with Dunmore's Proclamation, an early draft of the document blamed King George III for slavery, stating that "The king has waged cruel war against human nature itself, by violating its most sacred rights of life and liberty in the persons of a distant people, who never offended him, captivating and carrying them into slavery in another hemisphere, or to incur miserable death in their

[205] Nash, *Unknown American Revolution*, 127, 128.

[206] Nash, *Unknown American Revolution*, 166.

transportation thither."[207] However, the drafting committee of the Congress deleted these statements from the final document for two reasons. First, all thirteen colonies that chose to rebel relied on slavery in some fashion. Secondly, even people like Thomas Jefferson envisioned a new nation of yeoman farmers supported by slavery, and colonists in Virginia and South Carolina would have seen an attack on slavery as an attack on private property. Even one of the most important founding documents of the United States could not ignore the implications of broadly defined freedom on the wider Atlantic world.

After the American Revolution, however, the same leaders who were so dedicated to freedom were the same leaders who let slavery expand under their watch. Patrick Henry, famous for his passionate patriotism, was staunchly opposed to any limits on slavery. He backed slavery in debates around the Constitution, arguing, "We ought to posses them in the manner we have inherited them from our ancestors, as their manumission is incompatible with the felicity of the country."[208] At one point during the debate, he thundered, "They'll take your niggers from you!"[209] He wanted slavery to be an internal matter for Virginians to decide.

After the Constitution was ratified, Thomas Jefferson saw 1803's Louisiana Purchase as a way to secure an American agrarian culture in which the will of their owners would abolish slavery. In reality, slavery became a major tool of that society, and large-scale slave-owning planters controlled expansion instead of small farmers.[210] The growing plantation complex expanded through

---

[207] Julian R. Boyd, ed., *The Papers of Thomas Jefferson. Vol. 1, 1760-1776,* (Princeton: Princeton University Press, 1950), 243-247.

[208] Robert Einhorn, "Patrick Henry's Case against the Constitution: The Structural Problem with Slavery," *Journal of the Early Republic 22,* (2002): 552.

[209] Robert Einhorn, "Patrick Henry's Case against the Constitution: The Structural Problem with Slavery," 554.

[210] Adam Rothman, Slave Country: American Expansion and the Origins of the Deep South (Cambridge: Harvard University Press, 2005).

violence, as indigenous armed resistance continued as it had for 200 years prior. Some Native groups, like the Cherokee, attempted to assimilate into plantation culture by adopting a planter lifestyle that included Black slave ownership. Cherokee attempts to fit in were unsuccessful, as the Indian Removal Act of 1830 eventually forced many Native American groups, and their enslaved African Americans, on a forced march westward. Enterprising plantation owners managed to dominate southern politics in order to manipulate state powers to their advantage. Fear of slave revolt from a Black demographic majority lingering from the Stono Rebellion caused many Americans to oppose the continuance of an international slave trade, which the Constitution set to expire in 1808. Southern planters and politicians seized this opportunity to expand a cotton culture supported by increased global demand.

Proponents of slavery believed the growing number of free Black people in the United States threatened slavery's westward expansion. States like Pennsylvania had adopted gradual emancipation laws in the 1780s that began to free enslaved people starting around 1808. Despite facing severe limits on citizenship, these newly freed individuals exercised at least enough political power to threaten politicians advocating for slavery in the lands gained in the Louisiana Purchase. Benjamin Banneker, a free-born and self-taught African American mathematician, and scientist from Baltimore Country, Maryland, was one of these vocal opponents of slavery. In 1791, as Banneker worked as a surveyor laying out the plan for Washington D.C., he directly confronted Thomas Jefferson in a letter disagreeing with Jefferson's assertion that African Americans lacked the mental competence for education. Jefferson, serving as Secretary of State at the time, responded to Banneker in a non-committal manner, explaining that no one was more interested in finding a remedy for slavery than he was. While the letters between the two may not have been public, several newspapers followed Banneker's work on the federal city and mentioned his intellect with regard to Jefferson's earlier public writings.

Jefferson's comments were typical of politicians of this period, reflecting a desire to solve a growing racial divide without acknowledging the role of slavery in shaping their views of Black inequality. The American Colonization Society (ACS), an anti-slavery organization formed in 1816, sought to remedy these debates by sending African Americans back into the Atlantic world by shipping them to West Africa to form the colony of Liberia. Racist antislavery organizations like this one believed that although slavery was a moral ill, free African Americans were not equal to White Americans and could never integrate into society. On the other hand, abolitionists opposed the ACS and generally argued for ending slavery, as well as for racial equality, and African American inclusion in the new nation. Conversations about ending slavery, however, were complicated by the world-wide cotton boom of the mid-nineteenth century.

Cotton, Expansion, and the Market Revolution

The 1840s were close to the peak of a world-spanning empire with cotton at its center, reigniting Atlantic world exchanges. This time, slave-produced products, instead of the enslaved themselves, drove Atlantic economics. Expanding long-staple cotton throughout places like Louisiana and Mississippi brought considerable wealth to northern business people who exported the commodities overseas. Cotton elevated American slavery to a global economic engine, uniting slave and wage labor and connecting American plantations to British factories. As a global commodity, cotton helped spark the industrial revolution through American inventions like the cotton gin to the construction of textile factories in Britain. Historian Sven Beckert elegantly described this worldwide process, stating that:

> millions of people spent their lives working the acres of cotton that slowly spread across the world, plucking billions of bolls from resistant cotton plants, carrying bales of cotton from cart to boat and from boat to train, and working, often at very

young ages, at satanic mills from New England to China. Countries fought wars for access to these fertile fields, planters put untold numbers of people into shackles, employers abbreviated the childhoods of their operatives, the introduction of new machines led to the depopulation of ancient industrial centers, and workers, both slave and free, struggled for freedom and a living wage.[211]

As a crop that at its peak relied on slave labor, it is no wonder that the few decades leading up to 1860 are known as the Great Divergence, the beginning of a seemingly permanent divide between the economic development of North America and Western Europe, and the rest of the world.

Frederick Douglass and the Atlantic Currents of Abolition

Cotton linked the United States and Western Europe across the Atlantic, but other transatlantic conversations threatened the slave system that produced cotton. Parliament abolished slave trading in the British Empire in 1807, and most slaves in territories governed by Britain were freed in 1838. These actions corresponded with growing abolitionist sentiment in the United States and coincided with an American religious revival movement known as the Second Great Awakening. The religious fervor incited by this rapid growth of Christianity also led to a reexamination of American society that included the many arguments against slavery at the time, from the sloth and laziness it encouraged, to the kidnapping and breaking of families it caused, to the racist inequality it fueled. Groups like the American Anti-Slavery Society, who had previously focused on societal reform, now turned to more active means to resist slavery by creating an American network assisting enslaved people in escaping, to international coalitions intended to pressure the

---

[211] Sven Beckert, *Empire of Cotton: A Global History* (New York: Vintage Books, 2015), xii.

United States to abolish slavery internationally. Frederick Douglass, another African American man from Maryland, was essential to both efforts.

Born on the eastern shore of Maryland in 1818, Douglass escaped slavery in 1838. Eventually settling in Massachusetts, he became a well-known preacher at the time when the White abolitionists of the American Anti-Slavery Society were gaining popularity. Prominent abolitionists like William Lloyd Garrison were more than happy to elevate Douglass' profile through their networks, particularly the abolitionist newspaper *The Liberator*. This newspaper blamed the ratification of the Constitution a chief source of slavery's evil and promoted the idea of northern states breaking away from the American south, even inspiring public burnings of copies of the Constitution. The promotional efforts of Garrison and his newspaper afforded to Douglass also had the side effect of wealthy White citizens strongly suggesting talking points to Douglass. Fitting his compelling story within their own platform was important, as they would not offend the elite New Englanders on whom they relied for financial support. These edited speeches formed Douglass' wildly popular autobiography, outlining his life as an enslaved person and his escape from enslaved status. The text was immediately translated into French and Dutch and printed across Europe thanks to nineteenth-century innovations in printing technology and transatlantic travel. Douglass soon traveled to Europe to speak to abolitionist groups captivated by his gift of passionate oration in Britain and Ireland.

Despite the international recognition of Frederick Douglass, many African American abolitionists disagreed with his views. Douglass firmly believed that the Constitution was an antislavery document. Where Douglass hoped that slavery's end would bring an end to racial categorization and African Americans assimilated into White society, other Black abolitionists called for the recreation and preservation of the Black communities strained by the limitations of enslavement. Henry Highland Garnet, yet another Black man from Maryland, grew into one of Douglass' rivals in the public sphere. Garnet's held militant views when compared to Douglass, challenging the enslaved populations (though most of his speeches were given in the North, far away from the enslaved audience he addressed) that resistance to slavery was a better plan than hoping for a political solution. A strong Black nationalist, Presbyterian minister, and international orator in his own right, he once defended his classmates with a gun when White farmers attempted to destroy the school he attended in New Hampshire after they admitted black students. In his 1843 "Address to the Slaves," he called for enslaved Africans to resist by ceasing to work. Knowing that enslavers would react harshly, Garnet believed the struggle it would instigate, African Americans fighting for themselves, was the best path to end slavery. Unlike Douglass, Garnet did not advocate for White abolitionist partnerships.

In many ways, Frederick Douglass brings the purpose of this chapter into focus by questioning the ways in which the currents of the Atlantic world, wrought with colonial encounters and expansion, the exchange among – and of – people, along with experiments in liberty, all work to shape perspectives knowing and understanding freedom. While the Second Great Awakening called for reform and action, it was not a means of reflection on the past errors of American society when it came to race. Aware of the conflicts between White philanthropy and Black freedom, Douglass broke his association with William Lloyd Garrison when he returned from Europe. He then started his own abolitionist newspaper, *The North Star*, in 1847. *The North Star* promoted the idea that the northern states should not secede but stick with the southern states until slavery was ended. Douglass thought that since the Constitution did not mention the word "slave," that the "We the people" in the preamble applied to everyone, the Constitution could not support slavery.

In 1852, Douglass delivered his famous speech, "What to the Slave is the Fourth of July," to the Rochester Anti-Slavery Society in New York, forcing freedom-loving Americans to reconcile their civic ideals with the reality of enslavement and calling White American society to confront its compromises on race at the founding of the nation. Douglass berated the audience for the hypocrisy and misuse of religion that allowed slavery to persist, calling out Christians who argued for their own religious liberty, but remained silent in protesting legislation like the Fugitive Slave Act of 1850. Part of the larger Compromise of 1850, the Fugitive Slave Act was part of a package of bills passed by Congress to deescalate tension between free and slave states. It allowed any suspected runaway slave to be captured in free states and returned to servitude in the South, essentially opening the door to state sponsored kidnapping and abduction. Assisting fugitive slaves was also prohibited. Because of this, simply crossing the Mason-Dixon line, or the Ohio River, no longer guaranteed freedom for enslaved people escaping bondage.

The Fugitive Slave Act was a symbol of desperation from southern states, whose external supply of enslaved humans ended with the ban of international slave trading. In its place, a domestic slave trade which sold enslaved children away from their families at an average age of seven, rose in its place. Even worse, slavers used slave breeding farms in places like Virginia's Shenandoah Valley to force enslaved people to create and bare children, before marching those children southward towards slave markets in Louisiana. For Douglass, White society, abolitionists or not, was far too quiet on this issue because it did not impact them. He identified their separation from these events as a barrier to the racial reconciliation he sought. "What to the Slave is the Fourth of July," was a direct critique of White society from which Douglass disassociated himself by using the word "you" and "your."[212] In doing so, Douglass worked as a historian to highlight the idea that Black and White Americans have a different historical memory, that is to say, different collective attachments to historical narratives that form the basis of culture and belonging. Recognizing the sins present at the founding of the United States

---

[212] Trisha Posey, "Frederick Douglass's Fourth of July Speech, Lament, and Historical Memory," *in Lament and Justice in African American History: By the Rivers of Babylon*, Timothy David Fritz and Trisha Posey eds. (New York: Lexington Books, 2023), 14-17.

by living up to the ideals of the Constitution was his preferred path forward.

Reconciliation was far from the minds of enslaved African Americans in a slave system which grew harsher every day, and from the minds of those free Black people who endured a violent brand of patriotism in the North. Though festive Independence Day speeches had become major public events during this period, the Fourth of July was also a day of anti-Black violence. Outside of the halls of supposedly supportive abolitionists, the holiday also marked a time for many Black citizens to stay home. African Americans were barred from many parades and public celebrations on the Fourth itself, leading many in New York to celebrate July 5th as the day of New York's gradual emancipation legislation. Other African Africans celebrated January 1, 1808, for the end of the transatlantic slave trade.[213] All these alternatives proved Douglass' point that the Black experience was not yet one of full citizenship, and the end of slavery would not be enough to herald an era of equality, yet also validates the perspective of Garnet, who saw a White society not truly interested in liberty for all. The breakout of the Civil War, less than a decade later, put these debates on citizenship to the test.

---

[213] Derrick Spires, *The Practice of Citizenship: Black Politics and Print Culture in the Early United States* (Philadelphia: University of Pennsylvania Press, 2019.

Sources

Letter to Luis Santangel (1493)

Christopher Columbus
Translated by Gregory Murry, All Rights Reserved

Dear Sir, because I know that you will be pleased with the great victory that Our Lord has granted me on my journey, I write to inform you about how I sailed from the Canary Islands to the Indies with the fleet provided me by the illustrious King and Queen. During this voyage, I encountered numerous inhabited islands with countless people, and I have claimed possession of all of them on behalf of their Highnesses. I made this claim with a proclamation and by displaying the royal flag, without opposition.

I named the first island San Salvador in honor of Our Savior, who granted us this success. The natives of this island call it Guanahaní. I named the second island Santa María de Concepción, the third Fernandina, the fourth Isabela, and the fifth island, I called Juana.

Upon reaching Juana, I followed its western coast, and it was so vast that I thought it might be mainland China. However, I did not find any towns or settlements on the seashore, only scattered groups of people, who quickly fled, making it impossible to communicate with them. Nevertheless, I explored this path, hoping to discover large cities or villages.

I had learned much from other Indians I had encountered, which led me to believe that this land was an island. So, I continued along its eastern coast for one hundred and seven leagues until it came to an end. From this point, I saw another island to the east, about eighteen leagues away, which I named La Española. I traveled there and then followed the northern part, about 188 leagues eastward in a straight line from Juana. This island, along with the others, is incredibly fertile. It has numerous ports along the coastline, unlike any I have seen in Christian lands, as well as a number of large rivers.

The terrain is mountainous, with peaks higher than those of Tenerife. The beauty of these mountains, covered with countless varieties of trees that reach seemingly to the heavens, is truly awe-inspiring. The lush vegetation remains evergreen, seemingly never losing its leaves, as I observed them to be as vibrant and beautiful as the greenest of Spanish landscapes in May.

La Española boasts exceptional pine forests, vast plains, and an abundance of honey, various bird species, and diverse fruits. It is rich in mineral mines and home to a considerable number of people. The natural beauty of La Española is truly remarkable, with fertile lands that offer ideal conditions for cultivation, livestock rearing, and establishing towns and villages. The coastal ports are almost beyond belief. The island is also blessed with numerous large rivers, most of which carry gold...

The people of these islands walk around completely naked, just as they are born, although some women cover one part of themselves with a grass leaf or a cotton headscarf, which they make for this purpose. They do not possess iron, steel, or any weapons, nor do they seem inclined to have them. Not because they lack physical strength or shapely stature, but because they are exceedingly fearful. Their only weapons are cane spears, which they dare not even use. On numerous occasions, I have sent two or three men ashore to some village in an attempt to communicate, but the natives would flee upon seeing them. Despite my efforts to provide them with various goods, including cloth and other valuable items, without asking for anything in return, they remain unshakably fearful.

Nevertheless, once they overcome their fear, they are incredibly generous with whatever they have...

They would even take the broken pieces of our bows and pipes in exchange for whatever we wanted, almost like animals. This did not sit well with me, so I prohibited it. Instead, I would give them many good things that I had brought, hoping to win their affection and lead them to become Christians. I desired them to embrace the love and service of Their Highnesses, and to share with us the abundant resources they possess. They have no concept of idols or any form of idolatry, but rather believe that strength and goodness reside in the heavens. They firmly believed that I and my ships came from the heavens, and they welcomed me with great respect and hospitality after overcoming their fear.

Now they believe without a doubt that I come from the heavens, despite my having spoken with them extensively. When I arrived, the locals were the first to proclaim this, and others would run from house to house and nearby villages, shouting loudly, inviting everyone to come and see the people from the heavens. Once they felt secure in our presence, they all came, without exception, young and old, bringing food and drink with a marvelous display of love and hospitality.

Throughout these islands, I observed little diversity in the appearance, customs, or language of the people. They all understand one another, a fact that holds great promise for Their Highnesses' efforts to convert them to our holy faith, to which they seem very open and willing....

In the island of Española, which is the most suitable and advantageous place for gold mines and all kinds of trade, both from here and from the mainland and Gran Can, where there will be significant trade and profit, I have taken possession of a large village, which I named Villa de Navidad. There, I have constructed a fort that should be completed by now, and I have left behind a well-armed and well-provisioned group of people for such an undertaking. Additionally, I have brought carpenters skilled in shipbuilding and established a friendly relationship with the local king, to the extent that he prides himself in calling me his brother.

In these islands, I have not found any monsters, as many believed we'd find here. On the contrary, the people are beautiful, not as dark-skinned as those from Guinea, although their hair is curly...I have found no evidence of monstrous beings, except on an island called Quaris... It is inhabited by a fierce people known to consume human flesh. These people raid and plunder the surrounding Indian islands. Although they are more aggressive than other groups, who tend to be quite cowardly, I regard them no differently than the others.

There is another island, which they assure me is larger than Española, where the people have no hair. This island is abundant in gold, and I have brought some of these natives with me as witnesses.

Speaking of this journey only, Their Highnesses can see that with just a little assistance, I can provide them with as much gold, spices and mastic as they require. I can also provide slaves from among the idolaters. I believe I have found rhubarb and cinnamon, as well as many other valuable things. I have wasted no time, sailing wherever the wind allows me to, stopping only at the Villa de Navidad to secure and establish it. Indeed, I would have accomplished much more if the ships had sailed tolerably well.

This is the work of Our Lord, God who gives victory over the impossible to those who walk in his ways. Though others have written about these lands, no one has yet seen them. The majority judged more from hearsay than from actual knowledge. Therefore, as our Redeemer has granted this victory to our illustrious king and queen, it is a cause for great celebration, joy, and solemn prayers of thanks to the Holy Trinity. The conversion of so many people to our holy faith and the temporal benefits will not only bring joy and gain to Spain but to all Christians as well.

This is the account of the events, summarized briefly.

Written aboard the caravel, near the Canary Islands, on the 15th of February, in the year 1493.

I will do as you command, The Admiral.

On the Just War Against the Indians (1550)

Juan Gines Sepulveda
Translated by Gregory Murry, All Rights Reserved

There are many causes for undertaking a just war; some are more clear (like defense) and some less clear and less frequent, but they are not for that reason less founded upon natural and divine law. One just cause for war involves forcing submission (as a last resort) from those who by their natural condition should obey others but refuse to. The greatest philosophers declare that this type of war is justified by natural law... Indeed, you have to remember that dominion and power...are a type of law that commands a child to obey his parents, a wife her husband, servants their lords, citizens their public officials, and the people their king. Even though all these powers are different, they are all based on natural law, which can be reduced to one principle: the more perfect needs to rule the less perfect, and the more excellent need to rule over the less excellent. This state of affairs is so natural that in everything that consists of multiple parts, one thing rules over the others, as the philosophers declare.

For instance, in inanimate things, the form is more perfect than matter; so form rules, and matter obeys. This is much clearer in animals, in which the soul rules the body, which is the slave of the soul. In the soul, the rational part rules, and the irrational part obeys and submits. All of this is consistent with the divine and natural law that commands the more perfect and more powerful to rule the less perfect and less powerful. This is true of objects with uncorrupted natures and men who are healthy in soul and body, for it frequently happens that in vicious and depraved men, the appetites dominate the body and the reason, but this is contrary to nature. Only in men does the soul exercise dominion over the body and the civil and royal power of reason exercise dominion over the appetites. It is clearly natural and just when the soul rules the body and the reason rules the appetites, for when the parts are equal or the inferior part rules the superior, this is harmful to the whole. Man and all the other animals submit to this law, for on account of it, the beasts are domesticated and submitted to the dominion of man. Because of this, the man rules over his wife, the adult rules over children, the father rules over his sons, that is to say, the more powerful and perfect rule over the weaker and less perfect. Even among adults this is true since some are naturally lords and others naturally servants. Those who are more intelligent (even if they have weaker bodies) are natural lords. Less intelligent people (even if they are physically strong) are naturally servants, and it is just and right that they be, and this is sanctioned by divine law. It is written in Proverbs: "the stupid shall serve the wise." By the word 'stupid,' the scriptures refer to barbarous and inhumane peoples who do not live a civil life with peaceful customs. And it will always be just and natural that such men submit to the power of princes and nations that are more cultured and humane, so that they may benefit from the virtues and prudence of civilized laws, give up barbarism, and live a more humane and cultivated life of virtue. If they reject this, it can be imposed by force of arms, for such a war will be just according to natural law. Aristotle writes, "It seems that wars arise from nature when they are in accordance with the craft of a hunter, which can be used equally against beasts and against men. When such men are born to obey but refuse servitude, war is justified." Saint Augustine says, "Do you think that no one can be compelled to do justice? Have you not read what the father of the family said to his servants—'compel them to enter, all those whom you meet.' In another place:

You can do much even to those who resist: you can treat them with a beneficial harshness, looking more to their benefit than what they want. Even when a father treats his son harshly, he does not therefore give up his paternal love. Do what needs to be done, even if you need to cause harm because this is the only thing that can help.

In summary, it is just, suitable, and in conformity with the natural law that lords who are upright, humane, virtuous and intelligent command those who do not have these qualities.... Though God approves of the power of a prince or republic over clients and subjects, he does not therefore approve of the sins committed by officials and ministers. Thus, even though unjust men have given examples of cruelty and greed and other vices in the conquest of the New World (and I have heard many examples of this), this does not change the fact that the prince and other good men had good intentions in undertaking this conquest. The prince did not permit these outrages nor were they due to his negligence (in which case God would have judged the prince as equally guilty)...It is true that the conquest of New Spain has been carried out in this way, as I have read...It is also true that we should conquer with as little bloodshed as possible. If the leadership of this enterprise were given to virtuous men, they would accomplish it without cruelty and crimes, and certainly this would be good for the Spaniards but much better for the barbarians...

It is just and natural that prudent, upright, and humane men have lordship over those who are not, and it is for this reason that the Romans established their legitimate and just empire over many nations, a fact that is affirmed by Saint Augustine in various places in his On the City of God, and by Saint Thomas in various places in his On the Regime of Princes. Since this is the case, anyone who knows the customs and nature of both the Spaniards and the natives will know that it is perfectly right that the Spaniards should rule over the barbarians of the New World and the adjacent islands because in prudence, intelligence, virtue, and humanity the natives are as inferior to the Spaniards as children are to adults and women are to men. For there is as much difference between Spaniards and natives as there is between clement men and cruel men or between self-controlled men and wild men. That is to say, as much difference as there is between men and apes...

Sepulveda proceeds to a lengthy explanation of the causes of the conquest, demonstrating why he thinks they are just. I have included just the summary here.

In summary, the causes that make the war against the barbarians legitimate are as follows. First, the Indian barbarians are naturally slaves because they are barbarous, uncultured, inhumane, and they refuse to submit to the lord-ship of more prudent, powerful, and perfect men, a lordship that would be very useful for them, for natural law declares it just that matter obey form, the body obey the soul, the appetite obey the reason, beasts obey men, the wife obey the husband, sons obey the father, the imperfect obey the perfect, the worse obey the better, and so on for all things. This is the natural order that the divine and eternal law commands. Moreover, this doctrine has been confirmed by Aristotle, whom all philosophers and theologians venerate as the most excellent teacher of justice and the other moral virtues, and as a wise interpreter of natural law. It has also been confirmed by Saint Thomas, who is considered the prince of scholastic philosophers and as weighty an authority as Aristotle.

The second just reason for this war is that the Spaniards need to root out the nefarious and wicked crime of cannibalism amongst these people, a crime that offends nature because it is part of their religion and by it, they give to demons the glory that belongs to God. These monstrous rites and human sacrifices provoke the wrath of God. Moreover, the just war against the Indians will save many victims, whom the Indians would otherwise be able to sacrifice in future years. Of course, it is part of the divine and natural law that all men are obliged, if they are able, to punish crimes and prevent harm to innocent people.

The third just reason for this war is that the Christian religion needs to spread by means of evangelism whenever there is an opportunity for it, and now there is an open and secure path in the New World for preachers [in the text, Sepulveda had cited the examples of several missionaries who had been killed in the New World]. The New World is so secure now that not only are preachers able to preach, which they would not have been able to do if the Spaniards had not freed the Indians from the fear of their own princes and priests, but the Indians can receive the Christian religion freely, since the Spaniards have removed all the obstacles, especially the cult of idols.

On the War Against the Indians 1552

Bartolommeo De las Casas
Translated by Gregory Murry, All Rights Reserved

On whether war can be undertaken in order to punish idolatry and sins against the natural law.

On this question, one needs to hear the true opinion of the canon lawyers. The first reason one can undertake such a war is to defend Christian lands that have been violently seized, like North Africa and the Holy Land. The second is if the infidels contaminate our faith, sacraments, temples or images with the grave sins of idolatry: like how Constantine forbid the pagans to keep idols where they might scandalize the Christians....[Only on these conditions can we attack the infidels, not to punish just any crime against nature]. The third case is if the infidels blaspheme the name of Jesus Christ, the saints, or the Church with full knowledge of what they are doing. The fourth is when with full knowledge, they impede the preaching of the faith, but they must know what it is that they are impeding. We cannot make war against them when they kill the preachers if they only do so because they are afraid that the preachers are going to harm them or are really men-at-arms dressed as preachers. The fifth case is to make war against the Turks. The sixth is to protect the innocent, for everyone is commanded to protect their neighbor. We are not commanded to protect our neighbor from sinning against the natural law, but divine law does entrust some to the protection and care of the church. I might add that if one cannot protect the innocent without resorting to war, it is better to forgo such protection because we should always choose the lesser of two evils, and the harm that war brings to innocent people is much greater than the death of a few innocent people. In all these cases, one should respect the opinions of the canonists and deny the first justification of Doctor Sepulveda, which is that the war against the Indians is just because they practice idolatry and sin against nature...

On whether or not we should be able to make war to spread the Christian religion more easily.

First, faith cannot be spread by a simple demonstration of natural reason, but only by subjecting the understanding...to the one who preaches faith and introduces it; thus, the preacher's example becomes a testament to the true God whom he serves and the truth of the faith that he preaches. If the preacher is good, he is more easily believed. It does not help if the preacher's work is preceded by war; for war does not dispose the natives to like the Christians; rather, it causes the natives to abhor the God who allows such people to exist and makes them scorn the law that permits such war. In turn, they consider the faith which such men preach to be false, all of which [my] experience in the Indies confirms...Moreover, if a man only receives the faith in order to avoid the massacres, robberies and murders that he sees his neighbors has suffered, he receives an empty faith, without knowing what he receives.

Second, in the preaching of Christianity, one should include the preaching of penitence. Thus Luke writes, "It was right that Christ should suffer and die on the third day and preach penitence and the remission of sins to all men in his name...Because Jesus came to redeem us from our sins." Jesus wanted to preach repentance by baptism to all men, without punishing anyone; in baptism there is no punishment for the sins of the past. This rule is to be observed amongst all nations, for as Paul says in Romans 10 and Galatians 3: "There is no difference...between servant and free, nor man and women, but all are one in Christ." And Paul says that all are equally saved, both the Greeks and barbarians, as well as both the wise and unwise. Thus, we must preach the remission of past sins, and even if the natives deserve punishment, we should neither punish them nor make war against them, for all is forgiven in the waters of baptism. [It is written], "For Christ did not come to judge the world, but to save it."

It is true that we can make war on the infidel if they impede the teaching of our faith…but there are limitations to this, for this only holds good if they know what they are impeding, like the Moors, who know about our religion; however, if they impede it because they think we are going to rob and kill them as enemies, it is licit to defend ourselves but not to make war against them. The second limitation is this: when the princes and lords of the infidels ask their people to impede our preaching and the common consent of all the republic agrees that they do not want to hear us…we are not able to make war against them.

Even though it seems as if the Gospel of Mark, which tells us to preach the word of God to all the earth, gives us the right to preach anywhere and so to defend our preachers, this does not give us the right to force the Gentiles to hear us…For it is a very different thing to say that we have the right to preach than to say we have a right to force others to hear us…

On Making War to Protect the Innocent

Doctor Sepulveda also says that the Spaniards are right to make war against the Indians in order to protect the innocents who are sacrificed and eaten. Now, I concede that the Church needs to defend innocent people; however, I say that it is neither suitable nor decent to defend them by war. There are four reasons for this. First, one must always choose the lesser of two evils. Now, the

Indians kill some innocent people in order to eat them, which is even worse than just sacrificing them; however, this is not nearly as bad as what happens in war. For war kills far more people than the Indians sacrifice. Moreover, because of these wars, the Indians grow to hate our faith, which is even worse. The second reason is that we are commanded by Exodus not to kill the innocent, which is much more important than the command to defend the innocent. When one cannot follow the second without violating the first, one should choose not to kill rather than defend the innocent. Though it may happen that in just wars between cities, soldiers may accidently kill innocents, when we make war to punish delinquents, and we know that some people are innocent and it will be impossible to distinguish the innocent from the guilty; it is much better to forgo that war and conform to the precepts of Jesus Christ, which does not permit us to cut the wheat from the chaff. Rather, Christ commands us to wait for the Day of Judgment, when we might discern the good from the bad without difficulty or danger, and when we might punish the bad without harming the good.

Moreover, these people should not be punished for sacrificing men because they are not obliged to know their errors if we approach them armed for war rather than as friends who are there to teach them. Their ignorance is not their fault, and so they should not be punished for it...for the sacrifice of men was very common in antiquity. Eusebius claimed that it was common for princes to sacrifice their own sons to give greater reverence to the gods.

On the Barbarity of the Natives

On the question on the native's barbarity, which causes Doctor Sepulveda to say that the Indians are naturally servants and obliged to be the subjects of the Spaniards, I respond that in the scriptures and profane writers, one finds three types of barbarians. One kind refers to any people who have strange opinions or customs, but neither lack the prudence nor political wisdom to rule themselves. The second type are those people who do not have languages that can be represented with pictures or letters, as were the English at one point… Aristotle does not at all say that this type of barbarian is naturally a servant on whom one can make war; rather, in the third book of the Politics, he claims that among some barbarians there are true and natural kings, lords, and governors. The third type of barbarians are those who have perverse customs, are unintelligent, and have brutal inclinations. They are like wild animals who live in the fields, without cities, without houses, without political life, without laws, and even without the simple agreements that are part of the law of nations….and they live by robbing and fighting, as did the princes of the Goths and the Alans, and today as do the Arabs in Asia and the Alarabes in Africa. It is only these types that Aristotle says it is licit to hunt like wild animals, by which we should understand that it is licit to defend ourselves from the harm that they can bring us and reduce them to humane and civil life…

But though the Indians have some customs that are not very political, this alone does not make them barbarians; rather, they are sociable and civil people. They have large cities, houses, laws, crafts, lords, and governance; they punish crimes against nature with death. Thus, they have enough of a civil life that we cannot make war on them on account of their barbarity.

The False Saint Anthony (1711)

By: Bernard da Gallo
Translated by Gregory Murry, all rights reserved

In the year of the Lord 1701, I was ordered to go to the aid of the Bamba mission.

Some time later, a Negro who served the missions said to me, "A young woman claiming to be Saint Anthony has appeared before the king; she performs miracles. As she passed by, the twisted trees straightened and fell. Now she is in the King's palace, accusing you....She has changed the Salve Regina and makes them sing it in her way. I see that the people passing by are intimidated. Some say she might be a demon sent by God for our punishment. The King doesn't know what to do. She is preaching against you, against the Pope, and many other things against the Catholic Faith."

I cannot express the anguish of my soul, considering myself alone, abandoned by superiors, and lacking all human aid, in danger of losing the faithful of the Congo and witnessing the ultimate ruin of that poor kingdom, without any hope of remedy. It tormented me even more because I felt I might ruin the whole mission by not taking the right course of action....

The false St. Anthony stayed in the Ambrice valley-where she burned fetishes, idols, and crosses that were brought to her, as she had taken advantage of not being handed over to me by the King and had used the opportunity to present herself as a saint, preach, prophesy, and threaten as she pleased. Seeing that I had reconciled with the King and opened the church without mentioning her, she took another opportunity to ascend the mountain.

The King, partly out of courtesy to me and partly because he was concerned about the whispers among the people, sent her back to me, accompanied by his advisers and the chief interpreter, on a Sunday morning when it was time for the mass. I said to the advisers, "Ah! Are you already filled, or too full, with her superstitious and devilish lies? I thank my Son, the King, for the good deed done, but as it is already time for the mass, I cannot delay. Come tomorrow"

The following Monday, the advisers returned with the false St. Anthony, who entered where I was waiting. She went directly in front of the statue of the Madonna, which stood facing the door..

She knelt down and struck the ground three times with her forehead, then stayed in a prayer-like posture for a while, and finally, with a strange smile, she circled the room three times while I stood in the middle.

I asked the advisers the meaning of her action. They replied that it was a sign of joy and that she had done the same to the King. The Interpreter, who seemed somewhat foolish, added that she seemed to have died and then been resurrected. "Very well," I said, "you must be right because what you say makes no sense."

I confess that she did not seem as if she was faking, as I watched her walking on the tips of her toes without touching the ground, moving her hips and body like a snake, extending her neck as if in a trance, her eyes bulging, and her speech frenzied and delirious (I could barely understand what she was saying). Rather, I thought she might be possessed.

I began to question her in the local language to satisfy the advisers and the King, who had sent her for that purpose. First, I asked if she knew what she had been worshipping. She replied that it was the Madonna, covered with a cloth, and aside from that, there were statues of St. Francis and St. Anthony. One could easily distinguish between them, but the advisers were amazed, thinking she knew this information in some extraordinary way.

I asked her who she was. She said she was St. Anthony who had come from heaven. "Alright," I said, "and what news do you bring from up there? Tell me, are there Congolese people in heaven, and if there are, are they black like here?" She replied that there are Congolese people in heaven, both small baptized children and adults who have observed God's law, but they are neither black nor white because there is no color in heaven.

"So, in heaven, there are baptized Congolese children and adults who have kept God's law?" I repeated. "Therefore, I and the other missionaries, preaching the Faith of Christ, the divine law, and the observance of the Ten Commandments, which are necessary for eternal salvation, are not spreading lies but truth? By administering the holy sacraments of the Church, especially baptism, penance, and marriage, we are not deceiving the people? Therefore, the Holy Pope is not a liar or seducer, nor does he send us to deceive people, but rather to lead them on the path to eternal salvation?"

When she heard me reproaching her in this way, she began to tremble and cry, and excuse herself, saying that she had not said anything against me or the Pope, but that all the lies had been told about her to hinder the service of God. She insisted that she had spoken in my favor and in favor of the Holy Pope, teaching that the Pope is the Vicar of Christ on earth, and I, as a priest sent by the same Holy Pope to Congo, deserved all honor and reverence as their spiritual Father.

Meanwhile, the aforementioned interpreter, named D. Michel de Castro, came with advisers and, seeing the woman crying, started to console her and caress her (calling her daughter) and telling her to speak freely and not be afraid because I would not harm her, as she was under their protection.

When I saw how inappropriately this man was defending her, I raised my voice against him, calling him a bad, shameful heretic. For he had no shame in treating a sorceress of *marinda* as his daughter and defending a negro woman who was sowing discord among the poor Christians, not considering that his position in the church should always lead him to stand on my side.

He responded boldly that he could not deny she was his daughter because she was of his people, but he had never heard her say such things.

I countered by asking if she did not burn crosses together with her fetishes in the valley of Ambrice. Did she not want to remove the one from the royal square if the King allowed it?

He denied this, but emboldened by his defense, the false St. Anthony admitted that it was true, and that the crosses in the valley were also mixed with superstitions.

I asked her, "If you are a woman, how can you claim to be St. Anthony?" She replied that God had sent St. Anthony, the first holy son of the religion of St. Francis, who first entered the head of a woman in Mugeto. However, the people there did not receive him, so he left and entered the head of an old man in Sogno, where they wanted to beat him because they considered him a sorcerer, so he fled again. Then he went to Ambula, and the same happened. Finally, he entered her head to preach to the Chibango people and was received with applause and joy. Therefore, she preached the word of God to the people.

She explained that it happened this way: When she was on her deathbed, during her agony, a friar who claimed to be St. Anthony sent by God, appeared to her and commanded her to preach to the people and hasten the restoration of the kingdom, threatening severe punishments to anyone who resisted. After she died, St. Anthony entered her head (instead of her soul) without her knowing how. She suddenly felt revived and rose healthy and free to go and preach. She called her relatives and explained the divine command. To fulfill this command, she gave away all her belongings, just as the missionaries do.

Fed up with hearing such foolishness and nonsense, I dismissed the woman while pretending to remain calm…

The absurdities and follies of this woman are unworthy of being recounted, but her popularity continued to spread. And she did not stop from spreading her lies. I mention them only for the sake of the truth. It is essential that we look on these poor people with compassion. For they are deprived of judgment, reason, doctrine, and other spiritual aids due to their mental and spiritual poverty. They are like prey to hunger and thirst for spiritual nourishment.

In reality, the false St. Anthony was a black woman from Congo, named Kimpavita, who had been baptized as Beatrice. As she admitted before her execution, (which may not be trustworthy)…she had been a concubine of two men (though probably not at the same time) with whom she could not live peacefully due to her pride. She also acted as a Nganga Marinda, a priestess or healer of a certain superstition or witchcraft called Marinda, or perhaps even a demon by that name.

She spoke against the Pope, the church's sacraments, and was not a friend of the cross, as I mentioned before. She didn't want them to pray to any saint except herself. She also showed hostility towards vices, superstitions, fetishes, and other similar things, which she burned along with crosses. These campaigns against vices and witchcraft served as arguments for the slaves to believe she was a saint.

She also distorted the "Salve Regina" prayer with inappropriate and blasphemous words. I will mention a few, even though they are shameful and disordered.

You say 'Hail,' but you don't know why. You recite 'Hail,' but you don't know why. You beat yourself saying 'Hail,' but you don't know why. God wants the intention, and God takes the intention. Marriage serves no purpose; God takes the intention. Baptism serves no purpose; God takes the intention. Confession serves no purpose; God takes the intention. Prayer serves no purpose; God wants the intention. Good deeds serve no purpose; God wants the intention. The mother and the son kneel together. If it weren't for Saint Anthony, what would they do? Saint Anthony is compassionate, Saint Anthony is our remedy, Saint Anthony restores the kingdom of Congo, Saint Anthony consoles the kingdom of heaven. Saint Anthony is the gateway to heaven. Saint Anthony holds the keys to heaven. Saint Anthony is above the angels and the Virgin Mary. Saint Anthony is the second God... and many other nonsensical things that I don't remember.

...She pretended to be Saint Anthony to gain influence and started spreading absurd teachings and proclamations against me and the Catholic Church, causing confusion and turmoil among the Africans. She changed the words to the "Ave Maria" as well.

Her teachings and actions had a profound impact, and the Africans learned her chants and sang them everywhere. She prophesied falsely, made exaggerated threats, and sent followers known as "Antonij piccioli" to various places. She spread heretical beliefs, mocked the Catholic Church, and attempted to undermine the legitimate King's authority, resulting in a deteriorating situation in the region.

She claimed that Jesus Christ was born in S. Salvatore (Bethlehem) and baptized in Sundi (Nazareth). She said that both

Jesus Christ and the Virgin Mary, along with Saint Francis, had been born in Congo and were of the race of the negros (I write clearly, although with horror in my pen). According to her, Saint Francis was born from the lineage of the Marquis of Vunda, and the Virgin Mary, Mother of Jesus Christ, was the daughter of a slave of Marchioness Nzimba Npanghi.

She taught that white men originated from a certain soft white stone called "fuma," which is why they are white. On the other hand, black people originated from a tree called "musanda,"...thus they are black, or the color of the bark.

From this belief, she invented certain objects she called crowns, made from the bark of the Musanda tree. Those who wore these crowns were her most distinguished friends, supporters, and most important followers. Except for herself, women did not wear them. She had them wear these crowns on their heads, as a sign of being Antonians... She called it "yari," where their devotion to their false Saint Anthony would grant them victory and establish them in the kingdom. They believed that without any study or effort, they would gain knowledge; some would become priests, some friars, and some bishops....

She prophesied that the tree trunks left behind after cutting down the trees in S. Salvatore would turn into gold and silver. She claimed that there were also mines of gold, silver, precious stones, and other treasures beneath the stones, including various fabrics, silks, and other riches from the white people.

To make them believe this, she secretly had money buried, namely certain cowry shells, in different places inside the destroyed cathedral. Then she assigned the locations of the hiding spots and had the cowry shells publicly dug up, so people could see that she was telling the truth.

When she went to the church, whether to preach or perform other spiritual exercises, while singing the Antonian salve, she would climb onto the platform of the altar. Afterward, she would process out of the sacristy door, and when she arrived in front of her hut, people would approach a little tree that stood there and kiss her feet.

During meals, the noblemen held out the edges of their capes instead of aprons or tablecloths, and certain men could eat a bit of food given by her hand or put in their mouths any fragments that she dropped. When she drank, they held their hands under the cup, and if some drops of water or palm wine fell, they drank it with devotion.

The principal women swept the roads leading to her hut up to the door. The poor black people (born, raised, and aged in the forests), were even more ignorant than one can imagine. When they saw the ruined churches in S. Salvatore, many could not decide whether they were made by human hands or had come from heaven...

Due to the ignorance of the Congolese people, their love for their nation, the desire to see their destroyed homeland restored, the ambition to reign, and the fact that I was all alone, just one man among them—all combined with the diabolical foolishness of the false Saint Anthony, as well as the authority of the interpreters who were not very fond of me, as I had taken away their profits by learning the language myself—all this resulted in the ease with which these people fell into superstition. Once someone gives in to superstition, they easily believe anything, as is sometimes seen even among sensible white people, and much more among young girls, as I know from experience and can attest to.

I beg those who read these pages not to be scandalized by the poor people of Congo, who are deeply devoted to our Holy Faith. Rather, be moved to compassion for their miseries, especially since, as I will explain, they ultimately proved themselves to be true Catholics, though ignorant.

The glory prophesied by the Antonians and the sanctity of the false Saint Anthony did not last long, as within less than two years, it all fell apart.

The false Saint Anthony had a habit of dying every Friday, going to Heaven to dine with God and advocate for the cause of her black followers, particularly the restoration of Congo. Then she would resurrect on Saturday. However, an irreparable misfortune occurred during one of these episodes.

Trying to follow the example of the missionaries, she wanted to observe chastity and be considered chaste. However, she had a companion named Angelo, by whom she twice became pregnant and twice aborted the child. Unable to miscarry a third time, she sought a remedy to cover up the mistake. She thus began to tell her followers that she wanted to go to Heaven, and she would need to remain there to advocate for their cause with God and attend to their affairs. Instead of ascending to Heaven, she secretly descended from Mount S. Salvator, going into the bush to give birth to a male child. It was on this occasion that Divine Providence intervened to provide the remedy for everything.

At that same time, the Duke of Bamba and the old Queen of Congo sent ambassadors to the King. As these ambassadors passed near the slopes of Mount S. Salvatore, they heard the crying voice of a child...When the ambassadors reached the location, they found the false Saint Anthony, a man, and a small black woman serving the false saint. They questioned the man, inquiring about his destination and the identity of the woman carrying the baby. The man admitted that the woman with the baby was Saint Anthony herself.

The ambassadors were taken aback by this revelation. Saint Anthony among the straw and grass, nursing a baby and trying to soothe him with milk? They further questioned the man about the child's parentage, and he claimed that the baby was Saint Anthony's child. The ambassadors were puzzled and reminded the man that Saint Anthony was a Franciscan and could not have children. They asked if he was claiming to be the child's father, to which the man replied, "No." The ambassadors were infuriated and exclaimed, "How dare you! Are you claiming that these are divine secrets that cannot and should not be scrutinized?" They immediately ordered their servants to arrest both the man and the woman and vowed to determine whether they were truly saints or just wicked impostors.

The false Saint Anthony was arrested and brought before the King in Evululu. When I learned that they had been captured and were in the King's custody, I felt immense relief and gave thanks to God. Since I had already decided on the appropriate course of action for them, I sent word to ensure they were not left to starve but kept under close watch until a final decision could be made....

Later that Saturday evening, the King issued a proclamation that every man should bring a piece of wood to the square on the following Sunday. On that day, the false Saint Anthony confessed and abjured privately. She was willing to make a public confession, but the King, who was already displeased, did not permit it, saying that everyone already knew her lies to be from the devil.

Gathered, on the first day of July 1706, the people assembled in the square, and the condemned were brought before them. The judge appeared and publicly declared the sentence: they were to be thrown alive into the flames. He explained the awfulness of their crimes against the king and the church and why they deserved such a dreadful punishment. Meanwhile, Father Lucca and I were waiting, intending to console the souls of the poor condemned. However, it was not possible because as soon as the judge finished his speech and left, the mob attacked her like a pack of hounds. Dragging the accused on the ground, through the dust, they nearly killed her before reaching the pyre. Once they arrived, more dead than alive, they were tightly bound and thrown onto two piles of wood, not far from each other. The fire was lit, and within a short time, roughly the time it takes to say a creed, they surrendered their souls. One of them pronounced the name of Jesus, and the other the name of the Virgin Mary, as I was told, and they quickly turned to ashes.

The poor false Saint Anthony, who was accustomed to dying and resurrecting, died this time but did not come back to life. Nevertheless, her followers were so bold that they spread a rumor that the spots where their saints were burnt turned into two deep wells, with a beautiful star appearing in each of them. They further claimed that the form of Saint Anthony had died, but not Saint Anthony (I truly don't know what they meant by this). This shows that they remained stubborn, even after witnessing the unfortunate and infamous end of their saint and her false and diabolical madness. From this, one can guess what could have happened if she had lived.

Spiritual Visions

Teresa of Avila (1512-1582)
Translated by Gregory Murry, All Rights Reserved

Our Lord was pleased that I should sometimes see the vision of an angel close by me, on my left side, in bodily form. This did not usually happen to me, except when God miraculously allowed it. Though I frequently was in the presence of angels, I usually did not literally see them. It was the Lord's will that I should see this one in the flesh; he was not large, but short and most beautiful. His face was afire, and he seemed to be a Cherubim, a very high angel who seems to be made of fire. The angels never tell me their names; but I see that in heaven there is so great a difference between one angel and another, and between these and the others, that I cannot explain it.

I saw a long spear of gold in the Cherubim's hand, and at the point there seemed to be a little fire. He seemed to be thrusting it into my heart and to pierce my bowels themselves; when he removed it, he seemed to draw them out also, and to leave me all on fire with a great love of God. The pain was so great that I moaned, and yet the sweetness of this pain brought me such ecstasy that I did not want it to end nor for my soul to be satisfied by anything but God alone. The pain is not bodily, but spiritual, though there is a sharp bodily pain as well. The tenderness between God and the soul is so sweet that I pray God will give the same experience to whomever may think that I am lying.

During the days that this lasted, I went around as if beside myself. I did not wish to see or speak with anyone, but only to embrace my pain, which was to me a greater glory than any earthly thing. I was in this state from time to time, whenever it was our Lord's pleasure to throw me into a deep trance. I could not stop them from coming on even if others were present, even though it bothered me that they became publicly known... May He be blessed forever, who hath given such great graces to one who has not been worthy of them.

...When I went to receive communion, I remembered this vision, in which I had seen the majesty of the Lord directly. I saw that the same majesty was present there in the host (indeed, many times the Lord desired that I should physically see him in the host). Then, my hair stood on end, and I seemed to be completely overwhelmed. O my Lord. If you did not cover up your greatness in the host, what wretched and miserable creature would dare to combine with your majesty in Holy Communion? Blessed be the Lord. Let all the angels and creatures praise him! You measure all things by our weakness, veiling your sovereign majesties in the Eucharist, so that we weak and miserable beings do not grow too afraid of your great power and therefore fear to enjoy your presence in communion.

If God were to reveal himself openly to us in all his majesty, we might become like a certain peasant I know, who found a treasure that was too large to fit inside his lowly soul. Not knowing how to spend it, the peasant fell into a great sadness, from which he eventually died. If he had been given the treasure little by little, rather than all at once, he would have been relieved of his poverty without losing his life....

How can I keep silent about these miracles? How shall I feel? A soul so heavy with sin and having shown so little fear of God in this life. How shall I feel when I see God's great majesty and see that he wants to join with me? How shall I put that glorious, pure, and compassionate body in a mouth that has so often spoken words against my Lord? To a soul that has not served the Lord, the love that shines through his faith is more painful than all of his terrible majesty.

What must I have felt, then, on the two occasions that I am about to describe?

...Once when I arrived at communion, the eyes of my soul saw two hideously shaped demons. They were clearer to me than if I had seen them with my bodily eyes. It seemed to me that their horns encircled the throat of the poor priest, and I saw my Lord in the wafer that the priest was about to give me. By this, I saw clearly that the priest had offended Christ, and I understood that his soul was in mortal sin.

Oh, to see your beauty between two such hideous figures, Lord! They seemed to be so frightened and alarmed by your presence, that it seemed they would have left willingly if you had given them leave to do so. The whole episode disturbed me so greatly that I did not know how I would take communion. I stood there, petrified by fear. However, since the vision came to me from God, I knew he would not let me be harmed by it. The Lord told me to pray for the priest, and that he had allowed me to see the vision so that I would know just how powerful the words of consecration are. God's presence in communion does not fail just because of the sins of the priest who says the words. In his great goodness, God surrenders himself to the hands of his enemy, and all for my good and the good of others.

I understood how important it is for priests to live holy lives. I understood how evil it is to take this Holy Sacrament unworthily. Finally, I understood how powerfully a demon can become the master of a soul in mortal sin. It was of great profit to me and made me understand my debts to God. Blessed be God forever...

On another occasion, I experienced a similar vision that frightened me very much. I was visiting a place, and in this place, a man whom I knew to have lived a very evil life had just died. He had been sick for the last two years, and towards the end, he had begun making some amends for his sins. Even though he had died without confession, I still thought there was a chance that he might have escaped the hell fires. However, when he died, I saw a throng of demons come for his body, and it seemed to me as if they were playing with it, tossing it amongst themselves with their large claws. This vision terrified me, and when I saw the body buried with great honor and ceremony, I was thinking of the goodness of God, and how he preferred to hide the fact that this man was his enemy rather than to dishonor him openly.

I was driven half-crazy by this vision. During the rest of the service, I did not see any demons, but when they put the body in the ground, there was such a horde of demons in the grave waiting to take him that I was nearly driven mad just looking at them, and it took all my courage to hide my fear from others. When I saw them make themselves the lords of his body, I considered what they would do to his soul. Let it please God to give such a terrifying vision to all who live such evil lives, for it would be a great spur for them to live better, it seems to me.

All this was done to make me recognize how much I owe the Lord and to see what he had saved me from. I kept this fear in my heart until I spoke of the matter with my confessor, thinking that it could perhaps be a demonic trick to defame the reputation of that man, even though he was not known for his Christianity. Illusion or not, it still terrifies me to think about it.

I have begun to speak about visions of the dead. I want to briefly share some visions of the dead that the Lord has wanted me to see. Once, I was told of the death of a prelate from another province. He was a very virtuous person who had done me many favors. When I heard that he had died, I was very disturbed because I feared for his salvation. He had been a prelate for twenty years and for all that time had the care of souls, which seems to me a dangerous and heavy responsibility. I prayed hard for him, offering up all the little merits that I had earned in my life and asking the Lord to supply what was still lacking with his own merits, so that the prelate's soul might ascend through purgatory.

As I was asking this of the Lord the best I could, the prelate seemed to rise from the ground on my right, and I saw him joyfully ascend to heaven. At the time he died, he had been very old, but in my vision he appeared to be about thirty years old or younger, and his face shone with a radiant glow. The vision was brief, but I remained consoled. His death gave me no more cause for pain, even though I saw many people very distressed by it because he was very well-liked. My soul was so consoled that I was no longer disturbed by his death, certain as I was that this was a true vision, and not an illusion.

By the time we heard of his death, he had been gone for more than fifteen days; nevertheless, I continued to pray for his soul and encouraged others to do so, though not as fervently as before I had the vision since praying for a soul that I knew to be in heaven seemed to me like giving alms to the rich. I learned afterwards that he edified many by his death, and witnesses at his bedside left astonished by the composure, tears, and humility with which he died.

There was a nun in our house who was a great servant of God. About a day and half after her death, we were reading an Office for the Dead, and I was helping with the verses. In the middle of the reading, I saw her: it seemed to me that her soul rose up from the ground and went to heaven. This was no vision of the soul, like the last, but rather like the others I have described. I cannot at all doubt what I saw.

Once a younger nun died in our convent; she was a great friend of the house and a virtuous servant of God. I thought that she would go right to heaven because she had often been sick, and I thought that her tribulations would give her the merit to pass quickly through purgatory. While we were praying the liturgy of the hours (it would have been about four hours after she died), I saw her rise from the ground and ascend to heaven.

One time, I was visiting a Jesuit college and suffering in both soul and body, so much so that I doubted my ability to have a single positive thought. That night, a young Jesuit died, and while I was praying for him at Mass, I saw him ascending to heaven in great glory with Christ by his side.

Once, when I was at Mass, I had a vision of a very holy Carmelite friar, and I saw how he had died and risen to heaven without entering purgatory. He died the very same hour that my vision occurred, though I only learned of his death afterwards. I was amazed that he had not entered purgatory. I was given to understand that he had fulfilled his profession as a monk and had profited from the indulgences granted to the order by papal bull, so that he might be freed from purgatory. I did not understand why I understood this. It seemed to me that God showed me this vision to teach me that clothes alone do not make one a true friar. The Lord has given me other visions, which I choose not to share here.

But the only two souls that I knew who escaped purgatory completely were the friar that I mentioned and Father Peter Alcantara. It has pleased the Lord to show me the different grades of glory in heaven and the places in heaven that he has assigned to each. And there is a great difference between one and the other.

Nican Mopua (1649)

Translated from Nahuatl by Chat GPT

Here it is told, how a great lady, the honored and venerable lady, the Mother of God, the one who is our mother, appeared. It happened on the hill called Tepeyac, she is called Guadalupe.

Ten years after the conquest, when the water, the mountain, and the city of Mexico were already subdued, when the arrows and shields were laid down, and peace reigned in all the villages, their waters, and their mountains. Just as it sprouted and grew green, the faith, the knowledge of the Giver of life, the true God, opened its petals.

Then, in the year 1531, a few days into December, there was an Indian, a commoner, a poor man from the people. His name was Juan Diego, as it is said, a resident of Cuauhtitlán, and he belonged to Tlatelolco in matters of God.

It was early Saturday morning, and he came seeking God and His commandments. When he approached the hill called Tepeyac, the dawn was already shining on the earth. There, he heard singing on the hill, as if various precious birds were singing. When their songs ceased, it was as if the hill echoed in response. Their melodies were exceedingly sweet and delightful, surpassing the songs of the coyoltototl and the tzinitzcan, and other precious singing birds.

Juan Diego stopped and wondered, "Am I worthy, deserving of what I hear? Am I perhaps only dreaming? Could I be seeing this only as if in a dream?

Where am I? Where do I find myself? Is it possible, as the elders, our ancestors, our grandparents said, that I am in the land of flowers, the land of maize, our flesh, our sustenance, perhaps in the heavenly land?"

He was looking in that direction, towards the top of the hill, where the sun rises, towards the place from where the celestial and precious singing emanated.

And when the singing suddenly stopped, when it was no longer heard, he heard someone calling him from the top of the hill, saying, "Juanito, Juan Dieguito."

He then dared to go where he was being called. His heart was not troubled, and nothing disturbed him. On the contrary, he felt exceedingly joyful and content. He climbed the hill to find out who was calling him.

When he reached the top of the hill, he beheld a noble Maiden standing there. She called him to come close to Her.

When he stood before Her, he was greatly amazed by Her incomparable beauty and grandeur. Her dress radiated like the sun, shining brightly. The stones and rocks on which She stood emitted rays like precious jade, gleaming like jewels. The earth reflected brilliant colors like those of a rainbow in the mist. And the mesquite trees and the nopales (cacti) and all the other various little plants that usually grow there appeared like quetzal feathers, their foliage shone like turquoise, and their trunks, thorns, and little thorns gleamed like gold.

In Her presence, he prostrated himself, listening to Her venerable breath, Her venerable words that were extremely gentle, exceedingly noble, as if they were attracting him and showing him love.

She said to him, "Listen, my son, the youngest, Juanito, where are you going?"

And he replied, "My Lady, my Queen, my little girl, I am going to your venerable house in Mexico Tlatelolco, to follow the teachings of God that are given to us by our priests, who are the images of Our Lord, our God."

Immediately, She spoke to him and revealed Her precious will.

She said, "Know for certain, my son, the smallest one, that I am truly the ever-perfect Virgin Mary, who has the honor and joy of being the Mother of the true God, the giver of life, the Creator of all people, the Owner of heaven and earth. I desire greatly, and I want very much, that a sacred little house be built for me here, where I will show Him, exalt Him by making Him manifest, and give Him to the people in all my personal love. He is my compassionate gaze, my help, my salvation. For in truth, I take pride in being your compassionate Mother, yours and of all the people living on this land, and also of all the other various lineages of men, those who love me, call upon me, seek me, and trust in me.

For there, I will hear their weeping, their sorrow, and will remedy and alleviate all their different sufferings, their miseries, their pains. And to carry out the compassionate and merciful intent of my gaze, go to the palace of the Bishop of Mexico, and you will tell him how I send you to reveal my great desire that a temple be built for me here in the plain. You will tell him everything you have seen and admired, and what you have heard.

And be assured that I will greatly thank and reward you; I will enrich and glorify you. And from there, I will grant you much with which I may repay your weariness, your service in carrying out the task I am sending you on. You have heard, my youngest son, my breath, my word; go now and do what is within your power.

Immediately, in Her presence, he prostrated himself and said, "My Lady, my little girl, I will now fulfill your venerable breath, your venerable word. For now, I leave, I, your humble servant."

Then he went down to carry out his mission: he came to the road and went straight to Mexico. When he arrived in the city, he went straight to the palace of the bishop, who had recently arrived. The Ruling Priest's name was Friar Juan de Zumárraga, a priest of San Francisco.

As soon as he arrived, he attempted to see him and begged those who served him, his servants, to go and inform him. After a long while, they came to call him, and the bishop ordered him to enter. As soon as he entered, he immediately knelt before him, prostrated himself, and then revealed to him the precious breath and precious words of the Queen of Heaven.

So they went to tell the Lord Bishop, and they filled his mind with doubts, telling him not to believe Juan Diego, that he only told lies and invented the things he came to tell, or that he dreamt or imagined what he said or asked for. They decided that if he came back again, they would catch him and punish him severely so that he would stop telling lies and disturbing the people.

Meanwhile, Juan Diego was with the Most Holy Virgin, telling her the response he received from the Lord Bishop. She heard him and said, "My little son, it's good. You will come back here tomorrow to bring the sign that he asked for. With that, he will believe you and will no longer doubt or suspect you. And know, my little son, that I will reward you for your care and the work and tiredness you have endured for me. Now go, for I will wait for you here tomorrow."

The next day, on Monday, when Juan Diego was supposed to bring some proof to be believed, he did not return. When he reached his home, his uncle, named Juan Bernardino, was gravely ill. He called for a doctor, who attended to him, but it was too late, as he was already in agony. That evening, his uncle asked him to go to Tlatelolco and call one of the priests to come and confess him and prepare him for death.

On Tuesday, while it was still very dark, Juan Diego left his home to call the priest in Tlatelolco. As he approached the hill, at the foot of Tepeyac, the end of the mountain range, where the road leads toward the setting sun, the same path where he had previously gone, he said to himself, "If I continue on this path, the Noble Lady may see me and, for sure, like before, detain me to take the sign to the ruling priest as she commanded. Let our affliction first be resolved. I must quickly call the religious priest, as my poor uncle is eagerly waiting for him."

He then went around the hill, climbed through the middle, and from there, crossing over, he went toward where the sun rises. He wanted to quickly reach Mexico City so that the Queen of Heaven would not detain him. He thought that by taking this detour, she would not be able to see him as she sees everything perfectly.

But she saw him and came down from the top of the hill where she had been watching him since before. She intercepted him on the side of the hill and said, "My little son, what's happening? Where are you going, where are you heading?"

Juan Diego, perhaps feeling a little embarrassed or ashamed, or maybe even frightened or startled, prostrated himself before her, greeted her, and replied.

"My Young Lady, my little Daughter, my Child, I hope you are well. How did you wake up? Is your beloved little body feeling fine, my Lady, my Child? With sorrow, I distress your face, your heart: I want to let you know, my little Girl, that a relative of yours, my uncle, is very sick. He has a severe illness, and it is likely that he will soon die from it. Now, I will hurry to your venerable house in Mexico to call one of the beloved servants of Our Lord, one of our priests, so that he may come and confess him and prepare him. Because this is why we were born, to wait for the task of our death. But if I am to carry it out, I will come back here again to bring your venerable breath, your venerable word, Lady, my Child. Forgive me, have a little patience with me because I am not deceiving you, my little Daughter. Tomorrow, without fail, I will come back in a hurry."

As soon as she heard Juan Diego's words, the Compassionate, the Perfect Virgin, responded:

"Listen, put it in your heart, my little Son, that you should not be frightened or afflicted by anything. Do not let your face or heart be disturbed. Do not fear this illness or any other painful and distressing thing.

Am I not here, I who have the honor and joy of being your mother? Are you not under my shadow and protection? Am I not the source of your happiness? Are you not in the hollow of my mantle, in the crossing of my arms? Do you need anything else? Let nothing else worry you or disturb you. Let the illness of your uncle not grieve you, for he will not die from it now. Be certain that he has already recovered."

(And indeed, at that moment, his uncle was healed, as it was later confirmed).

Juan Diego, upon hearing the venerable breath, the venerable word of the Queen of Heaven, was greatly comforted and his heart was calmed. He immediately asked her to send him as a messenger to see the ruling Bishop, to bring him the sign of verification so that he would believe him. The Celestial Queen then instructed him to go up to the top of the hill where he had seen her before. She said, "Go up, you, the youngest of my sons, to the top of the hill and to the place where you saw me and where I gave you my command. There, you will find various flowers spread out. Cut them, gather them all together, and then come down quickly. Bring them here to me."

Then he came down immediately, bringing the different flowers he had cut to the Heavenly Lady. When she saw them, she took them with her venerable hands. Then she placed them back in the hollow of Juan Diego's tilma and said to him:

"My little Son, these various flowers are the proof, the sign you will take to the Bishop. On my behalf, you will tell him to see in them my desire and to fulfill my will. And you, who are my messenger, in you, absolute trust is placed. I strongly command you to show the contents of your tilma to the Bishop only in private, in his presence. You will tell him everything precisely, about how I sent you to the top of the hill to cut the flowers, and everything you saw and admired. This way, you will convince the ruling Priest in his heart, and he will make the sacred house I have asked for to be built and erected."

As soon as the Heavenly Queen gave him her command, he took the road, heading straight to Mexico, feeling content, his heart calm because he was going to do well, carrying the flowers successfully. He was very careful with what was in the hollow of his tilma, afraid that something might fall. He enjoyed the aroma of the precious different flowers.

When he arrived at the Bishop's palace, the gatekeeper and the other servants of the ruling Priest met him. He pleaded with them to let him see the Bishop, but none of them wanted to. They didn't want to listen to him, maybe because it was still very dark. Or perhaps because they already knew him, and he only bothered and annoyed them. His companions who had followed him before had already told them about him. He waited there for a long time, hoping for a reason.

And when they saw that he had been standing there for a long time, head down, doing nothing, waiting to be called, they approached him to see what was in the hollow of his tilma and satisfy their curiosity.

When Juan Diego realized that he couldn't hide what he was carrying, and they might bother or even hit him because of it, he showed them a little that he had flowers. And when they saw that they were all beautiful, various flowers like those of Castile, even though it was not the season for them to grow, they were greatly surprised by their freshness, the open petals, the pleasant smell, and their beauty. They tried to pick a few, and they attempted it three times, but they couldn't do it. Because whenever they tried, the flowers appeared as if painted, embroidered, or sewn into the tilma.

Immediately, they went to tell the ruling Bishop what they had seen, and about the indigenous man who had come before and had been waiting there for a long time to see him. And when the ruling Bishop heard it, he was convinced in his heart that this was the sign he needed to carry out the task requested by the humble man. He immediately ordered Juan Diego to come and see him.

Upon entering, Juan Diego prostrated himself before the Bishop, just as he had done before. Once again, he recounted everything he had seen, admired, and the message he had received. He said: "My Lord, Ruler, I have indeed done as you commanded. I went to tell my Lady, the Heavenly Child, Holy Mary, the Beloved Mother of God, that you requested a sign to believe me, and that you would build her sacred house where she asked you to. I also told her that I had given you my word to bring you a sign, a proof of her venerable will, as you charged me to do. She listened attentively to your venerable desire and petition for a sign, so that her loving will may be fulfilled. She commanded me to come and see you again while it was still night. I asked her for the sign as she promised, and she immediately fulfilled her promise. She ordered me to go to the top of the hill where I had seen her before and cut various flowers like those of Castile. I went to cut them and brought them down to her. She took them with her venerable hands and placed them back in the hollow of my tilma, telling me to bring them to you personally.

Even though I knew that the top of the hill is not a place where flowers grow, as it is rocky with thorns, wild cacti, and mesquite trees, I did not doubt or hesitate. I approached the top of the hill and saw the Earth covered with various flowers, beautiful roses of Castile, the finest, full of dew, splendid. I cut them and brought them to her.

She told me to give them to you as her sign and proof, so that you may see the evidence you requested to fulfill her venerable will, and to confirm the truth of my message. Here they are; please receive them."

Juan Diego then spread out his white tilma, where he had placed the flowers.

As the various flowers of Castile fell to the ground, suddenly, there appeared the Beloved Image of the Perfect Virgin, Holy

Mary, Mother of God, in the same form and figure as she is now, where she is preserved in her beloved house, her sacred house in Tepeyac, called Guadalupe.

When the ruling Bishop and everyone present saw the miraculous image, they kneeled and were greatly amazed. Their hearts were moved, and their minds were uplifted. With tears and sadness, the ruling Bishop begged for forgiveness for not having fulfilled her venerable will and word.

He stood up, untied the tilma from Juan Diego's neck, in which the Heavenly Queen had appeared.

He then took it and placed it in his oratory.

Juan Diego stayed at the Bishop's house for an entire day. The next day, he asked for permission to go back home to see his uncle, Juan Bernardino, who had been very ill when he left him, and had called a priest from Tlatelolco to confess and prepare him, as the Heavenly Queen had told him that he was already healed. He was not allowed to go alone; they accompanied him to his house.

When they arrived, they found his venerable uncle in good health, with no pain at all. His uncle was astonished and asked why he was honored and accompanied in such a way. Juan Diego told him that when he left to call a priest to confess him, the Heavenly Lady appeared to him on Tepeyac Hill. She sent him to Mexico to see the ruling Bishop and tell him to build her house on Tepeyac Hill. His uncle confirmed that it was true and that she had healed him right at that moment. His uncle also mentioned that she had sent him to Mexico to see the Bishop.

He told the Bishop everything he had seen and how miraculously he had been healed.

She wanted to be called, she wanted her name to be: THE PERFECT VIRGIN SAINT MARY OF GUADALUPE, her Beloved Image.

The Bishop invited them to stay in his house for a few days while the sacred house of the Heavenly Queen was being built on Tepeyac Hill, where she had shown herself to Juan Diego. After a while, the Bishop transferred the precious, revered Image of the

Beloved Heavenly Child from his oratory to the main church for everyone to see and admire.

And absolutely everyone, the whole city, without exception, was filled with awe when they came to see and admire her precious Image.

They recognized her as something divine. They came to offer their prayers to her. They marveled at the miraculous way in which she had appeared, for no man on earth had painted her beloved Image.

Letter to the Grand Duchess Christina, 1615

Galileo Galilei

Translated by Gregory Murry, All Rights Reserved

As you know, a few years ago, I discovered many bodies in the heavens that had not been visible before our age. Whether because of the novelty of my discoveries or because their existence contradicts commonly received scientific opinions, this discovery made me a target for many professors, almost as if I had placed those stars in the heavens with my own hands in order to upset science and nature. Forgetting that the discovery of facts strengthens rather than weakens the discipline of science and showing more affection for their own opinions than for truth, they rushed to deny my findings, which they would have seen were true if they had cared to look for themselves. Instead, they wrote a number of vain discourses and made a grave error by invoking Holy Scripture, citing passages that have nothing to do with science and which they did not fully understand. Perhaps they would not have made this error if they had known of a most useful tract written by Saint Augustine concerning matters that are difficult to understand. Speaking of certain conclusions about the stars, Augustine wrote, "Practicing moderation and a pious gravitas, we should not rush to conclusions about scientific matters, since we might later discover that we are in error and that the truths of science are not at all contrary to the Old and New Testament."

Other astronomers who investigated the matter honestly have confirmed my findings, and the rancor has gradually died down. Many skilled astronomers were persuaded immediately, and the opponents who refused to believe me, either because of the novelty of my findings or because they had not had a chance to observe those bodies themselves, have quieted down as well. Others, however, seem to have a perverse vendetta against either myself or my discoveries. Because they can no longer deny my findings, they have grown even more bitter and try to attack me in any way they can. I would simply laugh at them, but they do not limit their attacks to my work as a scientist; rather, they have called me a name that I consider worse than death: heretic. Thus, I cannot sit idly by while they try to smear my reputation.

My opponents know that I believe the sun to be motionless and fixed in the center of the celestial orbs, and I believe that the Earth moves around the sun. They also know that I support my position not only by challenging Ptolemy and Aristotle, but by giving many reasons to support this opinion. Some of these are deduced from various aspects of nature, for the Copernican model explains many things about the natural world. Some of my reasons are astronomical and based on my new discoveries, which flatly contradict the Ptolemaic system and support Copernicus....Since my opponents cannot attack me on scientific grounds, they are determined to call me a heretic and use religion to dispute my findings. For this purpose, they have resorted to the authority of Holy Scripture, which they deploy with little intelligence and use to combat arguments that they cannot understand.

In the first place, my opponents have attempted to convince everyone that the heliocentric universe contradicts Sacred Scripture and thus is heretical. In doing this, they not only harm my ideas, they do injustice to mathematics and mathematicians everywhere. Thus, they grow ever more confident, hoping that the seeds that they have insincerely planted will grow and spread their branches everywhere, and the people go around murmuring that soon the heliocentric model will be condemned by the Pope. My opponents know that if this happens, it will not only destroy the heliocentric model but will make all the connected observations heretical, so they have tried to make it seem as if the heliocentric model is some new opinion that is only held by me alone. They intentionally ignore the fact that this idea was first proposed by Nicolas Copernicus, a Catholic priest and cathedral canon, who was so esteemed that during the Lateran Council under Leo X, he was called to Rome to help reform the calendar, which at that time was flawed because we did not know the exact length of the year and the lunar month. Bishop Sempronese gave him the task of overseeing the reform of the calendar and better understanding the motions of the celestial bodies. With his almost miraculous and amazing genius, he gave himself over to study, advanced his knowledge of astronomy, and uncovered the secrets of the celestial motions with such exactitude that he won the title of highest astronomer. Not only was the calendar reformed according to his findings, but so was the table of all the movements of the planets. And having compiled his learning, he published it in a book at the request of the Cardinal Capuano and Bishop Culmense. Because he had undertaken this work at the request of the Pope, he dedicated it to the Pope's successor, Paul III. After publication, the work was received by the Holy Church and read and studied by all the world without anyone expressing even a slight worry about his ideas. Now, it has been discovered that the idea is supported by clear observation and necessary proofs; nonetheless, there are many people, though they have never read the book, who reward Copernicus's efforts by declaring him a heretic, and this only to satisfy their unreasonable grudge against me, who has no other connection to Copernicus but to approve of his ideas.

Now I have thought it necessary to defend myself from these false accusations in the court of public opinion, which I value far more than the few who attack me and want to see Copernicus condemned. For these men not only want the heliocentric model to be declared false but even heretical; thus, they feign concern for religion and insincerely enlist the support of scriptures. By doing this (if I understand the doctors of the church correctly), they extend and abuse the authority of the Bible by making it to decide questions about the natural world rather than questions of faith and by forcing us to completely abandon our senses and our reason because of a few passages in scripture that might be interpreted in a contradictory way. I wish to demonstrate how much more pious and religious is my method when I suggest that Copernicus's book should not be condemned without under - standing it, hearing it, or even seeing it, especially since he never treated matters of religion or faith, and none of his conclusions depend on Sacred Scripture. Rather, he based his conclusions on a study of nature: observing celestial motion, using astronomical and geometrical demonstration, and utilizing sense experience and careful observation. It is not that he completely disregarded Sacred Scripture, but he understood acutely that the conclusions that he had demonstrated could not be contrary to scripture, as long as those scriptures were perfectly understood...

Some wish to see this author condemned without even reading his book, and they persuade themselves it is licit and even good to use passages of Holy Scripture and the Sacred Councils out of context. I revere scripture and the councils as the supreme authority, and I would consider it impudent and rash to contradict them in the senses that they have been adopted by the Holy Church. However, I do not commit an error by publishing my discoveries if all my opponents do is cite some passages from scripture and use them in ways that the Holy Church never intended. However, with self-evident sincerity, let me declare that I will remove from my writings any errors of religion into which I might have fallen. Also, let me declare that I do not want to engage in religious disputes with anyone, even on disputable points...Interpreting scripture is not my field of expertise, so if the Holy Church finds anything useful in my writings, let it do so. If not, let my writings be torn to pieces and burned since I do not want to earn anything from my writings if they are not pious and Catholic. Moreover, though I have heard many of these accusations with my own ears, I freely admit and concede to those who have said them that they may not have said them; perhaps, I have misunderstood them. Thus, I am not responding to anyone specifically, but to whomever holds such opinions.

The reason that some people condemn the heliocentric model is that they read in many parts of the Bible that the Sun moves, and the Earth stands still. Because the scriptures can never lie or error, it necessarily follows that the assertion that the Sun is immobile and the Earth moves is erroneous and condemnable.

I piously and prudently agree that Sacred Scripture can never lie, but only insofar as the true meanings of its words are understood. Frequently, the true sense of its meaning is obscure and very different from the plain sense of the words. Thus, it follows that in trying to understand Holy Scripture, we might error if we always understand the words in their plain, literal sense. If we did this, the Bible would not only contain contradictions and falsehoods, but also grave heresies and blasphemies, since we would need to say that God has feet and hands and eyes, as well as bodily needs and human emotions, such as wrath, penitence, and hatred. We would also need to affirm that God sometimes forgets things that happened in the past or does not know what will happen in the future. On the contrary, all these ideas were inspired by the Holy Spirit and were articulated with words that could be understood by the most uneducated and unintelligent men. Thus, if you want to be different than the common people, you must rely on wise theologians who can clarify the true sense of scripture and explain the reasons why it uses the words it does. This point is so well accepted in theology that it is hardly worth citing authorities on the point. Thus, it seems reasonable to suggest that whenever the Holy Bible seems to make any conclusions about the natural world, especially in matters that are obscure and difficult to understand, it uses common language, so as to not cause confusion in the minds of simple people and make them doubt the truths of the higher mysteries…Given this, why should we assume that scripture requires us to interpret the words land, water, sun and other creatures in the restricted, literal sense? Especially since these things have nothing to do with the primary concern of Sacred Scripture: the divine cult and the salvation of souls…

Thus, it seems to me that we should not begin scientific disputes by appealing to the authority of Sacred Scripture. Rather, science should be argued on the basis of sense experience and demonstrative proofs. Both sacred scripture and nature are dictated by the Holy Spirit, and both observe the laws of God; however, in scripture there are many things that are accommodated to the understanding of the common person and thus mean something different than the pure, literal sense of the words. On the other hand, because nature is unchangeable, never transcends the limits of the laws imposed on it, and does not care at all whether its hidden operations are knowable or not, it seems that we should make our conclusions based on the natural effects that sense experience and necessary demonstration put before our eyes. These should not be doubted, much less condemned, by scriptural passages that have obscure meanings...Nor is it less excellent to discover God in the effects of nature than in the sacred words of scripture. As Tertullian writes, "We argue that God is first known through nature, then he is known by revelation: nature by its works, revelation, by preaching."

By asserting this, I do not want to imply that we should not value those parts of Sacred Scripture that speak of natural things; rather, once science has made conclusions about the natural world, we should use those conclusions to accommodate the true sense of scripture to the investigation of our sense experience. For the Bible must agree with scientific truth. Now, I think that scripture's primary purpose is to persuade men of the doctrines that mankind cannot discover by science because they exceed our intellectual capacity. We can only learn these truths from the mouth of the Holy Spirit herself. Even concerning those matters that are not properly matters of faith, we should prefer the authority of the Bible to all other human authorities that argue by narrative and probabilities rather than demonstrations and proofs, for the divine wisdom surpasses all human judgment and conjecture. Nevertheless, I do not believe that the same God who has given us sense, speech, and intellect forbids us to use them to acquire knowledge. I do not believe that God wants us to deny our senses, reason, intellect, experiences, and demonstrative proofs, especially in a field of science that is hardly mentioned in scripture at all. For the Bible doesn't even mention the names of the planets, except the sun, the moon, and Venus. If the sacred writers were trying to teach us about the planets and force us to get our knowledge of astronomy from the Bible, they would have said more about it, for the astronomy contained in the Bible is a tiny fraction of the discoveries to be made in the field.

It is the opinion of the Holy Fathers that the writers of scripture did not mean to teach us about the make-up and movement of the heavens and the stars, or their shape, size, and distance. Though all of these things were known to them, they said nothing about them. In Saint Augustine we read the following words:

> *People have begun to ask about what form and figure of the heavens Christians must believe based on our scriptures. Many authors have debated about these things, but the most prudent of our authors do not speak about them at all, inasmuch as they have nothing to do with the question of everlasting life, and debating them takes up valuable time and impedes more salubrious things. What does it matter to me whether the heavens surround the earth on all sides like a sphere or whether they cover it like a disc? I have noted many times that the scriptures speak [only] about matters of faith in order to prevent anyone who does not understand the divine words to find anything in our scripture or hear anything in our doctrine that seems to contradict precepts or assertions that are not matters of faith and thus cause him to ignore scripture's many useful warnings and stories.*

Briefly put, our authors do not get the truth from the stars but from the Holy Spirit, and she only uses the scriptures to teach men things that are useful for their salvation.

...If the Holy Spirit did not mean to teach us whether the heavens move or not, nor whether the earth is a sphere or a disc, nor if the Earth is in the middle or on the side, she certainly did not mean to teach us other conclusions of this type...

And if the Holy Spirit has decided not to teach us about natural science, since it has nothing to do with our salvation, how can we then affirm that holding to this or that natural conclusion is necessary because of faith? Can an opinion be heretical if it has nothing to do with the salvation of souls? I repeat a saying that I have heard from an eminent priest: "The Holy Spirit meant to teach us how to go to heaven, not how the heavens go."

Let us consider how much we should value sense experience and demonstrative proofs in scientific matters. The doctors and theologians have given great weight to these matters when they say, amongst a hundred other things:

We should diligently avoid affirming propositions that contradict manifest experiments or philosophical reason merely because we think we learned them from the teachings of Moses. Since truth can never contradict truth, the doctrine of the Bible can never be contrary to true reason and human learning.

And in Augustine we read:

If a man uses the authority of sacred scripture against clear and certain reason, he does not understand what he does, for he sets up the sense of Sacred Scripture that he does not understand in contradiction to truth, so he does not use what is actually in Sacred Scripture but what he finds in himself through scripture.

Because two truths can never contradict one another, wise men must study and explain scripture in order to understand the true senses of the words; the true sense of the words will certainly agree with the conclusions of the sciences, when clear experience and demonstrative proof have rendered science's own conclusions certain. Because of all this, I believe it imprudent to limit scientists to the conclusions of Sacred Scripture or to force them to believe conclusions about the natural world that may be contrary to demonstrative proof and necessary reason. For, who would limit human ingenuity? Who would assert that he knows all there is to know...

On Cannibals (1580)

By Michel Montaigne
Translated by Gregory Murry

I don't see anything barbarous or savage about the Indians of Brazil, at least from what I can gather. The only reason people call them barbarians is that people call whatever is strange to them by that name. Our perception of what is true is usually governed by the examples and customs of the place where we live. We consider our own religion, government, and way of doing things perfect, while labeling others as savages simply because they are different. However, I believe that those we call "wild" or "savage" possess genuine and useful virtues and properties that we have lost or diminished due to our corrupted ways.

These people live a simple and natural life, close to their original state, with little influence from human inventions. They follow the laws of nature. They possess strengths, which we have forsaken in our pursuit of pleasure and comforts..

They are in constant war with neighboring nations on the mainland beyond their mountains. They fight without much clothing and only use bows and wooden swords shaped like javelins. Their battles are fierce and often result in bloodshed because they never retreat. As a trophy, each person brings home the head of an enemy they've killed and hangs it over their door.

When they capture enemies, they treat them well for a while, offering them hospitality. Then, the captor invites their friends for a gathering. During this event, they tie a rope to the prisoner's arm, with one end held by the captor and the other by their closest friend. In front of everyone, they kill the prisoner with their swords. After that, they roast and eat the body, even sending some parts to absent friends. This act is not for nourishment, but as an act of revenge. They decided to adopt this method after witnessing the Portuguese, who were in league with their enemies, use cruel and painful methods to kill prisoners.

Such actions are cruel, but are they any more cruel than our own? In my view, eating a person alive or subjecting them to torturous deaths is far more barbaric than consuming their remains after death.

Chrysippus and Zeno, leaders of the Stoic sect, believed that there was no harm in using dead bodies for necessities, including eating them if needed. Our ancestors once faced famine during a siege and resorted to consuming the bodies of the elderly, women, and others who couldn't fight.

On Miracles (1748)

David Hume

A miracle is a violation of the laws of nature; and as a firm and unalterable experience has established these laws, the proof against a miracle, from the very nature of the fact, is as entire as any argument from experience can possibly be imagined. Why is it more than probable, that all men must die; that lead cannot, of itself, remain suspended in the air; that fire consumes wood, and is extinguished by water; unless it be, that these events are found agreeable to the laws of nature, and there is required a violation of these laws, or in other words, a miracle to prevent them? Nothing is esteemed a miracle, if it ever happen in the common course of nature. It is no miracle that a man, seemingly in good health, should die on a sudden: because such a kind of death, though more unusual than any other, has yet been frequently observed to happen. But it is a miracle, that a dead man should come to life; because that has never been observed in any age or country. There must, therefore, be a uniform experience against every miraculous event, otherwise the event would not merit that appellation....

The plain consequence is (and it is a general maxim worthy of our attention), 'That no testimony is sufficient to establish a miracle, unless the testimony be of such a kind, that its falsehood would be more miraculous, than the fact, which it endeavours to establish....' When anyone tells me, that he saw a dead man restored to life, I immediately consider with myself, whether it be more probable, that this person should either deceive or be deceived, or that the fact, which he relates, should really have happened. I weigh the one miracle against the other; and according to the superiority, which I discover, I pronounce my decision, and always reject the greater miracle. If the falsehood of his testimony would be more miraculous, than the event which he relates; then, and not till then, can he pretend to command my belief or opinion.

In the foregoing reasoning we have supposed, that the testimony, upon which a miracle is founded, may possibly amount to an entire proof, and that the falsehood of that testimony would be a real prodigy: But it is easy to shew, that we have been a great deal too liberal in our concession, and that there never was a miraculous event established on so full an evidence

The Divine Right of Kings (1609)

By: James I

The State of MONARCHIE is the supremest thing upon earth: For Kings are not only God's lieutenants upon earth, and sit upon God's throne, but even by God himself, they are called Gods. There be three principal similitudes that illustrate the state of monarchy: One taken out of the word of GOD; and the two other out of the grounds of politics and philosophy.

In the scriptures kings are called gods, and so their power after a certain relation compared to the divine power. Kings are also compared to fathers of families: for a King is truly Parens patriæ, the political father of his people. And lastly, kings are compared to the head of this microcosm of the body of man.

Kings are justly called Gods, for that they exercise a manner or resemblance of divine power upon earth: For if you will consider the attributes of God, you shall see how they agree in the person of a King. God hath power to create, or destroy, make, or unmake at his pleasure, to give life, or send death, to judge all, and to be judged, nor is accountable to none: To raise low things, and to make high things low at his pleasure, and to God are both soul and body due. And the like power have Kings: they make and unmake their subjects: they have power of raising, and casting down: of life, and of death: Judges over all their subjects, and in all causes, and yet accountable to none but God only. They have power to exalt low things, and abase high things, and make of their subjects like men at chess; A pawn to take a bishop or a knight, and to cry up, or down any of their subjects, as they do their money. And to the king is due both the affection of the soul, and the service of the body of his subjects: And therefore that reverend Bishop here amongst you, though I hear that by different people, he was mistaken or not well understood, yet did he preach both learnedly and truly on this point concerning the power of a king: For what he spoke of a king's power in abstract, is most true in divinity: For to emperors, or kings that are monarch, their subjects bodies & goods are due for their defense and maintenance. But if I had bene in his place, I would only have added two words, which would have cleared all: For after I had told as a preacher, what was due by the subjects to their kings in general, I would then have concluded as an Englishman, shewing this people, That as in general all subjects were bound to relieve their King; So to exhort them, that as wee lived in a settled state of a Kingdome which was governed by his own fundamental laws and orders, that according thereunto, they were now (being assembled for this purpose in Parliament) to consider how to help such a King as now they had; And that according to the ancient form, and order established in this Kingdome: putting so, a difference between the general power of a King in divinity, and the settled and established state of this crown and kingdom. And I am sure that the Bishop meant to have done the same, if he had not been straited by time, which in respect of the greatness of the presence preaching before me, and such an auditory, he durst not presume upon.

As for the Father of a family, they had of old under the law of nature Patriam potestatem [fatherly power], which was Potestatem vitæ & necis [the power of life and death], over their children or family, (I mean such fathers of families as were the lineal heirs of those families whereof kings did originally come:) For kings had their first original from them, who planted and spread themselves in colonies through the world. Now a father may dispose of his inheritance to his children, at his pleasure: yea, even disinherit the eldest upon just occasions, and prefer the youngest, according to his liking; make them beggars, or rich at his pleasure; restrain, or banish out of his presence, as he finds them give cause of offence, or restore them in favor again with the penitent sinner: So may the king deal with his subjects.

And lastly, as for the head of the natural body, the head hath the power of directing all the members of the body to that use which the judgement in the head thinks most convenient. It may apply sharp cures, or cut off corrupt members, let blood in what proportion it thinks fit, and as the body may spare, but yet is all this power ordained by God to edification not to destruction. For although God have power as well of destruction, as of creation or maintenance; yet will it not agree with the wisdom of God, to exercise his power in the destruction of nature, and overturning the whole frame of things, since his creatures were made, that his glory might thereby be the better expressed: So were he a foolish father that would disinherit or destroy his children without a cause, or leave off the careful education of them; And it were an idle head that would in place of physick so poison or phlebotomize the body as might breed a dangerous distemper or destruction thereof…

I conclude then this point touching the power of kings, with this axiom of divinity, That as to dispute what God may doe, is blasphemy… So is it sedition in subjects, to dispute what a king may do in the height of his power: But just kings will ever be willing to declare what they will do, if they will not incur the curse of God. I will not be content that my power be disputed upon: but I shall ever be willing to make the reason appear of all my doings, and rule my actions according to my laws.

Second Treatise of Civil Government (1690)

By: John Locke

On the State of Nature

To understand political power right, and derive it from its original, we must consider what state all men are naturally in and that is, a state of perfect freedom to order their actions, and dispose of their possessions and persons, as they think fit, within the bounds of the law of nature, without asking leave, or depending upon the will of any other man.

A state also of equality, wherein all the power and jurisdiction is reciprocal, no one having more than another; there being nothing more evident, than that creatures of the same species and rank, promiscuously born to all the same advantages of nature, and the use of the same faculties, should also be equal one amongst another without subordination or subjection, unless the lord and master of them all should, by any manifest declaration of his will, set one above another, and confer on him, by an evident and clear appointment, an undoubted right to dominion and sovereignty....

But though this be a state of liberty, yet it is not a state of license: though man in that state have an uncontrollable liberty to dispose of his person or possessions, yet he has not liberty to destroy himself, or so much as any creature in his possession, but where some nobler use than its bare preservation calls for it. The state of nature has a law of nature to govern it, which obliges every one: and reason, which is that law, teaches all mankind, who will but consult it, that being all equal and independent, no one ought to harm another in his life, health, liberty, or possessions: for men being all the workmanship of one omnipotent, and infinitely wise maker; all the servants of one sovereign master, sent into the world by his order, and about his business; they are his property, whose workmanship they are, made to last during his, not one another's pleasure: and being furnished with like faculties, sharing all in one community of nature, there cannot be supposed any such subordination among us, that may authorize us to destroy one another, as if we were made for one another's uses, as the inferior ranks of creatures are for our's. Every one, as he is bound to preserve himself, and not to quit his station wilfully, so by the like reason, when his own preservation comes not in competition, ought he, as much as he can, to preserve the rest of mankind, and may not, unless it be to do justice on an offender, take away, or impair the life, or what tends to the preservation of the life, the liberty, health, limb, or goods of another.

And that all men may be restrained from invading others rights, and from doing hurt to one another, and the law of nature be observed, which wills the peace and preservation of all mankind, the execution of the law of nature is, in that state, put into every man's hands, whereby everyone has a right to punish the transgressors of that law to such a degree, as may hinder its violation: for the law of nature would, as all other laws that concern men in this world 'be in vain, if there were no body that in the state of nature had a power to execute that law, and thereby preserve the innocent and restrain offenders. And if anyone in the state of nature may punish another for any evil he has done, every one may do so: for in that state of perfect equality, where naturally there is no superiority or jurisdiction of one over another, what any may do in prosecution of that law, everyone must needs have a right to do.

And thus, in the state of nature, one man comes by a power over another; but yet no absolute or arbitrary power, to use a criminal, when he has got him in his hands, according to the passionate heats, or boundless extravagancy of his own will; but only to retribute to him, so far as calm reason and conscience dictate, what is proportionate to his transgression, which is so much as may serve for reparation and restraint: for these two are the only reasons, why one man may lawfully do harm to another, which is that we call punishment. In transgressing the law of nature, the offender declares himself to live by another rule than that of reason and common equity, which is that measure God has set to the actions of men, for their mutual security; and so he becomes dangerous to mankind, the tie, which is to secure them from injury and violence, being slighted and broken by him. Which being a trespass against the whole species, and the peace and safety of it, provided for by the law of nature, every man upon this score, by the right he hath to preserve mankind in general, may restrain, or where it is necessary, destroy things noxious to them, and so may bring such evil on any one, who hath transgressed that law, as may make him repent the doing of it, and thereby deter him, and by his example others, from doing the like mischief. And in the case, and upon this ground, EVERY MAN HATH A RIGHT TO PUNISH THE OFFENDER, AND BE EXECUTIONER OF THE LAW OF NATURE…

Besides the crime which consists in violating the law, and varying from the right rule of reason, whereby a man so far becomes degenerate, and declares himself to quit the principles of human nature, and to be a noxious creature, there is commonly injury done to some person or other, and some other man receives damage by his transgression: in which case he who hath received any damage, has, besides the right of punishment common to him with other men, a particular right to seek reparation from him that has done it: and any other person, who finds it just, may also join with him that is injured, and assist him in recovering from the offender so much as may make satisfaction for the harm he has suffered…

thus it is, that every man, in the state of nature, has a power to kill a murderer, both to deter others from doing the like injury, which no reparation can compensate, by the example of the punishment that attends it from everybody, and also to secure men from the attempts of a criminal, who having renounced reason, the common rule and measure God hath given to mankind, hath, by the unjust violence and slaughter he hath committed upon one, declared war against all mankind, and therefore may be destroyed as a lion or a tiger, one of those wild savage beasts, with whom men can have no society nor security: and upon this is grounded that great law of nature, Whoso sheddeth man's blood, by man shall his blood be shed. And Cain was so fully convinced, that everyone had a right to destroy such a criminal, that after the murder of his brother, he cries out, Every one that findeth me, shall slay me; so plain was it writ in the hearts of all mankind.

...It is often asked as a mighty objection, where are, or ever were there any men in such a state of nature? To which it may suffice as an answer at present, that since all princes and rulers of independent governments all through the world, are in a state of nature, it is plain the world never was, nor ever will be, without numbers of men in that state. I have named all governors of independent communities, whether they are, or are not, in league with others: for it is not every compact that puts an end to the state of nature between men, but only this one of agreeing together mutually to enter into one community, and make one body politic; other promises, and compacts, men may make one with another, and yet still be in the state of nature. The promises and bargains for truck, &c. between the two men in the desert island, mentioned by Garcilasso de la Vega, in his history of Peru; or between a Swiss and an Indian, in the woods of America, are binding to them, though they are perfectly in a state of nature, in reference to one another: for truth and keeping of faith belongs to men, as men, and not as members of society.

I moreover affirm, that all men are naturally in that state, and remain so, till by their own consents they make themselves members of some politic society; and I doubt not in the sequel of this discourse, to make it very clear.

On the Beginning of Civil Society

If man in the state of Nature be so free as has been said, if he be absolute lord of his own person and possessions, equal to the greatest and subject to nobody, why will he part with his freedom, this empire, and subject himself to the dominion and control of any other power? To which it is obvious to answer, that though in the state of Nature he hath such a right, yet the enjoyment of it is very uncertain and constantly exposed to the invasion of others; for all being kings as much as he, every man his equal, and the greater part no strict observers of equity and justice, the enjoyment of the property he has in this state is very unsafe, very insecure. This makes him willing to quit this condition which, however free, is full of fears and continual dangers; and it is not without reason that he seeks out and is willing to join in society with others who are already united, or have a mind to unite for the mutual preservation of their lives, liberties, and estates, which I call by the general name— property.

The great and chief end, therefore, of men uniting into commonwealths, and putting themselves under government, is the preservation of their property; to which in the state of Nature there are many things wanting....

Men being, as has been said, by nature, all free, equal, and independent, no one can be put out of this estate, and subjected to the political power of another, without his own consent. The only way whereby anyone divests himself of his natural liberty, and puts on the bonds of civil society, is by agreeing with other men to join and unite into a community for their comfortable, safe, and peaceable living one amongst another, in a secure enjoyment of their properties, and a greater security against any, that are not of it. This any number of men may do, because it injures not the freedom of the rest; they are left as they were in the liberty of the state of nature. When any number of men have so consented to make one community or government, they are thereby presently incorporated, and make one body politic, wherein the majority have a right to act and conclude the rest.

For when any number of men have, by the consent of every individual, made a community, they have thereby made that community one body, with a power to act as one body, which is only by the will and determination of the majority: for that which acts any community, being only the consent of the individuals of it, and it being necessary to that which is one body to move one way; it is necessary the body should move that way whither the greater force carries it, which is the consent of the majority: or else it is impossible it should act or continue one body, one community, which the consent of every individual that united into it, agreed that it should; and so everyone is bound by that consent to be concluded by the majority. And therefore we see, that in assemblies, empowered to act by positive laws, where no number is set by that positive law which empowers them, the act of the majority passes for the act of the whole, and of course determines, as having, by the law of nature and reason, the power of the whole.

And thus every man, by consenting with others to make one body politic under one government, puts himself under an obligation, to every one of that society, to submit to the determination of the majority, and to be concluded by it; or else this original compact, whereby he with others incorporates into one society, would signify nothing, and be no compact, if he be left free, and under no other ties than he was in before in the state of nature. For what appearance would there be of any compact? what new engagement if he were no farther tied by any decrees of the society, than he himself thought fit, and did actually consent to? This would be still as great a liberty, as he himself had before his compact, or anyone else in the state of nature hath, who may submit himself, and consent to any acts of it if he thinks fit.

...Whosoever therefore out of a state of nature unite into a community, must be understood to give up all the power, necessary to the ends for which they unite into society, to the majority of the community, unless they expressly agreed in any number greater than the majority. And this is done by barely agreeing to unite into one political society, which is all the compact that is, or needs be, between the individuals, that enter into, or make up a commonwealth. And thus that, which begins and actually constitutes any political society, is nothing but the consent of any number of freemen capable of a majority to unite and incorporate into such a society. And this is that, and that only, which did, or could give beginning to any lawful government in the world.

On the Dissolution of Government

He that will with any clearness speak of the dissolution of government, ought in the first place to distinguish between the dissolution of the society and the dissolution of the government. That which makes the community, and brings men out of the loose state of nature, into one politic society, is the agreement which everyone has with the rest to incorporate, and act as one body, and so be one distinct commonwealth. The usual, and almost only way whereby this union is dissolved, is the inroad of foreign force making a conquest upon them…

The power that every individual gave the society when he entered into it can never revert to the individuals again, as long as the society lasts, but will always remain in the community; because without this there can be no community— no commonwealth, which is contrary to the original agreement; so as when the society hath placed the legislative in any assembly of men, to continue in them and their successors, with direction and authority for providing such successors, the legislative can never revert to the people whilst that government lasts; because, having provided a legislative with power to continue forever, they have given up their political power to the legislative, and cannot resume it. But if they have set limits to the duration of their legislative, and made this supreme power in any person or assembly only temporary; or else when, by the miscarriages of those in authority, it is forfeited; upon the forfeiture of their rulers, or at the determination of the time set, it reverts to the society, and the people have a right to act as supreme, and continue the legislative in themselves or place it in a new form, or new hands, as they think good.

The Declaration of the Rights of Man and Citizen (1789)

Translated by Gregory Murry, all rights reserved

Inasmuch as the ignorance, disregard, and scorn of the Rights of Man are the sole causes of public ill and governmental corruption, the representatives of the French people, duly constituted in the National Assembly, have resolved to solemnly declare the natural, inalienable, and sacred Rights of Man, so that all the members of this social body can see them and bring them to their mind at any time, constantly recalling their rights and their duties; so that all the acts of the legislative and executive power can be instantly compared to the ends of all political institutions and to be more respected; and so that the complaints of the citizens, founded now on simple and incontestable principles, redound always to the maintenance of the Constitution and the happiness of all.

Therefore, the National Assembly recognizes and declares, in the presence and under the auspices of the Supreme Being, the following rights of Man and Citizen:

Man is born and remains free and equal in rights. Social distinctions can only be founded on the common utility.

The goal of all political association is the maintenance of the natural and unwritten rights of man. These rights are life, liberty, security, and resistance to oppression.

Sovereignty remains with the Nation. No body or individual can exercise authority unless expressly authorized by the nation.

Liberty consists in being able to do all that does not harm others; thus, man is only limited in his natural rights when they infringe on the rights of other members of society. These limits can only be determined by law.

The law only has the right to forbid actions that harm society. All that is not forbidden by law cannot be impeded, and no one can be forced to do what the law does not command.

The law is the expression of the general will. All Citizens have the right to participate in the formation of the law, either personally or by their representatives. The law should be the same for all, whether it concerns what the law protects or what the law punishes. Because all citizens are equal in the eyes of the law, they are equally admissible to all dignities, stations, and public employments, according to no other measure than their capabilities, virtues, and talents.

No man can be accused, arrested, or detained, except in cases determined by the law and according to the forms that it has prescribed. Those who ask for, aid in, execute, or cause to be executed arbitrary orders should be punished, but all citizens called forth or seized by the power of the law must obey immediately. Those who do not render themselves guilty by their resistance.

The law should only establish penalties that are strictly and evidently necessary, and no one should be punished by a law established and promulgated after the crime.

Because all men are innocent until they have been declared guilty, anyone whom it is judged necessary to arrest shall have protection from any force or harm beyond that which is necessary to secure their person.

No one should be harassed for their opinions, including religious views, provided that the manifestation of said opinions not disturb the public order established by Law.

The free communication of thoughts and opinions is one of the most precious rights of Man. All citizens can thus, speak, write, and print freely, but shall be responsible for abuses of said liberty as determined by Law.

The guarantee of the rights of Man and Citizen necessitates a public force; this public force is thus instituted for the advantage of all, and not for the particular utility of those to whom it is entrusted.

A common contribution is necessary for the maintenance of this public force as well as for the expenses of public administration; it should be equally shared by all citizens in accordance with their faculties.

All Citizens, either by themselves or by their representatives, have the right to ascertain the necessity of the public contribution, to consent to it freely, to know what it is used for, and to determine its amount, assessment, collection method, and duration.

Society has the right to demand an account from every public agent of his administration.

A society in which the guarantee of rights is not assured, nor the separation of powers determined, has no constitution.

Property being a sacred and inviolable right, no one can be deprived of it, except when there is a legally-ascertained, manifestly-evident, public necessity and when a just indemnity has been made.

The Haitian Declaration of Independence (1804)

By: Jean-Jacques Dessalines

Translated by Gregory Murry, all rights reserved

It is not enough to have chased out the barbarians who bloodied our country for the last two centuries; it is not enough to have restrained those who would deceive us with the phantom of liberty promised to us by the French; it is necessary, by one last act of national authority, to protect the power of liberty in our homeland. The inhumane government that so long held our souls in despair must lose all hope of ever ruling here again. It is necessary to live free or die.

Independence or death. Let these sacred words unite us. Let them be for us the battle-cry of our assembly.

Citizens. My compatriots. I have gathered many courageous soldiers here on the solemn day, who on hearing the last sighs of a dying liberty, lavished their blood in order to save it. But these generals, who have led your fight against tyranny, have not yet done enough for your happiness--since the miserable name of France still haunts us.

Who can forget the barbarous cruelty of these people when our laws, our customs, and our towns all still carry their imprint? When there are still Frenchmen who live on our island? Do you believe that you are actually free from France, who has fought against all nations, though, it is true, has never defeated those who wanted to be free.

No! For 14 years we have been victims of our own credulity and our own indulgence; defeated, not by their armies, but by the piteous eloquence of their agents. How much longer must we breathe the same air as them? Compare their cruelty to our patience. The color of their skin to ours. Our avenging climate to theirs. Notice the sea that divides us. All of this should tell us that they are not our brothers; that they will never become our brothers, and that if they should find sanctuary among us, they will be the cause of all our troubles and divisions.

Native citizens: men, women, children, and infants. Look over this whole island. Look for your spouses, your husbands, your brothers, your sisters: what should I say? Look there for your infants, suckling at the breast. What have they become? I shudder to say it. The prey of these vultures. Do your eyes see these beloved victims? No, you can see only their murderers; the tigers engorged with their blood, whose very existence rebukes you for the slowness with which you avenge them. Why do you wait? Do you think you can descend to eternal rest with the bones of your fathers without having avenged them first? No. Their bones would vomit you out of the tomb.

And you, great men and brave generals, who with no thought for your own good, have shed so much blood; know that you have done nothing if you do not give the nation a terrible, but just, example of the vengeance that a bold people should exercise once they have recovered their liberty and sworn to be fierce in keeping it. Let us terrify all of those who would dare to take it away from us again. Let them shudder when approaching our coasts, if not for the remembrance of the cruelties that they have committed here, at least for the knowledge that we will put to death any Frenchmen who would dare to put his sacrilegious foot on the land of liberty.

We have dared to be free; let us dare to be by ourselves and for ourselves; let us imitate the growing child. His own weight breaks the boundaries that he no longer needs and that impede his march. What people have fought for us? What people would like to receive the fruits of our labor? And what absurd dishonor would we experience if we conquer only to remain being slaves? Slaves. Let us leave this name to the French; for they have conquered only in order to cease being free.

Let us go another route; let us imitate those people who, looking to the future and fearful of leaving an example of cowardice to posterity, have preferred to be wiped out rather than lose their freedom.

But don't let our proselytizing spirit destroy our work. Let us leave our neighbors in peace. Let them live peaceably under the power of the laws that they have made. Let us not claim to be lawmakers for all the Caribbean or let our glory trouble the peace of our neighboring islands. Their islands have not, as has ours, been reddened with the blood of their inhabitants. They have no vengeance to carry out against the authority that protects them.

Happy to have never known the scourge that has destroyed us, they will only be able to make vows for our prosperity. Peace to our neighbors! But cursed be the name of France! Eternal hatred toward France! That is our cry.

Natives of Haiti, my happy destiny is to be the watchman who guards the idol for which you have sacrificed; I have watched and fought, at times alone, and if I am lucky enough to put back into your hands the sacred trust that you have confided to me, know that it is now your task to conserve it. In fighting for your liberty, I have worked for my own happiness. Before consolidating your individual liberty by laws, I have assembled your chiefs here, with myself, and we owe you the last proof of our devotion.

Generals gathered here for the well-being of our country, the day has arrived, which will make your glory live in eternity.

If any of you should be tepid or unsure, let him depart and tremble to pronounce the words that shall unite us.

Let us swear to the entire universe, and to posterity, and to ourselves, to renounce France forever, and to die rather than to live under its dominion. And to fight until our last breath for the independence of our country.

And to you, my long-suffering people, witnesses to the words that we have spoken, remember that it is your constancy and your courage that have sustained me in our battle of liberty against tyranny and despotism.

Remember that I have sacrificed everything to tear down the defenses of tyrants: parents, children, and fortune. Remember that now I am only rich with liberty, that my name has become a horror to all those who would keep others in slavery, and that despots and tyrants only utter it to curse the day that I was born. If ever you refuse to obey the laws which the spirit who guides your destiny shall dictate to me for your happiness or grumble when you receive them, you will merit the lot of an ungrateful people.

But let this frightful idea be far from me. You will sustain the liberty you cherish and be the support of the chief who commands you.

Put your hands between mine, and swear the vow of a free and independent people: to choose death rather than submit to the yoke.

Swear, finally, to pursue forever the traitors and enemies of your independence.

Vindication of the Rights of Women, 1792

By: Mary Wollstonecraft

AFTER considering the historic page, and viewing the living world with anxious solicitude, the most melancholy emotions of sorrowful indignation have depressed my spirits, and I have sighed when obliged to confess, that either nature has made a great difference between man and man, or that the civilization which has hitherto taken place in the world has been very partial. I have turned over various books written on the subject of education, and patiently observed the conduct of parents and the management of schools; but what has been the result?—a profound conviction that the neglected education of my fellow-creatures is the grand source of the misery I deplore; and that women, in particular, are rendered weak and wretched by a variety of concurring causes, originating from one hasty conclusion. The conduct and manners of women, in fact, evidently prove that their minds are not in a healthy state; for, like the flowers which are planted in too rich a soil, strength and usefulness are sacrificed to beauty; and the flaunting leaves, after having pleased a fastidious eye, fade, disregarded on the stalk, long before the season when they ought to have arrived at maturity.—One cause of this barren blooming I attribute to a false system of education, gathered from the books written on this subject by men who, considering females rather as women than human creatures, have been more anxious to make them alluring mistresses than wives; and the understanding of the sex has been so bubbled by this specious homage, that the civilized women of the present century, with a few exceptions, are only anxious to inspire love, when they ought to cherish a nobler ambition, and by their abilities and virtues exact respect.

In a treatise, therefore, on female rights and manners, the works which have been particularly written for their improvement must not be overlooked; especially when it is asserted, in direct terms, that the minds of women are enfeebled by false refinement; that the books of instruction, written by men of genius, have had the same tendency as more frivolous productions; and that, in the true style of Mahometanism, they are only considered as females, and not as a part of the human species, when improvable reason is allowed to be the dignified distinction which raises men above the brute creation, and puts a natural sceptre in a feeble hand.

Yet, because I am a woman, I would not lead my readers to suppose that I mean violently to agitate the contested question respecting the equality or inferiority of the sex; but as the subject lies in my way, and I cannot pass it over without subjecting the main tendency of my reasoning to misconstruction, I shall stop a moment to deliver, in a few words, my opinion.—In the government of the physical world it is observable that the female, in general, inferior to the male. The male pursues, the female yields—this is the law of nature; and it does not appear to be suspended or abrogated in favor of woman. This physical superiority cannot be denied— and it is a noble prerogative! But not content with this natural pre- eminence, men endeavour to sink us still lower, merely to render us alluring objects for a moment; and women, intoxicated by the adoration which men, under the influence of their senses, pay them, do not seek to obtain a durable interest in their hearts, or to become the friends of the fellow creatures who find amusement in their society.

I am aware of an obvious inference:—from every quarter have I heard exclamations against masculine women; but where are they to be found? If by this appellation men mean to inveigh against their ardour in hunting, shooting, and gaming, I shall most cordially join in the cry; but if it be against the imitation of manly virtues, or, more properly speaking, the attainment of those talents and virtues, the exercise of which ennobles the human character, and which raises females in the scale of animal being, when they are comprehensively termed mankind;—all those who view them with a philosophical eye must, I should think, wish with me, that they may every day grow more and more masculine.

This discussion naturally divides the subject. I shall first consider women in the grand light of human creatures, who, in common with men, are placed on this earth to unfold their faculties; and afterwards I shall more particularly point out their peculiar designation.

I wish also to steer clear of an error which many respectable writers have fallen into; for the instruction which has hither been addressed to women, has rather been applicable to ladies, if the little indirect advice, that is scattered through Sanford and Merton be excepted; but, addressing my sex in a firmer tone, I pay particular attention to those in the middle class, because they appear to be in the most natural state. Perhaps the seeds of false refinement, immorality, and vanity, have ever been shed by the great. Weak, artificial beings, raised above the common wants and affections of their race, in a premature unnatural manner, undermine the very foundation of virtue, and spread corruption through the whole mass of society! As a class of mankind they have the strongest claim to pity; the education of the rich tends to render them vain and helpless, and the unfolding mind is not strengthened by the practice of those duties which dignify the human character.—They only live to amuse themselves, and by the same law which in nature invariably produces certain effects, they soon only afford barren amusement.

But as I purpose taking a separate view of the different ranks of society, and of the moral character of women, in each, this hint is, for the present, sufficient; and I have only alluded to the subject, because it appears to me to be the very essence of an introduction to give a cursory account of the contents of the work it introduces.

My own sex, I hope, will excuse me, if I treat them like rational creatures, instead of flattering their fascinating graces, and viewing them as if they were in a state of perpetual childhood, unable to stand alone. I earnestly wish to point out in what true dignity and human happiness consists—I wish to persuade women to endeavour to acquire strength, both of mind and body, and to convince them that the soft phrases, susceptibility of heart, delicacy of sentiment, and refinement of taste, are almost synonymous with epithets of weakness, and that those beings who are only the objects of pity and that kind of love, which has been termed its sister, will soon become objects of contempt.

Dismissing then those pretty feminine phrases, which the men condescendingly use to soften our slavish dependence, and despising that weak elegancy of mind, exquisite sensibility, and sweet docility of manners, supposed to be the sexual characteristics of the weaker vessel, I wish to show that elegance is inferior to virtue, that the first object of laudable ambition is to obtain a character as a human being, regardless of the distinction of sex; and that secondary views should be brought to this simple touchstone.

This is a rough sketch of my plan; and should I express my conviction with the energetic emotions that I feel whenever I think of the subject, the dictates of experience and reflection will be felt by some of my readers. Animated by this important object, I shall disdain to cull my phrases or polish my style;—I aim at being useful, and sincerity will render me unaffected; for, wishing rather to persuade by the force of my arguments, than dazzle by the elegance of my language, I shall not waste my time in rounding periods, nor in fabricating the turgid bombast of artificial feelings, which, coming from the head, never reach the heart.—I shall be employed about things, not words!—and, anxious to render my sex more respectable members of society, I shall try to avoid that flowery diction which has slided from essays into novels, and from novels into familiar letters and conversation.

These pretty nothings—these caricatures of the real beauty of sensibility, dropping glibly from the tongue, vitiate the taste, and create a kind of sickly delicacy that turns away from simple unadorned truth; and a deluge of false sentiments and overstretched feelings, stifling the natural emotions of the heart, render the domestic pleasures insipid, that ought to sweeten the exercise of those severe duties, which educate a rational and immortal being for a nobler field of action.

The education of women has, of late, been more attended to than formerly; yet they are still reckoned a frivolous sex, and ridiculed or pitied by the writers who endeavor by satire or instruction to improve them. It is acknowledged that they spend many of the first years of their lives in acquiring a smattering of accomplishments: meanwhile strength of body and mind are sacrificed to libertine notions of beauty, to the desire of establishing themselves,—the only way women can rise in the world,—by marriage. And this desire making mere animals of them, when they marry they act as such children may be expected to act:—they dress; they paint, and nickname God's creatures.—Surely these weak beings are only fit for a seraglio! —Can they govern a family, or take care of the poor babes whom they bring into the world?

If then it can be fairly deduced from the present conduct of the sex, from the prevalent fondness for pleasure which takes place of ambition and those nobler passions that open and enlarge the soul; that the instruction which women have received has only tended, with the constitution of civil society, to render them insignificant objects of desire—mere propagators of fools!—if it can be proved that in aiming to accomplish them, without cultivating their understandings, they are taken out of their sphere of duties, and made ridiculous and useless when the short-lived bloom of beauty is over, I presume that rational men will excuse me for endeavouring to persuade them to become more masculine and respectable.

Indeed the word masculine is only a bugbear. there is little reason to fear that women will acquire too much courage or fortitude; for their apparent inferiority with respect to bodily strength, must render them, in some degree, dependent on men in the various relations of life; but why should it be increased by prejudices that give a sex to virtue, and confound simple truths with sensual reveries?

Women are, in fact, so much degraded by mistaken notions of female excellence, that I do not mean to add a paradox when I assert, that this artificial weakness produces a propensity to tyrannize, and gives birth to cunning, the natural opponent of strength, which leads them to play off those contemptible infantile airs that undermine esteem even whilst they excite desire. Do not foster these prejudices, and they will naturally fall into their subordinate, yet respectable station, in life.

It seems scarcely necessary to say, that I now speak of the sex in general. Many individuals have more sense than their male relatives; and,as nothing preponderates where there is a constant struggle for an equilibrium, without it has naturally more gravity, some women govern their husbands without degrading themselves, because intellect will always govern.

Observations on the State of Degradation to Which Woman Is Reduced by Various Causes.

THAT woman is naturally weak, or degraded by a concurrence of circumstances, is, I think, clear. But this position I shall simply contrast with a conclusion, which I have frequently heard fall from sensible men in favor of an aristocracy: that the mass of mankind cannot be anything, or the obsequious slaves, who patiently allow themselves to be penned up, would feel their own consequence, and spurn their chains. Men, they further observe, submit everywhere to oppression, when they have only to lift up their heads to throw off the yoke; yet, instead of asserting their birthright, they quietly lick the dust, and say, let us eat and drink, for to-morrow we die. Women, I argue from analogy, are degraded by the same propensity to enjoy the present moment; and, at last, despise the freedom which they have not sufficient virtue to struggle to attain. But I must be more explicit....

I shall not go back to the remote annals of antiquity to trace the history of woman; it is sufficient to allow that she has always been either a slave, or a despot, and to remark, that each of these situations equally retards the progress of reason. The grand source of female folly and vice has ever appeared to me to arise from narrowness of mind; and the very constitution of civil governments has put almost insuperable obstacles in the way to prevent the cultivation of the female understanding:—yet virtue can be built on no other foundation! The same obstacles are thrown in the way of the rich, and the same consequences ensue.

Necessity has been proverbially termed the mother of invention—the aphorism may be extended to virtue. It is an acquirement, and an acquirement to which pleasure must be sacrificed—and who sacrifices pleasure when it is within the grasp, whose mind has not been opened and strengthened by adversity, or the pursuit of knowledge goaded on by necessity?—Happy is it when people have the cares of life to struggle with; for these struggles prevent their becoming a prey to enervating vices, merely from idleness!...

Pleasure is the business of woman's life, according to the present modification of society, and while it continues to be so, little can be expected from such weak beings. Inheriting, in a lineal descent from the first fair defect in nature, the sovereignty of beauty, they have, to maintain their power, resigned the natural rights, which the exercise of reason might have procured them, and chosen rather to be short-lived queens than labor to obtain the sober pleasures that arise from equality. Exalted by their inferiority (this sounds like a contradiction) they constantly demand homage as women, though experience should teach them that the men who pride themselves upon paying this arbitrary insolent respect to the sex, with the most scrupulous exactness, are most inclined to tyrannize over, and despise, the very weakness they cherish....

Ah! why do women, I write with affectionate solicitude, condescend to receive a degree of attention and respect from strangers, different from that reciprocation of civility which the dictates of humanity and the politeness of civilization authorize between man and man? And, why do they not discover, when 'in the noon of beauty's power,' that they are treated like queens only to be deluded by hollow respect, till they are led to resign, or not assume, their natural prerogatives? Confined then in cages like the feathered race, they have nothing to do but to plume themselves, and stalk with mock majesty from perch to perch. It is true they are provided with food and raiment, for which they neither toil nor spin; but health, liberty, and virtue, are given in exchange. But, where, amongst mankind has been found sufficient strength of mind to enable a being to resign these adventitious prerogatives;

one who, rising with the calm dignity of reason above opinion, dared to be proud of the privileges inherent in man? And it is vain to expect it whilst hereditary power chokes the affections and nips reason in the bud.

The passions of men have thus placed women on thrones, and, till mankind become more reasonable, it is to be feared that women will avail themselves of the power which they attain with the least exertion, and which is the most indisputable. They will smile,—yes, they will smile, though told that—

> 'In beauty's empire is no mean,
> And woman, either slave or queen,
> Is quickly scorn'd when not ador'd.'
> But the adoration comes first, and the scorn is not anticipated....

On National Education.

THE good effects resulting from attention to private education will ever be very confined, and the parent who really puts his own hand to the plow, will always, in some degree, be disappointed, till education becomes a grand national concern. A man cannot retire into a desert with his child, and if he did he could not bring himself back to childhood, and become the proper friend and play-fellow of an infant or youth. And when children are confined to the society of men and women, they very soon acquire that kind of premature manhood which stops the growth of every vigorous power of mind or body. In order to open their faculties they should be excited to think for themselves; and this can only be done by mixing a number of children together, and making them jointly pursue the same objects....

[T]o improve both sexes they ought, not only in private families, but in public schools, to be educated together. If marriage be the cement of society, mankind should all be educated after the same model, or the intercourse of the sexes will never deserve the name of fellowship, nor will women ever fulfil the peculiar duties of their sex, till they become enlightened citizens, till they become free by being enabled to earn their own subsistence, independent of men; in the same manner, I mean, to prevent misconstruction, as one man is independent of another. Nay, marriage will never be held sacred till women, by being brought up with men, are prepared to be their companions rather than their mistresses; for the mean doublings of cunning will ever render them contemptible, whilst oppression renders them timid. So convinced am I of this truth, that I will venture to predict that virtue will never prevail in society till the virtues of both sexes are founded on reason; and, till the affections common to both are allowed to gain their due strength by the discharge of mutual duties.

Were boys and girls permitted to pursue the same studies together, those graceful decencies might early be inculcated which produce modesty without those sexual distinctions that taint the mind. Lessons of politeness, and that formulary of decorum, which treads on the heels of falsehood, would be rendered useless by habitual propriety of behaviour. Not indeed, put on for visitors like the courtly robe of politeness, but the sober effect of cleanliness of mind. Would not this simple elegance of sincerity be a chaste homage paid to domestic affections, far surpassing the meretricious compliments that shine with false lustre in the heartless intercourse of fashionable life? But, till more understanding preponderate in society, there will ever be a want of heart and taste, and the harlot's rouge will supply the place of that celestial suffusion which only virtuous affections can give to the face. Gallantry, and what is called love, may subsist without simplicity of character; but the main pillars of friendship, are respect and confidence—esteem is never founded on it cannot tell what!...

To render this practicable, day schools, for particular ages, should be established by government, in which boys and girls might be educated together. The school for the younger children, from five to nine years of age, ought to be absolutely free and open to all classes.....

[I]n an elementary day school, ...boys and girls, the rich and poor, should meet together. And to prevent any of the distinctions of vanity, they should be dressed alike, and all obliged to submit to the same discipline, or leave the school. The school-room ought to be surrounded by a large piece of ground, in which the children might be usefully exercised, for at this age they should not be confined to any sedentary employment for more than an hour at a time. But these relaxations might all be rendered a part of elementary education, for many things improve and amuse the senses, when introduced as a kind of show, to the principles of which, dryly laid down, children would turn a deaf ear. For instance, botany, mechanics, and astronomy. Reading, writing, arithmetic, natural history, and some simple experiments in natural philosophy, might fill up the day; but these pursuits should never encroach on gymnastic plays in the open air. The elements of religion, history, the history of man, and politics, might also be taught, by conversations, in the socratic form.

After the age of nine, girls and boys, intended for domestic employments, or mechanical trades, ought to be removed to other schools, and receive instruction, in some measure appropriated to the destination of each individual, the two sexes being still together in the morning; but in the afternoon, the girls should attend a school, where plain-work, mantua- making, millinery, &c. would be their employment.

The young people of superiour abilities, or fortune, might now be taught, in another school, the dead and living languages, the elements of science, and continue the study of history and politics, on a more extensive scale, which would not exclude polite literature.

I have already inveighed against the custom of confining girls to their needle, and shutting them out from all political and civil employments; for by thus narrowing their minds they are rendered unfit to fulfil the peculiar duties which nature has assigned them.

Only employed about the little incidents of the day, they necessarily grow up cunning. My very soul has often sickened at observing the sly tricks practiced by women to gain some foolish thing on which their silly hearts were set. Not allowed to dispose of money, or call anything their own, they learn to turn the market penny; or, should a husband offend, by staying from home, or give rise to some emotions of jealousy—a new gown, or any pretty bauble, smooths Juno's angry brow.

But these littlenesses would not degrade their character, if women were led to respect themselves, if political and moral subjects were opened to them; and, I will venture to affirm, that this is the only way to make them properly attentive to their domestic duties.—An active mind embraces the whole circle of its duties, and finds time enough for all. It is not, I assert, a bold attempt to emulate masculine virtues; it is not the enchantment of literary pursuits, or the steady investigation of scientific subjects, that lead women astray from duty. No, it is indolence and vanity—the love of pleasure and the love of sway, that will rain paramount in an empty mind. I say empty emphatically because the education which women now receive scarcely deserves the name. For the little knowledge that they are led to acquire, during the important years of youth, is merely relative to accomplishments; and accomplishments without a bottom, for unless the understanding be cultivated, superficial and monotonous is every grace. Like the charms of a made up face, they only strike the senses in a crowd; but at home, wanting mind, they want variety. The consequence is obvious; in gay scenes of dissipation we meet the artificial mind and face, for those who fly from solitude dread, next to solitude, the domestic circle; not having it in their power to amuse or interest, they feel their own insignificance, or find nothing to amuse or interest themselves....

To render mankind more virtuous, and happier of course, both sexes must act from the same principle; but how can that be expected when only one is allowed to see the reasonableness of it? To render also the social compact truly equitable, and in order to spread those enlightening principles, which alone can meliorate the fate of man, women must be allowed to found their virtue on knowledge, which is scarcely possible unless they be educated by the same pursuits as men. For they are now made so inferiour by ignorance and low desires, as not to deserve to be ranked with them; or, by the serpentine wrigglings of cunning they mount the tree of knowledge, and only acquire sufficient to lead men astray.

It is plain from the history of all nations, that women cannot be confined to merely domestic pursuits, for they will not fulfil family duties, unless their minds take a wider range, and whilst they are kept in ignorance they become in the same proportion the slaves of pleasure as they are the slaves of man. Nor can they be shut out of great enterprises, though the narrowness of their minds often make them mar, what they are unable to comprehend....

....In short, in whatever light I view the subject, reason and experience convince me that the only method of leading women to fulfil their peculiar duties, is to free them from all restraint by allowing them to participate in the inherent rights of mankind.

Make them free, and they will quickly become wise and virtuous, as men become more so; for the improvement must be mutual, or the injustice which one half of the human race are obliged to submit to, retorting on their oppressors, the virtue of man will be worm-eaten by the insect whom he keeps under his feet.

Let men take their choice, man and woman were made for each other, though not to become one being; and if they will not improve women, they will deprave them!

....The conclusion which I wish to draw, is obvious; make women rational creatures, and free citizens, and they will quickly become good wives, and mothers; that is—if men do not neglect the duties of husbands and fathers.

What to a Slave is the Fourth of July? (1852)

By Frederick Douglass

Mr. President, Friends and Fellow Citizens:

He who could address this audience without a quailing sensation, has stronger nerves than I have. I do not remember ever to have appeared as a speaker before any assembly more shrinkingly, nor with greater distrust of my ability, than I do this day. A feeling has crept over me, quite unfavorable to the exercise of my limited powers of speech. The task before me is one which requires much previous thought and study for its proper performance. I know that apologies of this sort are generally considered flat and unmeaning. I trust, however, that mine will not be so considered. Should I seem at ease, my appearance would much misrepresent me. The little experience I have had in addressing public meetings, in country schoolhouses, avails me nothing on the present occasion.

The papers and placards say, that I am to deliver a 4th [of] July oration. This certainly sounds large, and out of the common way, for it is true that I have often had the privilege to speak in this beautiful Hall, and to address many who now honor me with their presence. But neither their familiar faces, nor the perfect gage I think I have of Corinthian Hall, seems to free me from embarrassment.

The fact is, ladies and gentlemen, the distance between this platform and the slave plantation, from which I escaped, is considerable — and the difficulties to be overcome in getting from the latter to the former, are by no means slight. That I am here to-day is, to me, a matter of astonishment as well as of gratitude. You will not, therefore, be surprised, if in what I have to say I evince no elaborate preparation, nor grace my speech with any high sounding exordium. With little experience and with less learning, I have been able to throw my thoughts hastily and imperfectly together; and trusting to your patient and generous indulgence, I will proceed to lay them before you.

This, for the purpose of this celebration, is the 4th of July. It is the birthday of your National Independence, and of your political freedom. This, to you, is what the Passover was to the emancipated people of God. It carries your minds back to the day, and to the act of your great deliverance; and to the signs, and to the wonders, associated with that act, and that day. This celebration also marks the beginning of another year of your national life; and reminds you that the Republic of America is now 76 years old. I am glad, fellow-citizens, that your nation is so young. Seventy-six years, though a good old age for a man, is but a mere speck in the life of a nation. Three score years and ten is the allotted time for individual men; but nations number their years by thousands. According to this fact, you are, even now, only in the beginning of your national career, still lingering in the period of childhood. I repeat, I am glad this is so. There is hope in the thought, and hope is much needed, under the dark clouds which lower above the horizon. The eye of the reformer is met with angry flashes, portending disastrous times; but his heart may well beat lighter at the thought that America is young, and that she is still in the impressible stage of her existence. May he not hope that high lessons of wisdom, of justice and of truth, will yet give direction to her destiny?...

Fellow-citizens, I shall not presume to dwell at length on the associations that cluster about this day. The simple story of it is that, 76 years ago, the people of this country were British subjects...You were under the British Crown. Your fathers esteemed the English Government as the home government; and England as the fatherland. This home government, you know, although a considerable distance from your home, did, in the exercise of its parental prerogatives, impose upon its colonial children, such restraints, burdens and limitations, as, in its mature judgment, it deemed wise, right and proper.

But, your fathers, who had not adopted the fashionable idea of this day, of the infallibility of government, and the absolute character of its acts, presumed to differ from the home government in respect to the wisdom and the justice of some of those burdens and restraints. They went so far in their excitement as to pronounce the measures of government unjust, unreasonable, and oppressive, and altogether such as ought not to be quietly submitted to. I scarcely need say, fellow-citizens, that my opinion of those measures fully accords with that of your fathers. Such a declaration of agreement on my part would not be worth much to anybody. It would, certainly, prove nothing, as to what part I might have taken, had I lived during the great controversy of 1776. To say now that America was right, and England wrong, is exceedingly easy. Everybody can say it; the dastard, not less than the noble brave, can flippantly discant on the tyranny of England towards the American Colonies. It is fashionable to do so; but there was a time when to pronounce against England, and in favor of the cause of the colonies, tried men's souls. They who did so were accounted in their day, plotters of mischief, agitators and rebels, dangerous men. To side with the right, against the wrong, with the weak against the strong, and with the oppressed against the oppressor! here lies the merit, and the one which, of all others, seems unfashionable in our day. The cause of liberty may be stabbed by the men who glory in the deeds of your fathers. But, to proceed.

Feeling themselves harshly and unjustly treated by the home government, your fathers, like men of honesty, and men of spirit, earnestly sought redress. They petitioned and remonstrated; they did so in a decorous, respectful, and loyal manner. Their conduct was wholly unexceptionable. This, however, did not answer the purpose. They saw themselves treated with sovereign indifference, coldness and scorn. Yet they persevered. They were not the men to look back.

As the sheet anchor takes a firmer hold, when the ship is tossed by the storm, so did the cause of your fathers grow stronger, as it breasted the chilling blasts of kingly displeasure. The greatest and best of British statesmen admitted its justice, and the loftiest eloquence of the British Senate came to its support. But, with that blindness which seems to be the unvarying characteristic of tyrants, since Pharaoh and his hosts were drowned in the Red Sea, the British Government persisted in the exactions complained of.

The madness of this course, we believe, is admitted now, even by England; but we fear the lesson is wholly lost on our present ruler. Oppression makes a wise man mad. Your fathers were wise men, and if they did not go mad, they became restive under this treatment. They felt themselves the victims of grievous wrongs, wholly incurable in their colonial capacity. With brave men there is always a remedy for oppression. Just here, the idea of a total separation of the colonies from the crown was born! It was a startling idea, much more so, than we, at this distance of time, regard it. The timid and the prudent (as has been intimated) of that day, were, of course, shocked and alarmed by it....

On the 2d of July, 1776, the old Continental Congress, to the dismay of the lovers of ease, and the worshipers of property, clothed that dreadful idea with all the authority of national sanction. They did so in the form of a resolution; and as we seldom hit upon resolutions, drawn up in our day whose transparency is at all equal to this, it may refresh your minds and help my story if I read it. "Resolved, That these united colonies are, and of right, ought to be free and Independent States; that they are absolved from all allegiance to the British Crown; and that all political connection between them and the State of Great Britain is, and ought to be, dissolved."

Citizens, your fathers made good that resolution. They succeeded; and to-day you reap the fruits of their success. The freedom gained is yours; and you, therefore, may properly celebrate this anniversary. The 4th of July is the first great fact in your nation's history — the very ring-bolt in the chain of your yet undeveloped destiny.

Pride and patriotism, not less than gratitude, prompt you to celebrate and to hold it in perpetual remembrance. I have said that the Declaration of Independence is the ring-bolt to the chain of your nation's destiny; so, indeed, I regard it. The principles contained in that instrument are saving principles. Stand by those principles, be true to them on all occasions, in all places, against all foes, and at whatever cost.

Fellow Citizens, I am not wanting in respect for the fathers of this republic. The signers of the Declaration of Independence were brave men. They were great men too — great enough to give fame to a great age. It does not often happen to a nation to raise, at one time, such a number of truly great men. The point from which I am compelled to view them is not, certainly, the most favorable; and yet I cannot contemplate their great deeds with less than admiration. They were statesmen, patriots and heroes, and for the good they did, and the principles they contended for, I will unite with you to honor their memory.

They loved their country better than their own private interests; and, though this is not the highest form of human excellence, all will concede that it is a rare virtue, and that when it is exhibited, it ought to command respect. He who will, intelligently, lay down his life for his country, is a man whom it is not in human nature to despise. Your fathers staked their lives, their fortunes, and their sacred honor, on the cause of their country. In their admiration of liberty, they lost sight of all other interests.

They were peace men; but they preferred revolution to peaceful submission to bondage. They were quiet men; but they did not shrink from agitating against oppression. They showed forbearance; but that they knew its limits. They believed in order; but not in the order of tyranny. With them, nothing was "settled" that was not right. With them, justice, liberty and humanity were "final;" not slavery and oppression. You may well cherish the memory of such men. They were great in their day and generation. Their solid manhood stands out the more as we contrast it with these degenerate times.

Friends and citizens, I need not enter further into the causes which led to this anniversary. Many of you understand them better than I do. You could instruct me in regard to them. That is a branch of knowledge in which you feel, perhaps, a much deeper interest than your speaker. The causes which led to the separation of the colonies from the British crown have never lacked for a tongue. They have all been taught in your common schools, narrated at your firesides, unfolded from your pulpits, and thundered from your legislative halls, and are as familiar to you as household words. They form the staple of your national poetry and eloquence.

I remember, also, that, as a people, Americans are remarkably familiar with all facts which make in their own favor. This is esteemed by some as a national trait — perhaps a national weakness. It is a fact, that whatever makes for the wealth or for the reputation of Americans, and can be had cheap! will be found by Americans. I shall not be charged with slandering Americans, if I say I think the American side of any question may be safely left in American hands.

I leave, therefore, the great deeds of your fathers to other gentlemen whose claim to have been regularly descended will be less likely to be disputed than mine!

My business, if I have any here to-day, is with the present. The accepted time with God and his cause is the ever-living now.

Trust no future, however pleasant, Let the dead past bury its dead; Act, act in the living present, Heart within, and God overhead.

We have to do with the past only as we can make it useful to the present and to the future. To all inspiring motives, to noble deeds which can be gained from the past, we are welcome. But now is the time, the important time. Your fathers have lived, died, and have done their work, and have done much of it well. You live and must die, and you must do your work. You have no right to enjoy a child's share in the labor of your fathers, unless your children are to be blest by your labors. You have no right to wear out and waste the hard-earned fame of your fathers to cover your indolence. Sydney Smith tells us that men seldom eulogize the wisdom and virtues of their fathers, but to excuse some folly or wickedness of their own. This truth is not a doubtful one. There are illustrations of it near and remote, ancient and modern. It was fashionable, hundreds of years ago, for the children of Jacob to boast, we have "Abraham to our father," when they had long lost Abraham's faith and spirit. That people contented themselves under the shadow of Abraham's great name, while they repudiated the deeds which made his name great. Need I remind you that a similar thing is being done all over this country to-day? Need I tell you that the Jews are not the only people who built the tombs of the prophets, and garnished the sepulchres of the righteous? Washington could not die till he had broken the chains of his slaves. Yet his monument is built up by the price of human blood, and the traders in the bodies and souls of men shout — "We have Washington to our father." — Alas! that it should be so; yet so it is.

> The evil that men do, lives after them, The good is oft-interred with their bones.

Fellow-citizens, pardon me, allow me to ask, why am I called upon to speak here to-day? What have I, or those I represent, to do with your national independence? Are the great principles of political freedom and of natural justice, embodied in that Declaration of Independence, extended to us? and am I, therefore, called upon to bring our humble offering to the national altar, and to confess the benefits and express devout gratitude for the blessings resulting from your independence to us?

Would to God, both for your sakes and ours, that an affirmative answer could be truthfully returned to these questions! Then would my task be light, and my burden easy and delightful. For who is there so cold, that a nation's sympathy could not warm him? Who so obdurate and dead to the claims of gratitude, that would not thankfully acknowledge such priceless benefits? Who so stolid and selfish, that would not give his voice to swell the hallelujahs of a nation's jubilee, when the chains of servitude had been torn from his limbs? I am not that man. In a case like that, the dumb might eloquently speak, and the "lame man leap as an hart."

But, such is not the state of the case. I say it with a sad sense of the disparity between us. I am not included within the pale of this glorious anniversary! Your high independence only reveals the immeasurable distance between us. The blessings in which you, this day, rejoice, are not enjoyed in common. — The rich inheritance of justice, liberty, prosperity and independence, bequeathed by your fathers, is shared by you, not by me. The sunlight that brought life and healing to you, has brought stripes and death to me. This Fourth [of] July is yours, not mine. You may rejoice, I must mourn. To drag a man in fetters into the grand illuminated temple of liberty, and call upon him to join you in joyous anthems, were inhuman mockery and sacrilegious irony. Do you mean, citizens, to mock me, by asking me to speak to-day? If so, there is a parallel to your conduct. And let me warn you that it is dangerous to copy the example of a nation whose crimes, lowering up to heaven, were thrown down by the breath of the Almighty, burying that nation in irrecoverable ruin! I can to-day take up the plaintive lament of a peeled and woe-smitten people!

> By the rivers of Babylon, there we sat down. Yea! we wept when we remembered Zion. We hanged our harps upon the willows in the midst thereof. For there, they that carried us away captive, required of us a song; and they who wasted us required of us mirth, saying, Sing us one of the songs of Zion. How can we sing the Lord's song in a strange land? If I forget thee, O Jerusalem, let my right hand forget her cunning. If I do not remember thee, let my tongue cleave to the roof of my mouth."

Fellow-citizens; above your national, tumultuous joy, I hear the mournful wail of millions! whose chains, heavy and grievous yesterday, are, to-day, rendered more intolerable by the jubilee shouts that reach them. If I do forget, if I do not faithfully remember those bleeding children of sorrow this day, "may my right hand forget her cunning, and may my tongue cleave to the roof of my mouth!" To forget them, to pass lightly over their wrongs, and to chime in with the popular theme, would be treason most scandalous and shocking, and would make me a reproach before God and the world. My subject, then fellow-citizens, is AMERICAN SLAVERY. I shall see, this day, and its popular characteristics, from the slave's point of view. Standing, there, identified with the American bondman, making his wrongs mine, I do not hesitate to declare, with all my soul, that the character and conduct of this nation never looked blacker to me than on this 4th of July! Whether we turn to the declarations of the past, or to the professions of the present, the conduct of the nation seems equally hideous and revolting. America is false to the past, false to the present, and solemnly binds herself to be false to the future. Standing with God and the crushed and bleeding slave on this occasion, I will, in the name of humanity which is outraged, in the name of liberty which is fettered, in the name of the constitution and the Bible, which are disregarded and trampled upon, dare to call in question and to denounce, with all the emphasis I can command, everything that serves to perpetuate slavery — the great sin and shame of America! "I will not equivocate; I will not excuse;" I will use the severest language I can command; and yet not one word shall escape me that any man, whose judgment is not blinded by prejudice, or who is not at heart a slaveholder, shall not confess to be right and just.

But I fancy I hear some one of my audience say, it is just in this circumstance that you and your brother abolitionists fail to make a favorable impression on the public mind. Would you argue more, and denounce less, would you persuade more, and rebuke less, your cause would be much more likely to succeed. But, I submit, where all is plain there is nothing to be argued. What point in the anti-slavery creed would you have me argue? On what branch of the subject do the people of this country need light? Must I undertake to prove that the slave is a man? That point is conceded already. Nobody doubts it. The slaveholders themselves acknowledge it in the enactment of laws for their government. They acknowledge it when they punish disobedience on the part of the slave. There are seventy-two crimes in the State of Virginia, which, if committed by a black man, (no matter how ignorant he be), subject him to the punishment of death; while only two of the same crimes will subject a white man to the like punishment. What is this but the acknowledgement that the slave is a moral, intellectual and responsible being? The manhood of the slave is conceded. It is admitted in the fact that Southern statute books are covered with enactments forbidding, under severe fines and penalties, the teaching of the slave to read or to write. When you can point to any such laws, in reference to the beasts of the field, then I may consent to argue the manhood of the slave. When the dogs in your streets, when the fowls of the air, when the cattle on your hills, when the fish of the sea, and the reptiles that crawl, shall be unable to distinguish the slave from a brute, then will I argue with you that the slave is a man!

For the present, it is enough to affirm the equal manhood of the Negro race. Is it not astonishing that, while we are ploughing, planting and reaping, using all kinds of mechanical tools, erecting houses, constructing bridges, building ships, working in metals of brass, iron, copper, silver and gold; that, while we are reading, writing and cyphering, acting as clerks, merchants and secretaries, having among us lawyers, doctors, ministers, poets, authors, editors, orators and teachers; that, while we are engaged in all manner of enterprises common to other men, digging gold in California, capturing the whale in the Pacific, feeding sheep and cattle on the hill-side, living, moving, acting, thinking, planning, living in families as husbands, wives and children, and, above all, confessing and worshipping the Christian's God, and looking hopefully for life and immortality beyond the grave, we are called upon to prove that we are men!

Would you have me argue that man is entitled to liberty? that he is the rightful owner of his own body? You have already declared it. Must I argue the wrongfulness of slavery? Is that a question for Republicans? Is it to be settled by the rules of logic and argumentation, as a matter beset with great difficulty, involving a doubtful application of the principle of justice, hard to be understood? How should I look to-day, in the presence of Americans, dividing, and subdividing a discourse, to show that men have a natural right to freedom? speaking of it relatively, and positively, negatively, and affirmatively. To do so, would be to make myself ridiculous, and to offer an insult to your understanding. — There is not a man beneath the canopy of heaven, that does not know that slavery is wrong for him.

What, am I to argue that it is wrong to make men brutes, to rob them of their liberty, to work them without wages, to keep them ignorant of their relations to their fellow men, to beat them with sticks, to flay their flesh with the lash, to load their limbs with irons, to hunt them with dogs, to sell them at auction, to sunder their families, to knock out their teeth, to burn their flesh, to starve them into obedience and submission to their masters? Must

I argue that a system thus marked with blood, and stained with pollution, is wrong? No! I will not. I have better employments for my time and strength than such arguments would imply.

What, then, remains to be argued? Is it that slavery is not divine; that God did not establish it; that our doctors of divinity are mistaken? There is blasphemy in the thought. That which is inhuman, cannot be divine! Who can reason on such a proposition? They that can, may; I cannot. The time for such argument is passed.

At a time like this, scorching irony, not convincing argument, is needed. O! had I the ability, and could I reach the nation's ear, I would, today, pour out a fiery stream of biting ridicule, blasting reproach, withering sarcasm, and stern rebuke. For it is not light that is needed, but fire; it is not the gentle shower, but thunder. We need the storm, the whirlwind, and the earthquake. The feeling of the nation must be quickened; the conscience of the nation must be roused; the propriety of the nation must be startled; the hypocrisy of the nation must be exposed; and its crimes against God and man must be proclaimed and denounced.

What, to the American slave, is your 4th of July? I answer: a day that reveals to him, more than all other days in the year, the gross injustice and cruelty to which he is the constant victim. To him, your celebration is a sham; your boasted liberty, an unholy license; your national greatness, swelling vanity; your sounds of rejoicing are empty and heartless; your denunciations of tyrants, brass fronted impudence; your shouts of liberty and equality, hollow mockery; your prayers and hymns, your sermons and thanksgivings, with all your religious parade, and solemnity, are, to him, mere bombast, fraud, deception, impiety, and hypocrisy — a thin veil to cover up crimes which would disgrace a nation of savages. There is not a nation on the earth guilty of practices, more shocking and bloody, than are the people of these United States, at this very hour.

Go where you may, search where you will, roam through all the monarchies and despotisms of the old world, travel through South America, search out every abuse, and when you have found the last, lay your facts by the side of the everyday practices of this nation, and you will say with me, that, for revolting barbarity and shameless hypocrisy, America reigns without a rival.

Take the American slave-trade, which, we are told by the papers, is especially prosperous just now. Ex-Senator Benton tells us that the price of men was never higher than now. He mentions the fact to show that slavery is in no danger. This trade is one of the peculiarities of American institutions. It is carried on in all the large towns and cities in one-half of this confederacy; and millions are pocketed every year, by dealers in this horrid traffic. In several states, this trade is a chief source of wealth. It is called (in contradistinction to the foreign slave-trade) "the internal slave trade." It is, probably, called so, too, in order to divert from it the horror with which the foreign slave-trade is contemplated. That trade has long since been denounced by this government, as piracy. It has been denounced with burning words, from the high places of the nation, as an execrable traffic. To arrest it, to put an end to it, this nation keeps a squadron, at immense cost, on the coast of Africa. Everywhere, in this country, it is safe to speak of this foreign slave-trade, as a most inhuman traffic, opposed alike to the laws of God and of man. The duty to extirpate and destroy it, is admitted even by our DOCTORS OF DIVINITY. In order to put an end to it, some of these last have consented that their colored brethren (nominally free) should leave this country, and establish themselves on the western coast of Africa! It is, however, a notable fact that, while so much execration is poured out by Americans upon those engaged in the foreign slave-trade, the men engaged in the slave-trade between the states pass without condemnation, and their business is deemed honorable.

Behold the practical operation of this internal slave-trade, the American slave-trade, sustained by American politics and America religion. Here you will see men and women reared like swine for the market. You know what is a swine-drover? I will show you a man-drover. They inhabit all our Southern States. They perambulate the country, and crowd the highways of the nation, with droves of human stock. You will see one of these human flesh-jobbers, armed with pistol, whip and bowie-knife, driving a company of a hundred men, women, and children, from the Potomac to the slave market at New Orleans. These wretched people are to be sold singly, or in lots, to suit purchasers. They are food for the cottonfield, and the deadly sugar-mill. Mark the sad procession, as it moves wearily along, and the inhuman wretch who drives them. Hear his savage yells and his blood-chilling oaths, as he hurries on his affrighted captives! There, see the old man, with locks thinned and gray. Cast one glance, if you please, upon that young mother, whose shoulders are bare to the scorching sun, her briny tears falling on the brow of the babe in her arms. See, too, that girl of thirteen, weeping, yes! weeping, as she thinks of the mother from whom she has been torn! The drove moves tardily. Heat and sorrow have nearly consumed their strength; suddenly you hear a quick snap, like the discharge of a rifle; the fetters clank, and the chain rattles simultaneously; your ears are saluted with a scream, that seems to have torn its way to the center of your soul! The crack you heard, was the sound of the slave-whip; the scream you heard, was from the woman you saw with the babe. Her speed had faltered under the weight of her child and her chains! that gash on her shoulder tells her to move on. Follow the drove to New Orleans. Attend the auction; see men examined like horses; see the forms of women rudely and brutally exposed to the shocking gaze of American slave-buyers. See this drove sold and separated forever; and never forget the deep, sad sobs that arose from that scattered multitude. Tell me citizens, WHERE, under the sun, you can witness a spectacle more fiendish and shocking. Yet this is but a glance at the American slave-trade, as it exists, at this moment, in the ruling part of the United States.

I was born amid such sights and scenes. To me the American slavetrade is a terrible reality. When a child, my soul was often pierced with a sense of its horrors. I lived on Philpot Street, Fell's Point, Baltimore, and have watched from the wharves, the slave ships in the Basin, anchored from the shore, with their cargoes of human flesh, waiting for favorable winds to waft them down the Chesapeake. There was, at that time, a grand slave mart kept at the head of Pratt Street, by Austin Woldfolk. His agents were sent into every town and county in Maryland, announcing their arrival, through the papers, and on flaming "hand-bills," headed CASH FOR NEGROES. These men were generally well dressed men, and very captivating in their manners. Ever ready to drink, to treat, and to gamble. The fate of many a slave has depended upon the turn of a single card; and many a child has been snatched from the arms of its mother by bargains arranged in a state of brutal drunkenness.

The flesh-mongers gather up their victims by dozens, and drive them, chained, to the general depot at Baltimore. When a sufficient number have been collected here, a ship is chartered, for the purpose of conveying the forlorn crew to Mobile, or to New Orleans. From the slave prison to the ship, they are usually driven in the darkness of night; for since the antislavery agitation, a certain caution is observed.

In the deep still darkness of midnight, I have been often aroused by the dead heavy footsteps, and the piteous cries of the chained gangs that passed our door. The anguish of my boyish heart was intense; and I was often consoled, when speaking to my mistress in the morning, to hear her say that the custom was very wicked; that she hated to hear the rattle of the chains, and the heart-rending cries. I was glad to find one who sympathized with me in my horror.

Fellow-citizens, this murderous traffic is, to-day, in active operation in this boasted republic. In the solitude of my spirit, I see clouds of dust raised on the highways of the South; I see the bleeding footsteps; I hear the doleful wail of fettered humanity, on the way to the slave-markets, where the victims are to be sold like horses, sheep, and swine, knocked off to the highest bidder.[25] There I see the tenderest ties ruthlessly broken, to gratify the lust, caprice and rapacity of the buyers and sellers of men. My soul sickens at the sight.

Is this the land your Fathers loved, The freedom which they toiled to win? Is this the earth whereon they moved?

Are these the graves they slumber in?

But a still more inhuman, disgraceful, and scandalous state of things remains to be presented. By an act of the American Congress, not yet two years old, slavery has been nationalized in its most horrible and revolting form. By that act, Mason and Dixon's line has been obliterated; New York has become as Virginia; and the power to hold, hunt, and sell men, women, and children as slaves remains no longer a mere state institution, but is now an institution of the whole United States. The power is coextensive with the Star-Spangled Banner and American Christianity. Where these go, may also go the merciless slave-hunter. Where these are, man is not sacred. He is a bird for the sportsman's gun. By that most foul and fiendish of all human decrees, the liberty and person of every man are put in peril. Your broad republican domain is hunting ground for men. Not for thieves and robbers, enemies of society, merely, but for men guilty of no crime. Your lawmakers have commanded all good citizens to engage in this hellish sport. Your President, your Secretary of State, our lords, nobles, and ecclesiastics, enforce, as a duty you owe to your free and glorious country, and to your God, that you do this accursed thing. Not fewer than forty Americans have, within the past two years, been hunted down and, without a moment's warning, hurried away in chains, and consigned to slavery and excruciating torture. Some of these have had wives and children, dependent on them for bread; but of this, no account was made. The right of the hunter to his prey stands superior to the right of marriage, and to all rights in this republic, the rights of God included! For black men there are neither law, justice, humanity, not religion. The Fugitive Slave Law makes mercy to them a crime; and bribes the judge who tries them. An American judge gets ten dollars for every victim he consigns to slavery, and five, when he fails to do so. The oath of any two villains is sufficient, under this hellblack enactment, to send the most pious and exemplary black man into the remorseless jaws of slavery! His own testimony is nothing. He can bring no witnesses for himself. The minister of American justice is bound by the law to hear but one side; and that side, is the side of the oppressor. Let this damning fact be perpetually told. Let it be thundered around the world, that, in tyrant-killing, king-hating, people-loving, democratic, Christian America, the seats of justice are filled with judges, who hold their offices under an open and palpable bribe, and are bound, in deciding in the case of a man's liberty, hear only his accusers!

In glaring violation of justice, in shameless disregard of the forms of administering law, in cunning arrangement to entrap the defenseless, and in diabolical intent, this Fugitive Slave Law stands alone in the annals of tyrannical legislation. I doubt if there be another nation on the globe, having the brass and the baseness to put such a law on the statute-book. If any man in this assembly thinks differently from me in this matter, and feels able to disprove my statements, I will gladly confront him at any suitable time and place he may select.

I take this law to be one of the grossest infringements of Christian Liberty, and, if the churches and ministers of our country were not stupidly blind, or most wickedly indifferent, they, too, would so regard it.

At the very moment that they are thanking God for the enjoyment of civil and religious liberty, and for the right to worship God according to the dictates of their own consciences, they are utterly silent in respect to a law which robs religion of its chief significance, and makes it utterly worthless to a world lying in wickedness. Did this law concern the "mint, anise, and cumin" — abridge the right to sing psalms, to partake of the sacrament, or to engage in any of the ceremonies of religion, it would be smitten by the thunder of a thousand pulpits. A general shout would go up from the church, demanding repeal, repeal, instant repeal! — And it would go hard with that politician who presumed to solicit the votes of the people without inscribing this motto on his banner. Further, if this demand were not complied with, another Scotland would be added to the history of religious liberty, and the stern old Covenanters would be thrown into the shade. A John Knox would be seen at every church door, and heard from every pulpit, and Fillmore would have no more quarter than was shown by Knox, to the beautiful, but treacherous queen Mary of Scotland. The fact that the church of our country, (with fractional exceptions), does not esteem "the Fugitive Slave Law" as a declaration of war against religious liberty, implies that that church regards religion simply as a form of worship, an empty ceremony, and not a vital principle, requiring active benevolence, justice, love and good will towards man. It esteems sacrifice above mercy; psalm-singing above right doing; solemn meetings above practical righteousness. A worship that can be conducted by persons who refuse to give shelter to the houseless, to give bread to the hungry, clothing to the naked, and who enjoin obedience to a law forbidding these acts of mercy, is a curse, not a blessing to mankind. The Bible addresses all such persons as "scribes, Pharisees, hypocrites, who pay tithe of mint, anise, and cumin, and have omitted the weightier matters of the law, judgment, mercy and faith."

But the church of this country is not only indifferent to the wrongs of the slave, it actually takes sides with the oppressors. It has made itself the bulwark of American slavery, and the shield of American slave-hunters. Many of its most eloquent Divines. who stand as the very lights of the church, have shamelessly given the sanction of religion and the Bible to the whole slave system. They have taught that man may, properly, be a slave; that the relation of master and slave is ordained of God; that to send back an escaped bondman to his master is clearly the duty of all the followers of the Lord Jesus Christ; and this horrible blasphemy is palmed off upon the world for Christianity.

For my part, I would say, welcome infidelity! welcome atheism! welcome anything! in preference to the gospel, as preached by those Divines! They convert the very name of religion into an engine of tyranny, and barbarous cruelty, and serve to confirm more infidels, in this age, than all the infidel writings of Thomas Paine, Voltaire, and Bolingbroke, put together, have done! These ministers make religion a cold and flintyhearted thing, having neither principles of right action, nor bowels of compassion. They strip the love of God of its beauty, and leave the throng of religion a huge, horrible, repulsive form. It is a religion for oppressors, tyrants, man-stealers, and thugs. It is not that "pure and undefiled religion" which is from above, and which is "first pure, then peaceable, easy to be entreated, full of mercy and good fruits, without partiality, and without hypocrisy." But a religion which favors the rich against the poor; which exalts the proud above the humble; which divides mankind into two classes, tyrants and slaves; which says to the man in chains, stay there; and to the oppressor, oppress on; it is a religion which may be professed and enjoyed by all the robbers and enslavers of mankind; it makes God a respecter of persons, denies his fatherhood of the race, and tramples in the dust the great truth of the brotherhood of man. All this we affirm to be true of the popular church, and the popular worship of our land and nation — a religion, a church, and a worship which, on the authority of inspired wisdom, we pronounce to be an abomination in the sight of God. In the language of Isaiah, the American church might be well addressed, "Bring no more vain ablations; incense is an abomination unto me: the new moons and Sabbaths, the calling of assemblies, I cannot away with; it is iniquity even the solemn meeting. Your new moons and your appointed feasts my soul hateth. They are a trouble to me; I am weary to bear them; and when ye spread forth your hands I will hide mine eyes from you. Yea! when ye make many prayers, I will not hear. YOUR HANDS ARE FULL OF BLOOD; cease to do evil, learn to do well; seek judgment; relieve the oppressed; judge for the fatherless; plead for the widow."

The American church is guilty, when viewed in connection with what it is doing to uphold slavery; but it is superlatively guilty when viewed in connection with its ability to abolish slavery. The sin of which it is guilty is one of omission as well as of commission. Albert Barnes but uttered what the common sense of every man at all observant of the actual state of the case will receive as truth, when he declared that "There is no power out of the church that could sustain slavery an hour, if it were not sustained in it."

Let the religious press, the pulpit, the Sunday school, the conference meeting, the great ecclesiastical, missionary, Bible and tract associations of the land array their immense powers against slavery and slave-holding; and the whole system of crime and blood would be scattered to the winds; and that they do not do this involves them in the most awful responsibility of which the mind can conceive.

In prosecuting the anti-slavery enterprise, we have been asked to spare the church, to spare the ministry; but how, we ask, could such a thing be done? We are met on the threshold of our efforts for the redemption of the slave, by the church and ministry of the country, in battle arrayed against us; and we are compelled to fight or flee. From what quarter, I beg to know, has proceeded a fire so deadly upon our ranks, during the last two years, as from the Northern pulpit? As the champions of oppressors, the chosen men of American theology have appeared — men, honored for their so-called piety, and their real learning....

Americans! your republican politics, not less than your republican religion, are flagrantly inconsistent. You boast of your love of liberty, your superior civilization, and your pure Christianity, while the whole political power of the nation (as embodied in the two great political parties), is solemnly pledged to support and perpetuate the enslavement of three millions of your countrymen. You hurl your anathemas at the crowned headed tyrants of Russia and Austria, and pride yourselves on your Democratic institutions, while you yourselves consent to be the mere tools and body-guards of the tyrants of Virginia and Carolina. You invite to your shores fugitives of oppression from abroad, honor them with banquets, greet them with ovations, cheer them, toast them, salute them, protect them, and pour out your money to them like water; but the fugitives from your own land you advertise, hunt, arrest, shoot and kill. You glory in your refinement and your universal education yet you maintain a system as barbarous and dreadful as ever stained the character of a nation — a system begun in avarice, supported in pride, and perpetuated in cruelty. You shed tears over fallen Hungary, and make the sad story of her wrongs the theme of your poets, statesmen and orators, till your gallant sons are ready to fly to arms to vindicate her cause against her oppressors; but, in regard to the ten thousand wrongs of the American slave, you would enforce the strictest silence, and would hail him as an enemy of the nation who dares to make those wrongs the subject of public discourse! You are all on fire at the mention of liberty for France or for Ireland; but are as cold as an iceberg at the thought of liberty for the enslaved of America. You discourse eloquently on the dignity of labor; yet, you sustain a system which, in its very essence, casts a stigma upon labor. You can bare your bosom to the storm of British artillery to throw off a threepenny tax on tea; and yet wring the last hardearned farthing from the grasp of the black laborers of your country. You profess to believe "that, of one blood, God made all nations of men to dwell on the face of all the earth," and hath commanded all men, everywhere to love one another; yet you notoriously hate, (and glory in your hatred), all men whose skins are not colored like your own. You declare, before the world, and are understood by the world to declare, that you "hold these truths to be self evident, that all men are created equal; and are endowed by their Creator with certain inalienable rights; and that, among these are, life, liberty, and the pursuit of happiness;" and yet, you hold securely, in a bondage which, according to your own Thomas Jefferson, "is worse than ages of that which your fathers rose in rebellion to oppose," a seventh part of the inhabitants of your country.

Fellow-citizens! I will not enlarge further on your national inconsistencies. The existence of slavery in this country brands your republicanism as a sham, your humanity as a base pretence, and your Christianity as a lie. It destroys your moral power abroad; it corrupts your politicians at home. It saps the foundation of religion; it makes your name a hissing, and a bye-word to a mocking earth. It is the antagonistic force in your government, the only thing that seriously disturbs and endangers your Union. It fetters your progress; it is the enemy of improvement, the deadly foe of education; it fosters pride; it breeds insolence; it promotes vice; it shelters crime; it is a curse to the earth that supports it; and yet, you cling to it, as if it were the sheet anchor of all your hopes. Oh! be warned! be warned! a horrible reptile is coiled up in your nation's bosom; the venomous creature is nursing at the tender breast of your youthful republic; for the love of God, tear away, and fling from you the hideous monster, and let the weight of twenty millions crush and destroy it forever!

But it is answered in reply to all this, that precisely what I have now denounced is, in fact, guaranteed and sanctioned by the Constitution of the United States; that the right to hold and to hunt slaves is a part of that Constitution framed by the illustrious Fathers of this Republic.

Then, I dare to affirm, notwithstanding all I have said before, your fathers stooped, basely stooped

To palter with us in a double sense:

And keep the word of promise to the ear,

But break it to the heart.

And instead of being the honest men I have before declared them to be, they were the veriest imposters that ever practiced on mankind. This is the inevitable conclusion, and from it there is no escape. But I differ from those who charge this baseness on the framers of the Constitution of the United States. It is a slander upon their memory, at least, so I believe. There is not time now to argue the constitutional question at length — nor have I the ability to discuss it as it ought to be discussed.

Fellow-citizens! there is no matter in respect to which, the people of the North have allowed themselves to be so ruinously imposed upon, as that of the pro-slavery character of the Constitution. In that instrument I hold there is neither warrant, license, nor sanction of the hateful thing; but, interpreted as it ought to be interpreted, the Constitution is a GLORIOUS LIBERTY DOCUMENT. Read its preamble, consider its purposes. Is slavery among them? Is it at the gateway? or is it in the temple? It is neither. While I do not intend to argue this question on the present occasion, let me ask, if it be not somewhat singular that, if the Constitution were intended to be, by its framers and adopters, a slave-holding instrument, why neither slavery, slaveholding, nor slave can anywhere be found in it. What would be thought of an instrument, drawn up, legally drawn up, for the purpose of entitling the city of Rochester to a track of land, in which no mention of land was made? Now, there are certain rules of interpretation, for the proper understanding of all legal instruments. These rules are well established. They are plain, common-sense rules, such as you and I, and all of us, can understand and apply, without having passed years in the study of law. I scout the idea that the question of the constitutionality or unconstitutionality of slavery is not a question for the people. I hold that every American citizen has a right to form an opinion of the constitution, and to propagate that opinion, and to use all honorable means to make his opinion the prevailing one. Without this right, the liberty of an American citizen would be as insecure as that of a Frenchman. Ex-Vice-President Dallas tells us that the Constitution is an object to which no American mind can be too attentive, and no American heart too devoted. He further says, the Constitution, in its words, is plain and intelligible, and is meant for the home-bred, unsophisticated understandings of our fellow-citizens. Senator Berrien tell us that the Constitution is the fundamental law, that which controls all others. The charter of our liberties, which every citizen has a personal interest in understanding thoroughly. The testimony of Senator Breese, Lewis Cass, and many others that might be named, who are everywhere esteemed as sound lawyers, so regard the constitution. I take it, therefore, that it is not presumption in a private citizen to form an opinion of that instrument.

Now, take the Constitution according to its plain reading, and I defy the presentation of a single pro-slavery clause in it. On the other hand it will be found to contain principles and purposes, entirely hostile to the existence of slavery.

I have detained my audience entirely too long already. At some future period I will gladly avail myself of an opportunity to give this subject a full and fair discussion.

Allow me to say, in conclusion, notwithstanding the dark picture I have this day presented of the state of the nation, I do not despair of this country. There are forces in operation, which must inevitably work the downfall of slavery. "The arm of the Lord is not shortened,"and the doom of slavery is certain. I, therefore, leave off where I began, with hope. While drawing encouragement from the Declaration of Independence, the great principles it contains, and the genius of American Institutions, my spirit is also cheered by the obvious tendencies of the age. Nations do not now stand in the same relation to each other that they did ages ago. No nation can now shut itself up from the surrounding world, and trot round in the same old path of its fathers without interference. The time was when such could be done. Long established customs of hurtful character could formerly fence themselves in, and do their evil work with social impunity. Knowledge was then confined and enjoyed by the privileged few, and the multitude walked on in mental darkness. But a change has now come over the affairs of mankind. Walled cities and empires have become unfashionable. The arm of commerce has borne away the gates of the strong city. Intelligence is penetrating the darkest corners of the globe. It makes its pathway over and under the sea, as well as on the earth. Wind, steam, and lightning are its chartered agents. Oceans no longer divide, but link nations together. From Boston to London is now a holiday excursion. Space is comparatively annihilated. Thoughts expressed on one side of the Atlantic, are distinctly heard on the other. The far off and almost fabulous Pacific rolls in grandeur at our feet. The Celestial Empire, the mystery of ages, is being solved.[49] The fiat of the Almighty, "Let there be Light," has not yet spent its force. No abuse, no outrage whether in taste, sport or avarice, can now hide itself from the all-pervading light. The iron shoe, and crippled foot of China must be seen, in contrast with nature. Africa must rise and put on her yet unwoven garment. "Ethiopia shall stretch out her hand untoGod."

In the fervent aspirations of William Lloyd Garrison, I say, and let every heart join in saying it:

God speed the year of jubilee
The wide world o'er!
When from their galling chains set free,
Th' oppress'd shall vilely bend the knee,
And wear the yoke of tyranny
Like brutes no more.
That year will come, and freedom's reign,
To man his plundered rights again
Restore.

God speed the day when human blood
Shall cease to flow!
In every clime be understood,
The claims of human brotherhood,
And each return for evil, good,

Not blow for blow;
That day will come all feuds to end,
And change into a faithful friend
Each foe.

God speed the hour, the glorious hour,
When none on earth
Shall exercise a lordly power,
Nor in a tyrant's presence cower;
But to all manhood's stature tower,
By equal birth!
That hour will come, to each, to all,
And from his Prison-house, to thrall
Go forth.

Until that year, day, hour, arrive,
With head, and heart, and hand I'll strive,
To break the rod, and rend the gyve,
The spoiler of his prey deprive —
So witness Heaven!
And never from my chosen post,
Whate'er the peril or the cost,
Be driven.

Early Modern Genres

By: Sean Lewis

The concept of genre is one that is vital for literate adults, but you may not have seen it addressed directly in courses you have taken. Genre simply means a "kind" or "type" of discourse, and you probably already have an intuition for genre even if you've never considered the term. Is the book you are reading fiction or non-fiction? Are you reading a lyric poem or a short story? Understanding the genre of discourse you are reading, hearing, or watching is vital to your interpretation of it, and misunderstanding genre can lead to profound misinterpretations.

Some genres have been so important to Western and global rhetoric and literature that they seem to be fixed and eternal. Aristotle's Poetics considers epic, tragedy, and comedy in this way, and given their importance in ancient Greek culture, that's not surprising. Human lives tend to have similar narrative patterns, regardless of time or place (birth, growth, death), so genres that focus on the fearful and pitiable aspects of the human condition (tragedy) or the joyous and funny aspects (comedy) might naturally arise in very different human cultures. Nevertheless, genres of written and spoken discourse develop over time and within specific cultures. Some scholars argue that we should instead speak of generic discourses, since a single literary work may engage in multiple generic discourses, and artists are always in dialogue both with the generic expectations of the audience as well as their own artistic vision. Amy J. Devitt has put the matter well:

The fact that others have responded to similar situations in the past in similar ways—the fact that genres exist—enables writers and readers to respond more easily and more appropriately themselves. This initial insight—that genres respond appropriately to their rhetorical situations—reveals the rhetorical nature of generic forms and provides the basis of a newly rhetorical theory of genre. Knowing the genre, therefore, means knowing such rhetorical aspects as appropriate subject matter, level of detail, tone, and approach as well as the expected layout and organization.

When analyzing genre, we need to consider what the audience was expecting, what the author provided, and to what extent the literary product conformed to those expectations or challenged them. Great art often pushes the prior boundaries of generic expectation by including a diversity of generic voices and perspectives. Still, for our purposes, the term genre will be fitting, so long as we understand it with all of the complexity above.

The Early Modern world (c. 1450-1850) saw the rise of many new genres, and this chapter provides only a brief introduction and overview. For the sake of clarity, I have grouped them into non-fiction (chronicle, essay, treatise, letter, declaration) and fiction (drama, novel), though the boundary between the two could be porous (travel writing/marvels). I tend to use "audience" rather than "reader" because many of these genres were read aloud: even illiterate people had access to many of these genres, though as literacy rates increased, so did the practice of silent reading. Considering how these genres developed in the period and how they interacted with audiences is key for considering how people's of picture of the world developed over this period: how you imagine the world affects how you act in the world.

Early Modern Genres: Nonfiction

Our first observation about genres in the Early Modern world should be on the distinction between nonfiction and fiction. Nonfictional works attempt to make statements about the primary, physical, and temporal world that we commonly inhabit. Fiction presents "secondary worlds," drawn from our primary world, but with no pretense to historical veracity. Fictional works can nevertheless be important ways of forming the mind and heart: fictional worlds reflect on our historical world, and comment on it in various ways. The first set of genres considered here, however, claim to be reports of our primary, historical world. I say "claim" and "report" because we humans are limited in our understanding, and bring our own biases and prejudices to our own narratives about the world. These nonfictional genres do have backstories that are worth delving into, but for the sake of time and space, I will simply consider their generic features.

Chronicles

Chronicles are the first genre to consider in an early modern context. The genre was widespread in antiquity and the Middle Ages, and simply means a "record of the times". Renaissance humanists were greatly interested in the past, particularly that of classical antiquity, and these historical chronicles provide valuable material for study. Moreover, they provided a model of how to record events in the current world: chronicles take a relatively objective tone, simply recording what happened and when it happened. This objective tone, of course, has to be balanced against the bias and perspective of the chronicler. When you read the Florentine Codex, for example, a 16th-century Native American account of the Spanish conquest of Mexico, you are given a definite perspective on the events, though those events are narrated in a direct and unadorned manner. Chronicles come closest to what we might consider history writing, a model for recording past and current events for future generations. Eventually in the early modern period, chronicles would also lead to news-writing, writing down present events for current people (rather than sharing the news only by word-of-mouth).

Travel Writing

Chronicles gave a picture of the world in time; a less lofty and more popular genre gave readers and listeners a picture of the world in space: travel writing. As with chronicles, travel writing existed since antiquity, with Pausanias' Description of Greece (2nd century BCE) being a noteworthy example. Medieval audiences loved to hear of the journey of Marco Polo to China (which he may or may not have actually made), as well as the land of Prester John, a Christian Priest-King in Asia whose kingdom contained fantastical beasts like cyclopes, unicorns, and elephants. This last detail discloses an overlap of generic discourses: travel writing often contains marvels, and mirabilia ("things to be wondered at") were a very popular genre at the beginning of the Early Modern period. Around 1450, most people were born, lived, and died in the same area: hearing about the wonders of far-off places is certainly an attractive way to pass the time and build one's world-picture.

As the Age of Encounter got underway, accounts of travels to new and exotic worlds remained popular, and we should note an interesting shift. Initial reports of the New World or the Far East initially retained this marvelous quality, with fact and fiction intertwined (Native Americans cannot, for example, breathe underwater or live for 300 years, both of which were claimed in a 1496 account). These marvelous accounts were in the minds of European explorers and merchants, and provided a fictionalized impetus for discovery. As time went on, travel writing lost its marvelous quality and led to the "disenchantment" of the world as past legends failed to live up to reality. Nevertheless, we enjoy a good travel story to this day, and marveling over the wonders of a foreign place may motivate us to visit it (consider this an official plug for Mount St. Mary's Study Abroad Programs).

Letters

Relatively few people wrote chronicles or travel accounts in the Early Modern period: just about every literate person, however, wrote letters. The genre of the letter might seem like an odd one, both because it is so apparently mundane and because our current culture no longer writes them. Throughout early modernity, however, the letter was understood as a distinct genre, and more famous and literary people often composed letters with the intent that they be published more widely than their immediate audience. Letters can be about literally anything, but mark their common generic features: they are usually addressed from one person to another, and this personal address gives them the quality of spoken discourse. Stylistically, they can be elevated or colloquial, and colloquial, intimate letters could make for very good reading. When you read letters in this course (like those of King Alfonso of Kongo or Galileo Galilei), consider their rhetoric: what is the matter at hand? What does the writer hope the reader with think or do? How does the writer disclose their character (ethos) through their language? The growing frequency of correspondence over the Early Modern period clearly shaped the linguistic and literary imagination of those living in the period.

Essays

Essays and treatises can have the feeling of a letter: a thoughtful, engaging treatment of an important subject by an intelligent writer, who simply happens to be addressing a wider audience. While Plutarch's writings include antecedents of the genre, the modern essay was the invention of French philosopher Michel de Montaigne (1533-92), and it was literally an "attempt" (essai) to understand some subject better. Montaigne's essays often have an easy, conversational feel to them, and he frequently drops in quotations from Classical Latin authors to reflect on contemporary subjects (such as New World encounters in his essay on Cannibals). Some essays have a clear point or thesis, while others do not, simply exploring their subjects without coming to a definite conclusion about them. Treatises, on the other hand, most certainly do have theses with supporting arguments, and might be considered longer, more thesis-driven versions of essays. A good early modern treatise writer, like John Locke or Mary Wollstonecraft, will still have an engaging tone, but treat their subject (hence "treatise") in a much more thorough and methodical manner. One stylistic point that early modern essays and treatises often retain from their Latin analogues is the use of "of" or "on" in the title (a feature common in Latin titles, as in Cicero's De Amicitia, "On/Of Friendship").

Declarations

All of the genres treated so far developed distinctive forms in the Early Modern period, but also clearly had sources and analogues from Antiquity and the Middle Ages. The declaration might be the most important genre invented in the period. Royal or ecclesial proclamations are issued by a monarch or a bishop; by contrast, declarations are texts that presume to speak for the people as a whole, either the people of a specific nation (as in the Haitian Declaration of Independence) or all people (as in the Declaration of the Rights of Man). Declarations are performative speech acts: by speech alone, they constitute a new reality, in most cases a political one. Two questions naturally arise from the nature of declarations: 1. Do the authors of the declaration really speak for all the people, or simply for a portion of them? 2. How much do these declarations actually change the nature of the sociopolitical world on which they are focused? While these questions should be addressed, it would be hard to imagine early modern Liberty without this genre.

Drama

This brief treatment of drama in the Early Modern era will focus on the London theater around 1600 and on Shakespeare, since a Shakespearean play is a required part of the course. An education in the English-speaking world without studying Shakespeare would have been unthinkable a generation ago, but this requirement might need some explaining. Justifications for Shakespeare in the curriculum often turn on his linguistic and literary influence: Shakespeare is the earliest witness to scores of now-common words and phrases in the English language, and his influence on subsequent drama, film, and television is hard to overstate. Besides influence, however, Shakespeare explored questions, problems, and themes in his work at the heart of the Early Modern period, and that remain with us to this day. Even without his monumental, canonical status, his greatest works still yield insights into our world and our selves.

Putting William Shakespeare (1564-1616) back into his historical context might actually help with this process, since drama in his day was popular entertainment, not prestige art. Born into a middle-class family in Stratford-upon-Avon, Shakespeare moved to London to become involved in the growing theater scene. While drama was an art in the Middle Ages, it was expressed either through small groups of travelling players or through large-scale urban dramatizations of the Bible. From the 1570's, drama emerged as a relatively stable profession in the city of London, with theatrical companies supported financially by nobility or even royalty. Renaissance Humanists had rediscovered ancient Greek and Roman drama, and acting in Latin-language dramas was a key element of Humanist grammar schools in England (such as the one Shakespeare attended as a boy). Members of companies were by nature versatile: male actors played both men and women on the stage, while also providing song, music, and dance in the productions, and some actors, like Shakespeare himself, were also playwrights. Writing plays was a highly collaborative art at the time: we know that Shakespeare collaborated with other London playwrights on a number of dramas (such as The Play of Sir Thomas More and Two Noble Kinsmen), and other artists likely contributed to the texts that now bear only Shakespeare's name. Shakespeare eventually became a shareholder in his company, which is how he ultimately made some comfortable money: playwrights and actors did not typically earn high salaries. While outbreaks of plague or moral panics might temporarily close the theatres, drama was highly popular: people of all walks of life attended them, and the stories they told shaped the popular imagination.

Aristotle opined in the Poetics that no playwright can do both comedy and tragedy well: Shakespeare proved Aristotle wrong. His works include great tragedies (Hamlet, Macbeth, King Lear,

Othello), comedies (Twelfth Night, Much Ado About Nothing, As You Like It), histories of both England and Rome (Henry V, Julius Caesar), and romances (The Winter's Tale, The Tempest). Shakespeare pushed the boundaries of genre and generic expectations as well, leading to the 19th-century term "problem plays": plays that do not fit neatly into any one of those genres (The Merchant of Venice, Measure for Measure). Through his drama, Shakespeare explored the length and breadth of the human experience. By necessity, Shakespeare's plays are "secular": in the Age of the Reformations, putting religious material on stage would be dangerous, if not outright illegal. Nevertheless, Shakespeare's plays show a keen interest in religious and spiritual material, though it is often treated in an oblique manner.

Particularly in his history plays, Shakespeare also shows an interest in political questions, which also could not be raised directly in the public sphere. Roman history (drawn largely from Livy and Plutarch) could provide lessons for how society should (or should not) be run, and his two tetralogies explore 15th-century English political developments during the War of the Roses (the war on which George R.R. Martin's Game of Thrones series is essentially based). Censorship was an ever-present reality (no commentary on the monarch or the Church was allowed), but London playwrights were often coy: a play about a current political crisis was forbidden, but set that same crisis in ancient Rome or a foreign land and it became acceptable. It is clear why Shakespeare's plays became a nexus for exploring and imagining topics that were taboo in other contexts, a role that art has provided throughout human history.

Drama is meant to be performed, and I hope that you see at least clips of performances (if not full performances) while reading the drama. When writing about Shakespeare, the standard convention is to cite Act, Scene, and Lines (Hamlet 1.2.133-64), but these are editorial; in his own era, Shakespeare would have performed his play straight through, with no intermissions. Public theatres performed dramas during the daytime, using natural light, with basic but effective stagecraft and special effects. More elite performances were private, performed for the royal court, Inns of Court (London Law Schools), or at the houses of nobility. In any context, the line between the actors and audience was permeable: while maintaining "the fourth wall" for much of the play, the close proximity of the audience meant that breaking "the fourth wall" was a likely occurrence. Consider this dynamic when reading and watching the play: how are the characters speaking not only to one another, but to you? How do you participate in the action of the play by observing it? Shakespeare was clearly fascinated by the philosophy of drama, commenting on his own art by staging plays within plays (A Midsummer Night's Dream, Hamlet).

Shakespeare's works will provide a lifetime of entertainment and wisdom to those who dwell in them, and this section will close with some of the more philosophical questions that Shakespeare returns to in multiple plays. How do appearances and realities relate to one another? If someone changes their external appearance and behavior, does that make a real change within them, and if so, in what way? What is gender? Is it essential or merely performed? Is human love genuine, or always a self-seeking pretense? How should society be structured and run? What voice should the common people have in government? Is popular government desirable or dangerous? How should we live, knowing that death is inevitable? How should we face our own death and the deaths of our loved ones? What, ultimately, is valuable about human life? All of these questions, and more, are explored through the works of William Shakespeare, and as long as there are humans, Shakespeare's works will remain relevant, "even until the edge of doom" (Sonnet 116).

The Novel

Novels are the most common genre of printed fiction available. When people flock to beaches in the summer, their beach reading tends to include a popular novel. Because the novel is the predominant genre of the modern era, many students assume that any literary work (particularly any long literary work) is a "novel." This is not, however, the case. If you take away nothing else from this chapter (and please do take more) it is this: not every literary work is a novel! Plato's Apology, Sophocles' Antigone, and Dante's Commedia are not novels (dialogue, tragedy, and epic, respectively). So where did the novel come from? Part of that story is a shift in reading practices during the Early Modern era.

When books were produced by hand (that is, for much of human history), it was common to own only a few books, and that was if one was lucky enough to be literate. In the Middle Ages, religious texts were the most frequently copied and owned, and thus read repeatedly, slowly, deliberately. The printing press changed this status, and from c. 1500 onwards there was a steady increase in reading material. In this period, people's reading lists would become more diverse (though the Bible remained central throughout Early Modernity). Early Modernity built on the long tradition of popular literature in the Middle Ages. Romance was a favorite genre, with tales of knights, ladies, monsters, and quests surviving in every classical and modern language from the period. Joke collections eventually become episodic and picaresque, following the adventures of a single character. Geoffrey Chaucer's Canterbury Tales, though written in verse, provide a set of tales set in the present age, with questions and concerns of a decidedly current flavor. All of these are important antecedents to the genre that would come to dominate the early modern period and Modernity.

Mikhail Bakhtin theorized that the novel is the modern, secular form of the epic, and while this formulation isn't perfect, the contrasts are telling. Rather than being told in some far-distant past, the novel is set in the world of the present. Instead of the gods of epic or the magic of romance, the world of the novel is inhabited primarily by humans, doing normal human things. The epic is written in verse, the novel in prose. One common factor, however, is scope: both genres tend towards long works that seek to give a sort of totalizing picture of their world. Reading novels can profoundly increase readers' capacity for empathy, since they encounter perspectives on reality different from their own, living vicariously through characters different from themselves.

Because they are set in the here-and-now, novels from Cervantes' Don Quixote (1605/1615) onwards are said to be marked by "realism." Part of this is due to their form. Novels often present themselves as "found" works—the author is merely presenting artefacts found in the real, historical world that tell some story. Novels as diverse as Don Quixote (1605/15), Frankenstein (1818), Moby-Dick (1851), Dracula (1897), The Lord of the Rings (1954-55), and The Name of the Rose (1980) frame themselves in this way. As such, modern, personal genres are often included in the novel, with personal letters, diaries, and private correspondence forming the text of the novel: Jane Austen is particularly good at building her novels through such genres. The fiction in many novels, then, is that they are actually historical, though obviously fictional (hence adding to the "realism"). These generic features make the novel quite popular, since people are reading discourse that they themselves use and are used to. The plots of novels, however, often have a structure more akin to Romance: a protagonist undergoes a set of trials and ultimately triumphs, though these trials are of a more ordinary or secular nature (making a fortune, finding a spouse).

While novels are generally praised for "realism," we should interrogate that term. What makes a novel "realistic"? Some novels are overtly moralistic or preachy, convinced that the universe (or at least society) has a stable moral order in which good is rewarded and evil punished. Is that "realistic"? In contrast, some novels depict worlds in which virtue is not rewarded, and evil often triumphs. Is this more "realistic"? Perhaps. What about miracles? Are those "real"? If so, we are in the South American genre of "Magical Realism" (Disney's Encanto is a cinematic example, an homage to the magnificent novels of Gabriel García Márquez). I hope that it is clear that while the novel often eschews overt magic or miracle, the question of how "realistic" it is depends upon both the author's vision as well as that of the audience. Contemporary novels like Toni Morrison's Beloved (1987), Juniot Díaz's The Brief and Wondrous Life of Oscar Wao (2007), and George Saunders' Lincoln in the Bardo (2017) present worlds that remain enchanted by spiritual and mystical realities, in contrast to our presumptions about our "secular" world. As readers read more novels, they encounter ever more views of the world, and it should be no surprise that the era of the novel is also the era of increased pluralism in our world.

The Lyric

All of the early modern genres treated so far are narrative in nature. Narrative is so powerful that arguably most aspects of human life have a narrative component, from psychology to Supreme Court cases. But there is a literary genre that is not necessarily narrative in nature: the lyric poem. Lyric takes its name from the lyre that ancient poets played to accompany their performances: lyrics are inextricably linked to song. What does one sing about? Anything imaginable. In rhetorical terms, lyric poetry might be termed epideictic: praising or blaming its subject. Lyric poetry is often deeply personal, with the reader of the poem identifying with the speaker of the poem—the lyric speaker becomes part of our own consciousness as we read or hear the lyric.

Sonnets are a popular Early Modern genre of lyric poetry, invented by Francesco Petrarcha (1304-1374) as a "secular" version of the Psalms: just as the speaker in a psalm praises, blames, and wrestles psychologically on spiritual matters, so the speaker of a sonnet does the same on secular matters (often erotic love). Reading lyric poetry and reading or singing lyrical ballads shapes our own minds and values, and is a process akin to prayer or meditation: how many of you have specific song lyrics that you find meaningful? People often say that lyrical music has helped them get through trauma or difficulties, and people have been using the lyric for this function throughout human time and space. It is fitting, then, that some consideration of lyric finish this chapter, since the songs we sing and the poems we read remain intimate parts of who we are as individuals and as a community.

Made in the USA
Middletown, DE
30 July 2023